AF614816

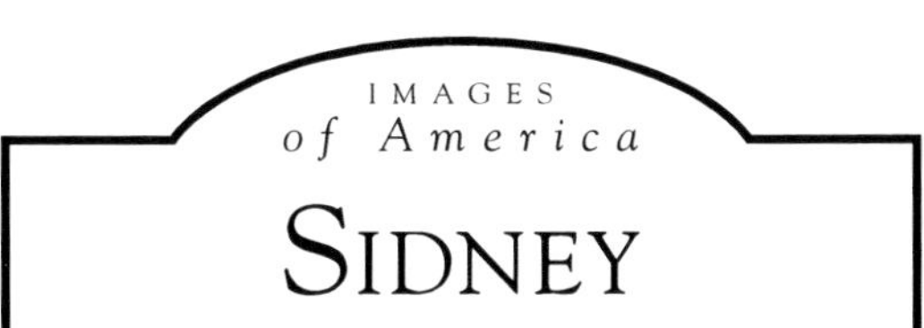
IMAGES
of America
SIDNEY

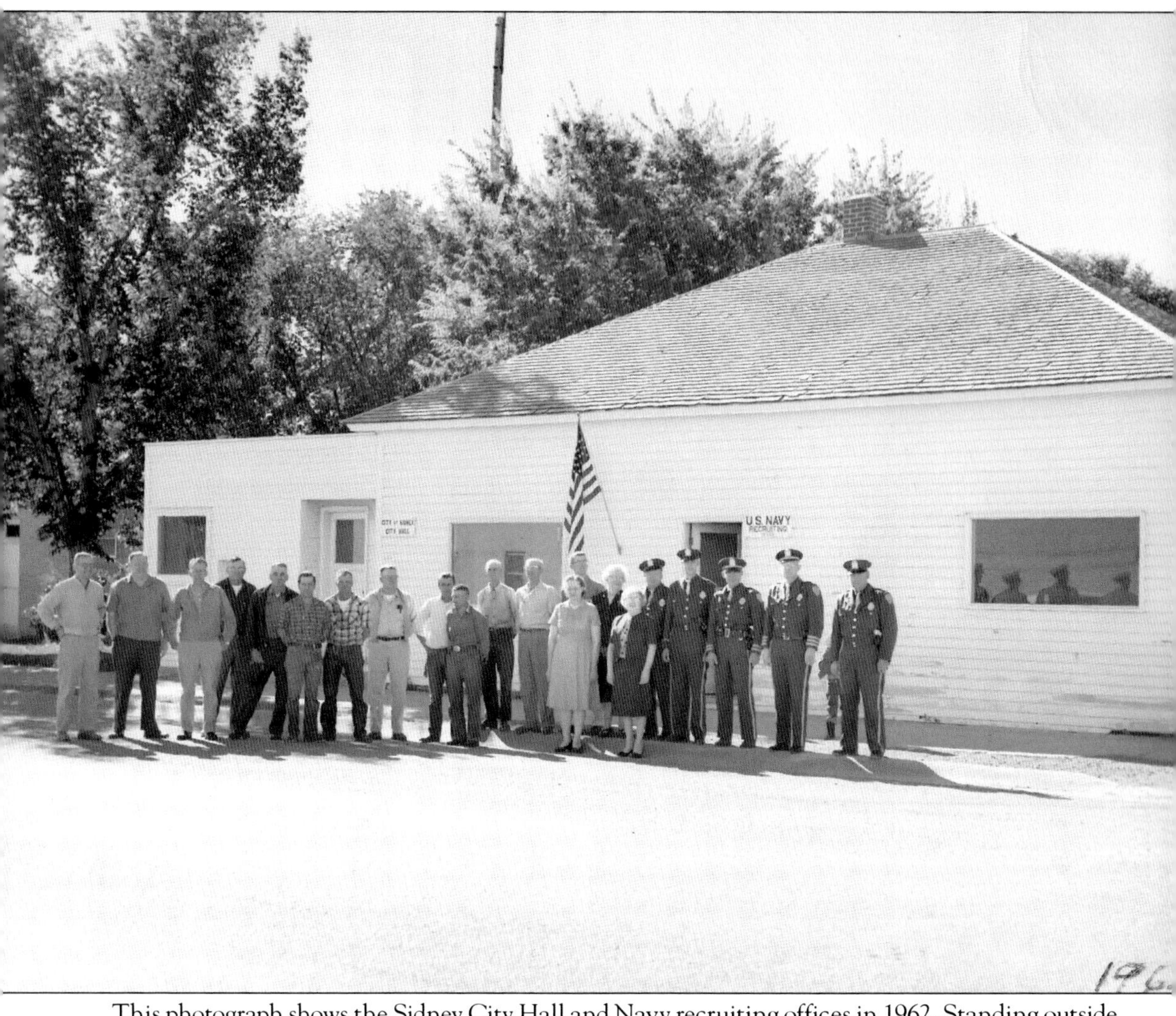

This photograph shows the Sidney City Hall and Navy recruiting offices in 1962. Standing outside are the staffs for both the city and the recruiting office. The city hall is still located on the same block, near Second Street SE and Second Avenue SE. There is no longer a Navy recruitment office in Sidney. (Courtesy of the MonDak Heritage Center.)

On the Cover: Taken by a photographer from Vic's Studio in Sidney, this image shows the Republican Party headquarters for the Montana gubernatorial campaign in 1960. Cars proclaim "Nutter for Governor" and men and women line Main Street. Sidney native Donald Nutter was elected the 15th governor of Montana that year. After serving just a year in office, however, Nutter was killed in an airplane crash during a blizzard on January 25, 1962. (Courtesy of the MonDak Heritage Center.)

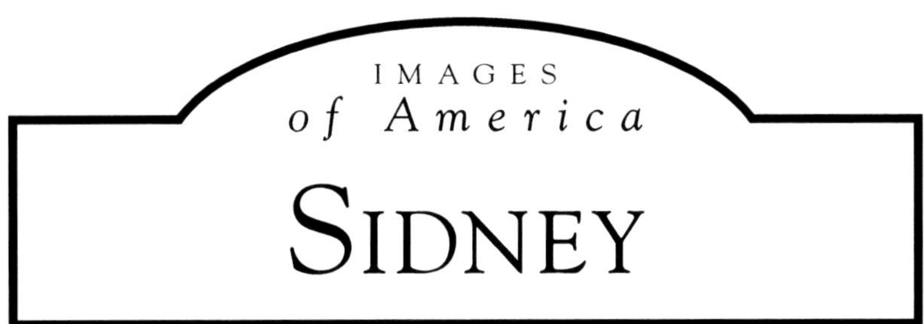

Kim Simmonds, Leann Pelvit,
and the MonDak Heritage Center

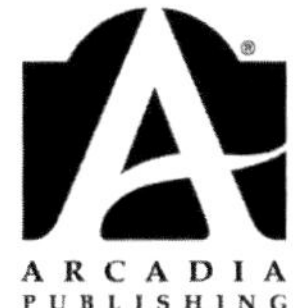

ISBN 978-1-4671-1560-5

Published by Arcadia Publishing
Charleston, South Carolina

Printed in the United States of America

Library of Congress Control Number: 2016936353

For all general information, please contact Arcadia Publishing:
Telephone 843-853-2070
Fax 843-853-0044
E-mail sales@arcadiapublishing.com
For customer service and orders:
Toll-Free 1-888-313-2665

Visit us on the Internet at www.arcadiapublishing.com

This book is dedicated to the pioneers, the homesteaders, the first settlers of Sidney, whose hearty spirit and everlasting determination continues to live on in the community today.

Contents

Acknowledgments

The authors together would like to first and foremost thank the MonDak Historical and Art Society's board of directors for their encouragement and support throughout the process of writing this book. Since the organization was formed in 1967, it has strived to preserve and share the arts, culture, and heritage of the eastern Montana and western North Dakota region. Without its excellent archives and history library, and the work done by countless volunteers and staff, our work and this book would not have been possible.

A special thank-you is also extended to Daneilia Benton and Ramona Raffaell for their work in the MonDak Heritage Center History Library and to Karen Redlin, who offered her editing skills for the project.

Additionally, without prior publications, including *Focus on Our Roots*, *Courage Enough*, *Courage Enough II*, and the *Sidney Herald*, this book would not have been possible. Thank you, to all of the writers and contributors to those publications.

Finally, the authors would like to thank Stacia Bannerman, title manager at Arcadia Publishing, for her support and encouragement throughout the project.

Unless otherwise noted, all images appear courtesy of the MonDak Heritage Center.

INTRODUCTION

This introduction will provide a quick overview of the history of Sidney, Montana. The rest of the book will go a little more in depth into the history, people, and places of the city. Please enjoy the historical photographs and narrative that are presented throughout, and note that even though Sidney has changed in the 140 years or so that people have settled here, the city is still filled with hardworking, friendly people who are willing to do whatever they can to help their neighbors.

In 1978, *Sidney Herald* reporter Ted Scherf wrote, "In terms of time, the history of Sidney is a mere drop in the bucket [compared to] the vast and ancient history associated with the primitive people who once lived here. Sidney's history spans the entire 20th century and part of the 19th, with the town founded in the days of stage coaches and fur traders."

In fact, were it not for Lewis and Clark leading their exploration of the Louisiana Territory through the region in 1805, one can only imagine when the area would have been settled. In their expedition journals, they made notes on the geography, the variety of plant life, and the types of wildlife that were in the area. Trappers from across the growing country read reports of the abundance of furry animals in the region and made their way into what would become northeastern Montana to take advantage of the possible fur trade. In 1828, near the confluence of the Missouri and Yellowstone Rivers, John Jacob Astor's American Fur Company built a trading post that would eventually become known as Fort Union Trading Post.

At least nine area tribes, including the Assiniboine, Plains Cree, Blackfoot, Plains Chippewa, Mandan, Hidatsa, Arikiara, Crow, and Sioux traded furs for goods at Fort Union. Trade business continued until 1867, when the US Army purchased Fort Union from its last owner, the Northwest Fur Company, and dismantled the fort. Salvaged timber was transported three miles down the road to expand Fort Buford, which had been built in 1866. Soon, little was left of Fort Union, and more and more settlements began to pop up in the territory as steamboats made their way up the Missouri River to the MonDak region.

Passage of the 1862 Homestead Act allowed immigrants and even single women to stake a claim on land in the West as long as they were 21 years of age and US citizens. The only requirements for homesteaders was that they had to live on the claim, build a home, make improvements, and farm for at least five years. Once the five years were up, the homesteaders could file for a deed of title for their land. Many of the early settlers took advantage of the act and began to put down roots in the late 1870s. However, most of the homesteaders began to settle south of Sidney because of an excluded settlement clause around Fort Buford that lasted until 1895.

Although people had passed through the future area of Sidney while traveling military roads, most of them kept moving due to increased tribal hostility throughout the Dakota Territory. Two reasons for the increase in hostility include the Sioux Uprising, which took place in 1862, and the Battle of Little Bighorn, which took place in southeastern Montana in 1876.

The first settlers in the area were bachelors. William Cheney came to Sidney in 1877. He earned a living for himself by cutting down wood on the banks of the Yellowstone River and selling it as fuel to passing steamboats that were traveling west.

Also in 1877, Jimmy Crain and Joe "French Joe" Seymore also made their homes in the region. Building a log cabin near Fox Creek (south of present-day Sidney), they made their living as trappers. Over 10 years later, the two trappers sold their log cabin to John O'Brien, who turned the cabin and several outbuildings he added to the property into a stagecoach stop. Travelers could buy supplies, eat a home-cooked meal, or sleep over for the night before heading on their way.

The arrival of families with children increased not only the population but also the need for a school. Annette Meadors taught the first classes in 1885 for six students in her home. Two years later, area residents built a log schoolhouse in order to hold classes in a central location.

Soon after that, in 1888, the settlers petitioned to get their own post office, which became known as the Sidney Post Office. Additionally, businesses began to pop up in the area, and the economy began to flourish. Sidney did not become official, however, until residents requested to become incorporated in 1911. Incorporation as a town was granted on April 21, 1911. The next big step for the town included removing Sidney from Dawson County. In 1914, Richland County was created, and Sidney was made the county seat.

The introduction of the Yellowstone Irrigation Project benefitted homesteaders, farmers, and ranchers, who were able to more easily grow their crops and their livestock, in addition to growing politically and economically. The railroad also made its way into Sidney in 1912, providing transportation for both people and crops. Taking advantage of the newly arrived railroad, larger businesses, including a flour mill and a sugar beet refinery, moved into town, providing jobs for townspeople and profits for farmers.

Electrical power and city water services, established in the 1910s, brought a taste of modernity to the community. A hospital was built in town to better serve residents, and it grew as the community grew. Beginning in 1920, the Richland County Fair brought entertainment and fun to established residents, newcomers, and visitors alike, as did the movies shown at the Princess Theatre on Central Avenue.

Sidney continued to grow steadily over the years. The sugar beet industry grew, and the livestock feed industry grew with it. Farms and ranches were also able to grow rapidly with the ability to irrigate land. The discovery of oil in the Bakken Formation beneath Montana, North Dakota, and Canada took place in 1951, but the technology to extract it easily did not yet exist. The oil created a boom in the late 1970s. As a result, people from around the country flocked to Sidney to seek their fortunes. Unfortunately, a bust did occur in the early 1980s, but the people of Sidney kept pressing on.

Once again, Sidney has continued to flourish, through good times and bad. Farming—especially the cash crop sugar beets—and ranching have provided a swift trade that encompasses many aspects of life in the region. The oil industry has boomed once again, and although processing of the natural resource has slowed down, it is still a large part of the economy. Longtime residents have had to deal with the growing pains of a new set of settlers, who, much like the explorers and homesteaders who made their way to Sidney in the late 1800s, are looking for their pieces of the pie.

One

The Municipality of Sidney

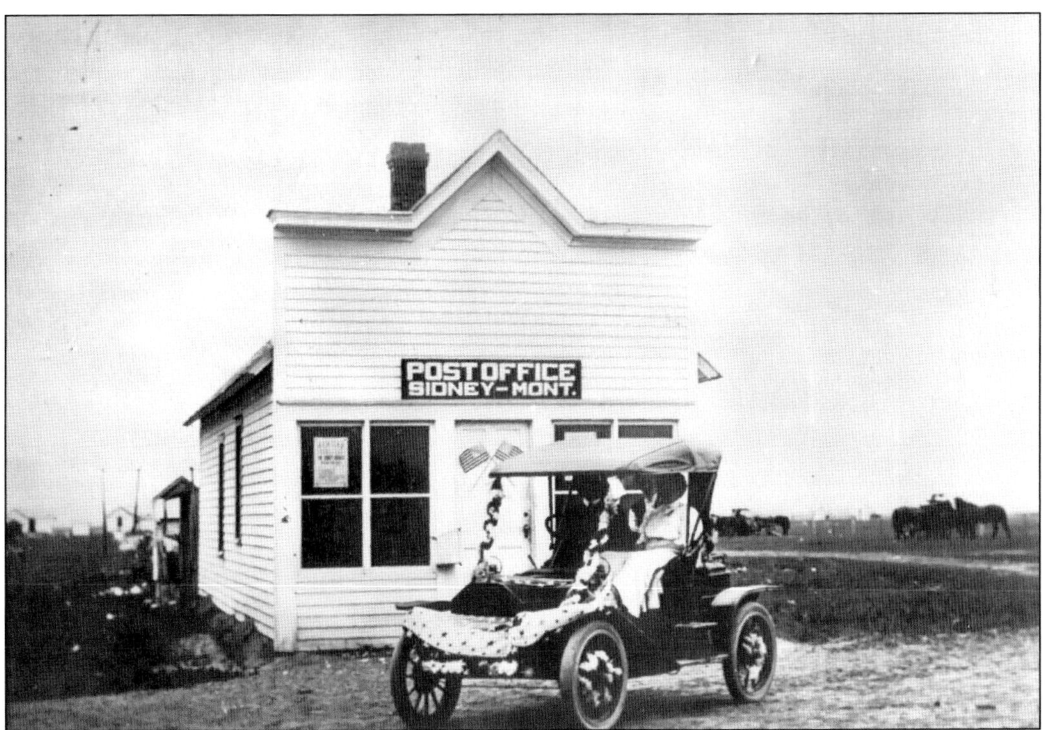

Maggie Crossen was made Sidney's first postmistress on October 22, 1888. Her home also served as the area's first post office. From January 23, 1893, to October 6, 1904, local dentist Charles Stockwell served as postmaster at his home near the corner of North Central Avenue and Holly Street. Edgar Kenoyer took over the position for just over a year, starting on October 6, 1904. The first official post office was built in 1905 by Bert Q. Blake, where he also served as postmaster starting on October 11, 1905. Other early postmasters included Phoebe Kemmis, who served from August 24, 1907, and Orra Kemmis, who took over as postmaster on June 3, 1910. The photograph above shows the frame post office in July 1909. There is a car out front that has been decorated for the Fourth of July parade.

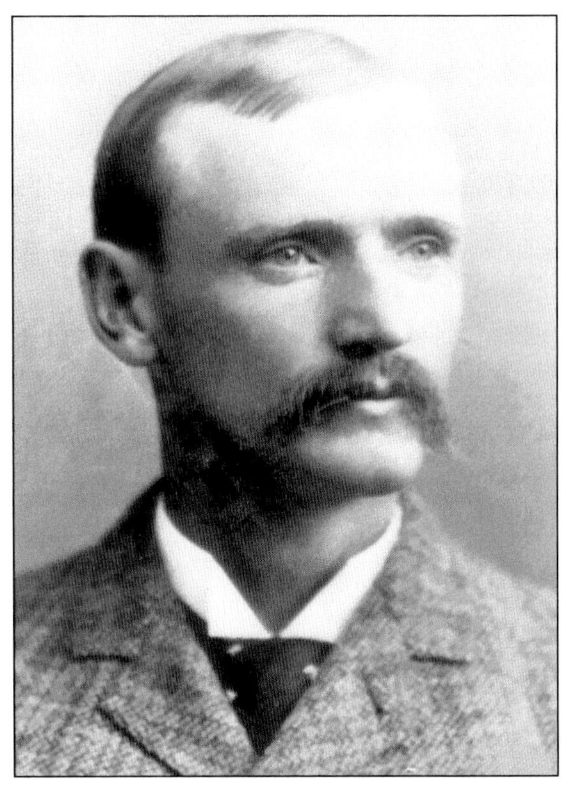

If it were not for the unique friendship of the local judge, Hiram Otis, and a six-year-old boy, Sidney may have been known by another name. Sidney Walters, the son of a family that Otis had in his employ, was well-liked by the judge and went with him nearly everywhere he went. The pair especially loved to go fishing together. When it came time to submit the petition for the first post office to be established in the city in 1888, the community selected the name of Eureka. Citizens were dismayed to find out, however, that Eureka had already been claimed by a city in northwestern Montana. Otis took it upon himself to resubmit the petition with the name Sidney for the post office. The name was approved, and so Sidney was born.

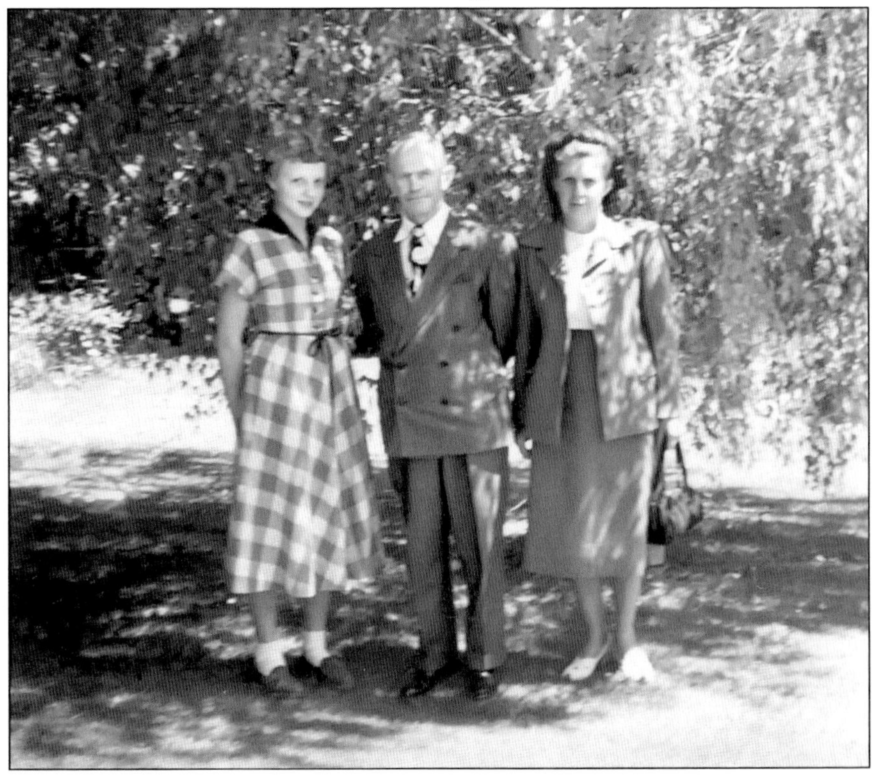

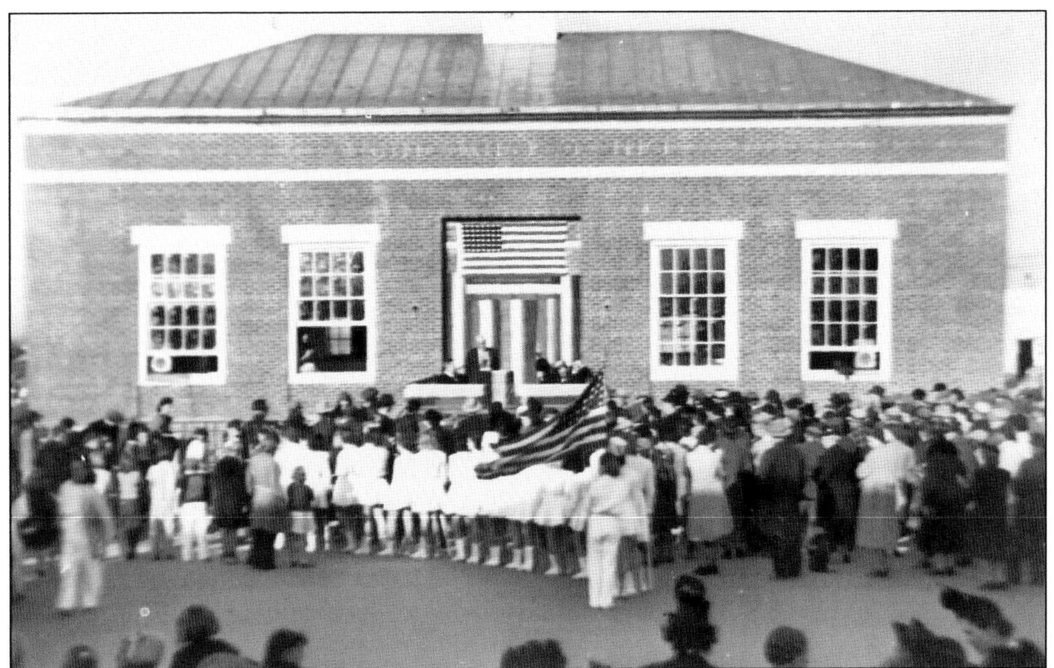

By 1940, the residents of Sidney had started planning for a new, one-story, Colonial-style building to replace the post office on North Central Avenue. The Sidney Post Office was dedicated before a large crowd, including local cheerleaders and a band. Artist J.K. Ralston was commissioned by the Treasury Department's Section of Fine Arts to paint a mural in the new post office, which was finished in 1941. The mural remains on display in the building today, though it no longer serves as a post office. In the 1980s, the building was renamed in memory of Donald G. Nutter, former resident and governor of Montana. The Nutter Building now houses several Richland County offices.

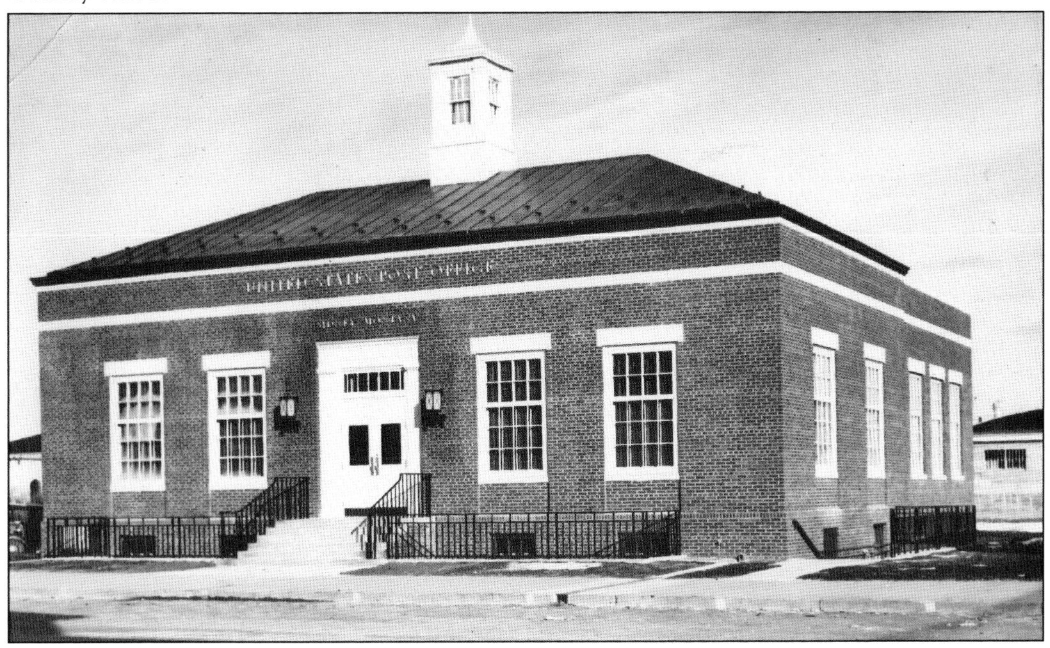

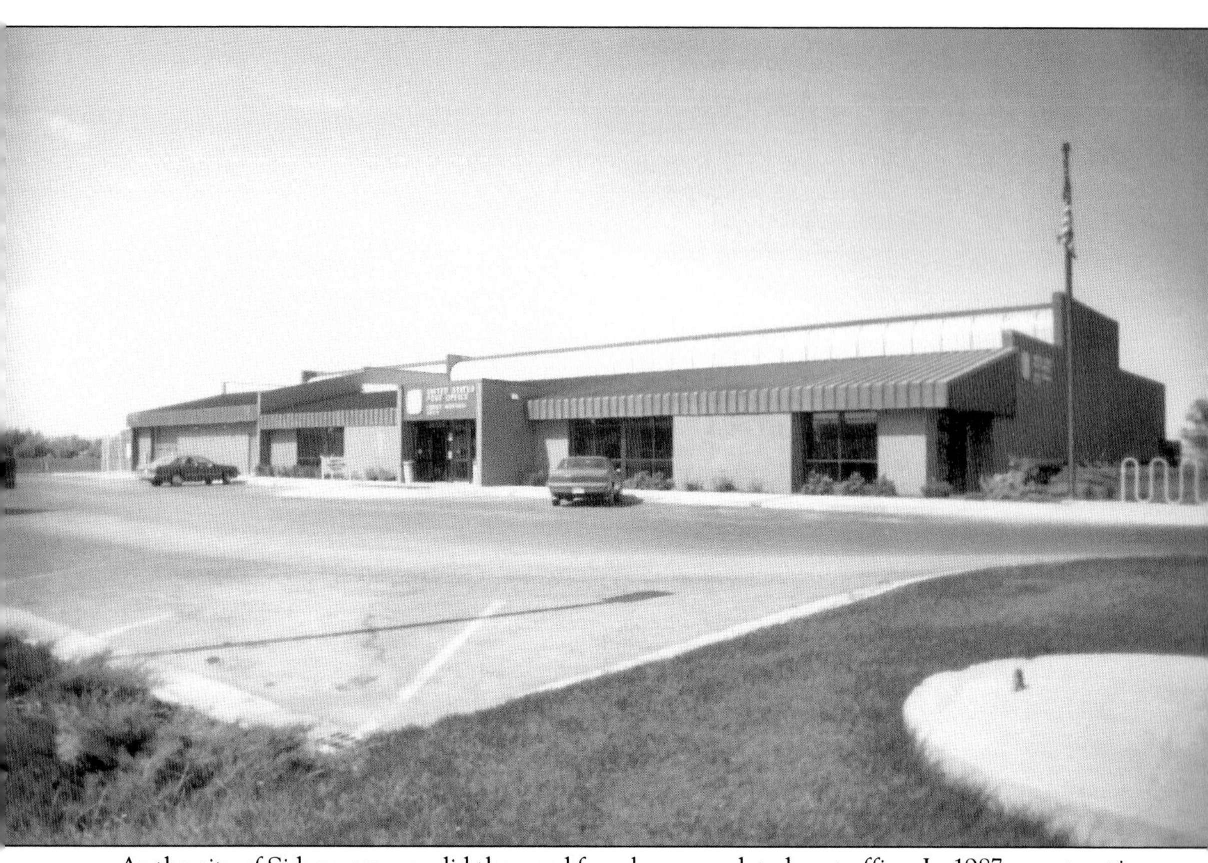

As the city of Sidney grew, so did the need for a larger, updated post office. In 1987, construction began on a brand-new post office at the corner of North Central Avenue and Holly Street on the north side of town. The building sits near the home of local dentist Charles Stockwell, who ran a post office from his house from 1894 to 1901. The new Sidney Post Office cost $1.3 million to build and is the largest post office the town has ever had. The post office built in 1987 is still utilized by the US Postal Service to process mail in Sidney.

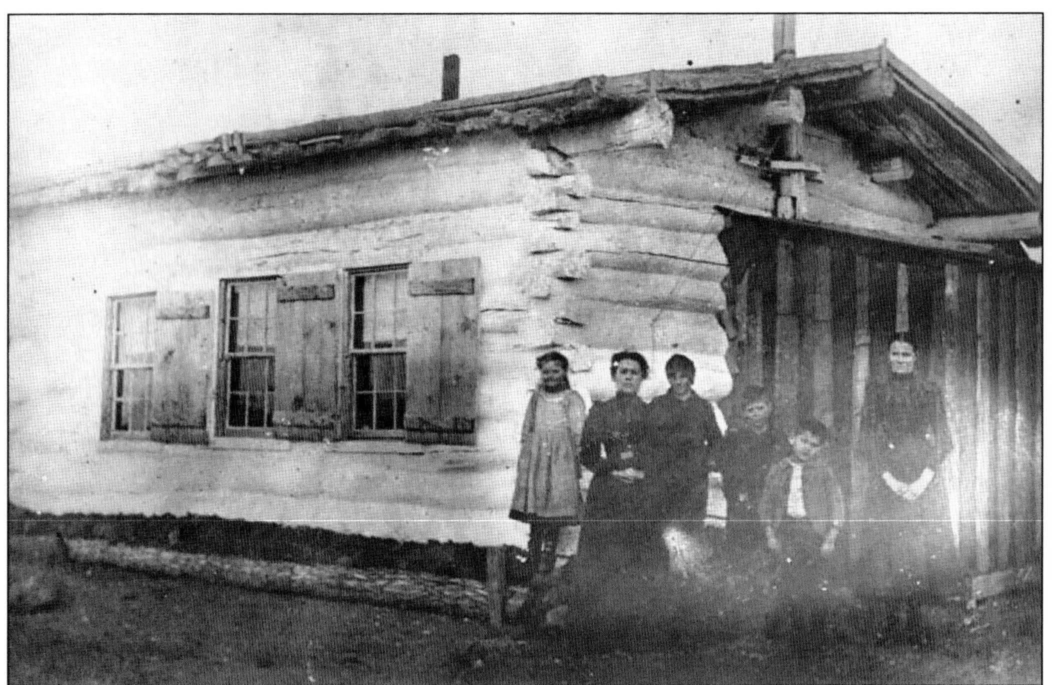

Built in 1887, a log building served as the first school in Sidney. By 1898, the school had grown to more than 14 students attending regular classes, and the townspeople decided it was time to construct a larger school. In 1902, a new school building was approved, and in 1903, the first frame school was completed with room to accommodate the growing population of students in Sidney and to allow for continued growth in the future. Posing outside the school are, from left to right, Nancy Stanhope, schoolteacher Alice Dyas, Lester Stanhope, Leonard Stanhope, Lawrence Smith, and Phoebe Kemmis.

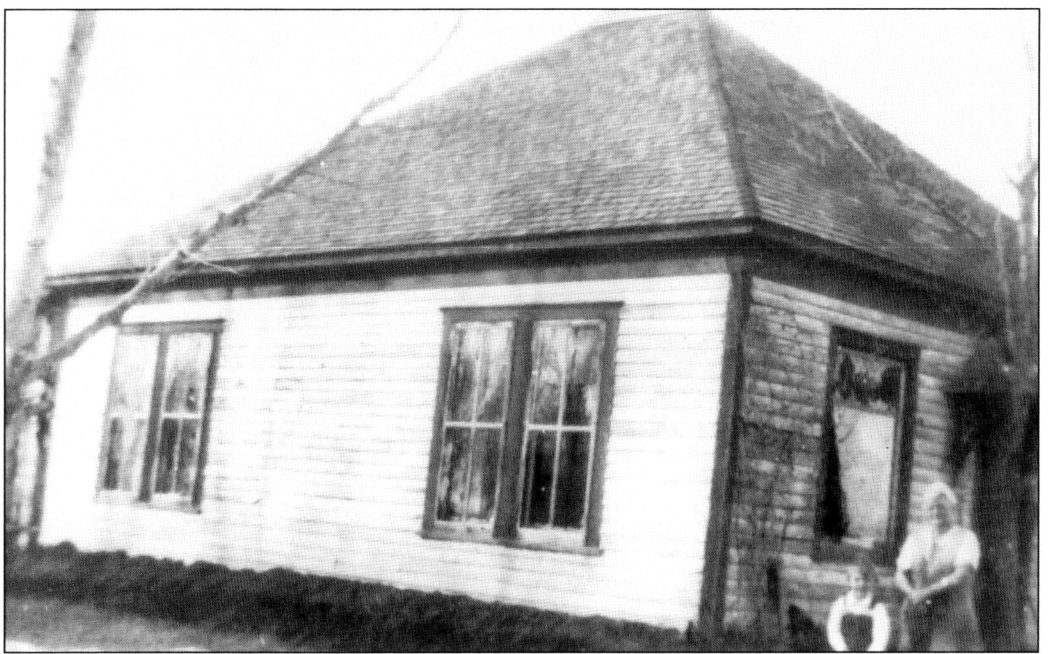

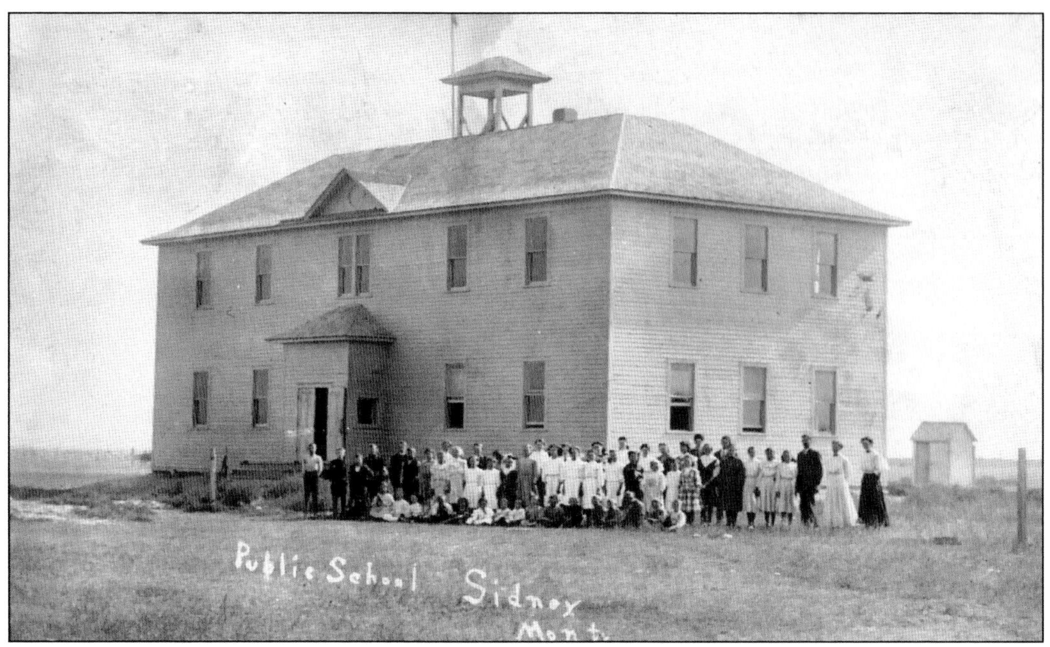

With planners having underestimated how fast the population of Sidney would grow, a new school was needed by 1908 to house all of the students. The school, which cost $4,000 to construct, was a two-story structure fitting the growing community. Unfortunately, four years later, on December 5, 1912, the school caught fire early in the morning. The townspeople, helpless without a fire department, formed a volunteer bucket brigade to no avail. The building was a total loss. Luckily, though, the school had been insured for $3,000 and its contents for $500, so the financial loss was minimal. The fire was also a wake-up call for the townspeople to take the time to form emergency services for the burgeoning community.

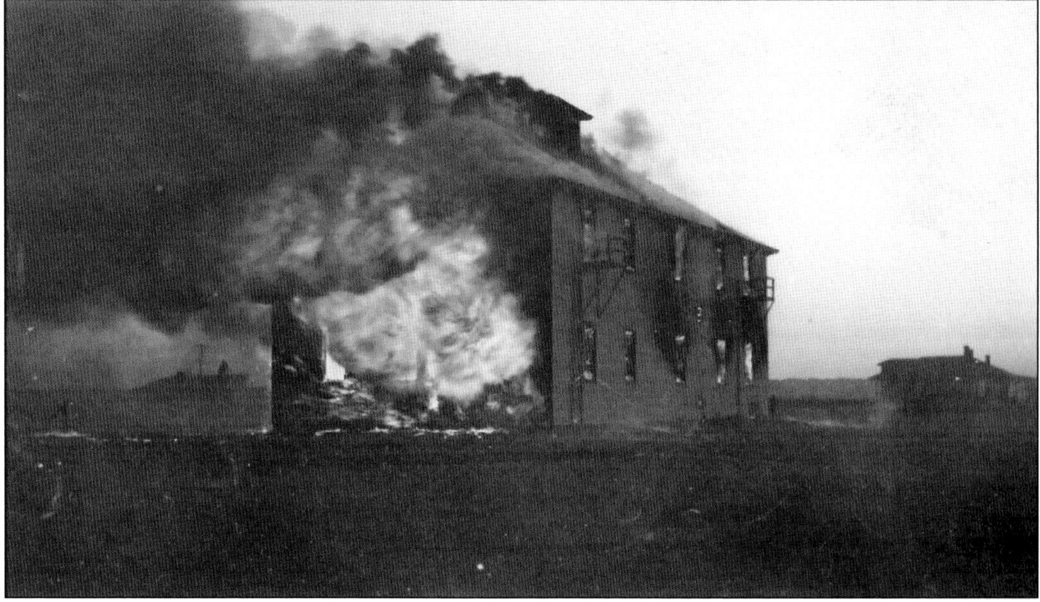

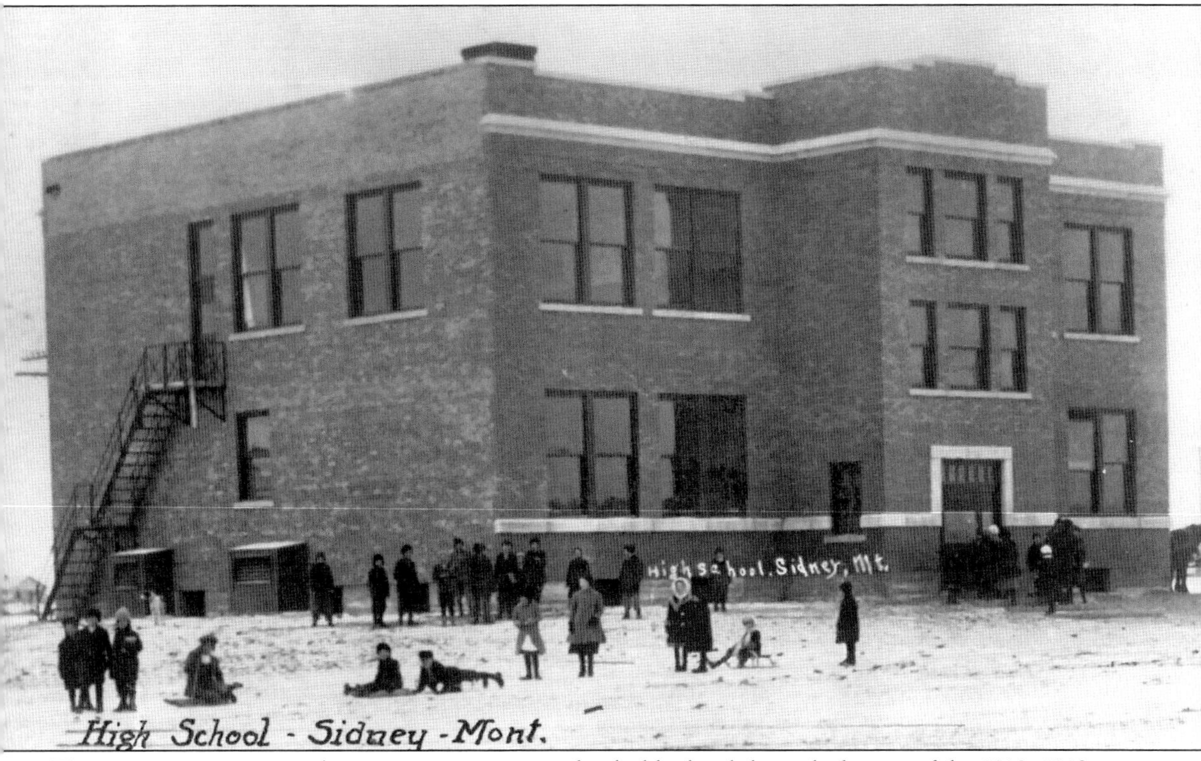

Temporary rooms across the community were used to hold school through the rest of the 1912–1913 school year, including the basements of churches and the Odd Fellows hall. Just before the start of the 1913–1914 school year, a temporary structure was built over one weekend to contain all of the students in one place until the new school building could be erected for the 1914–1915 school year. A contract was awarded to Bismarck Construction Company in June 1914 to build a 13-room school, featuring playrooms, classrooms, a library, and an auditorium. The plans included the use of two different kinds of brick, and additional wings could be added on as the need arose. With the promise of being modern in every detail, the school also had steam heat and electric lighting; it cost $22,500 when it was completed and furnished. Two years to the day after the old Sidney School burned down, the new school opened for class.

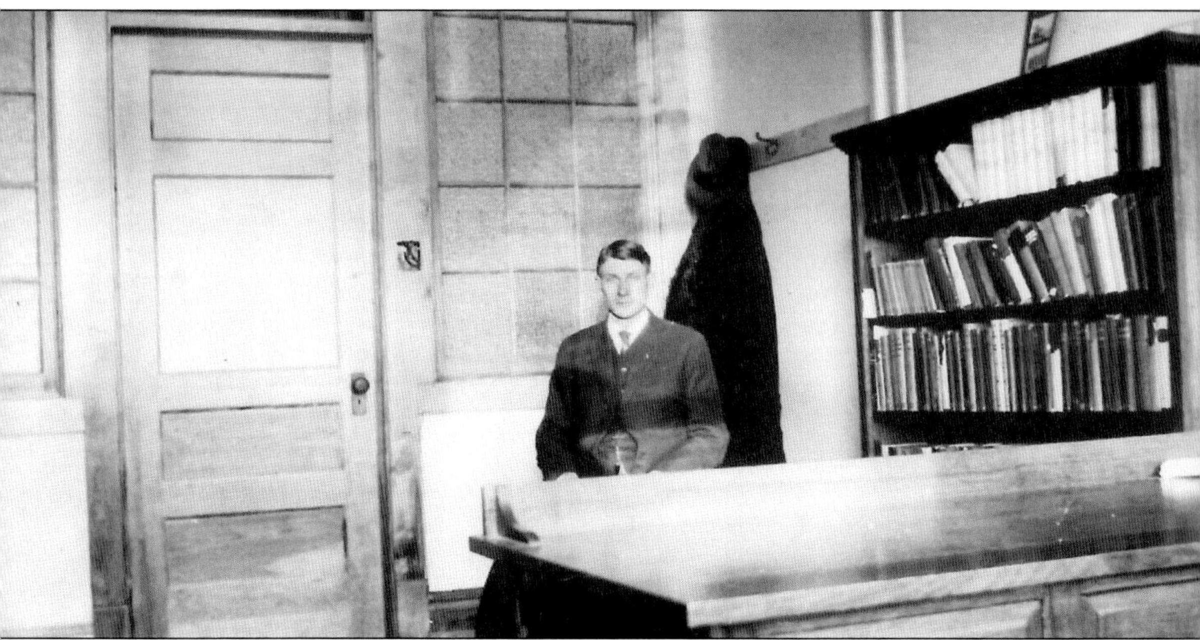

Due to the rising ages of children attending school in Sidney, Joseph Nevins founded the Sidney High School in 1910. Nevins served as the only high school teacher at that time, with just five students the first year. In addition to teaching all of the high school classes, he also taught all of the eighth-grade classes, as well as seventh-grade arithmetic and history. That was also the first year that the Sidney High School had an annual yearbook, called *The Crocus*. After the 1912 fire destroyed the public school that was built in 1908, Nevins was made the superintendent of Sidney Public Schools, but he still continued teaching agriculture. In this picture, Nevins is shown sitting in the school office. He served continuously as the superintendent of schools until his death in 1924.

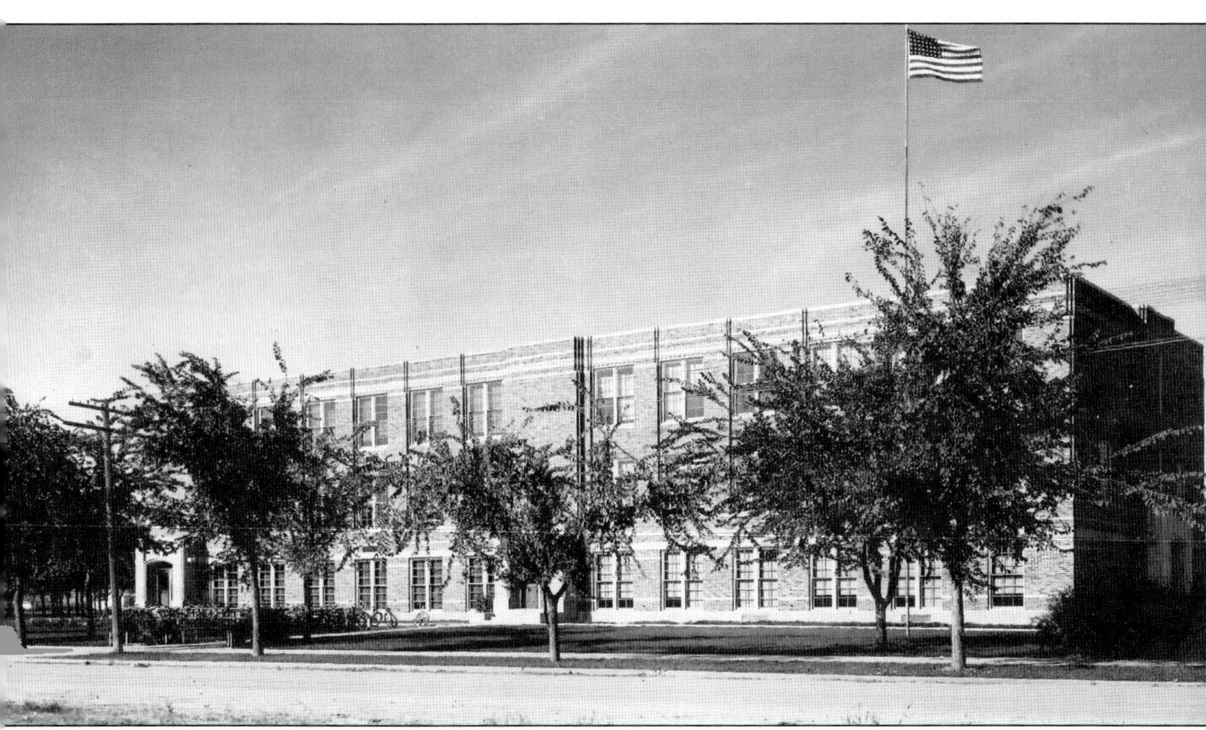

Over the years, additional wings were added on to the school to accommodate more students as Sidney grew. The north and south ends of the school were extended in each direction, just as the contractors and school officials had planned when it was built in 1914. By 1961, the school had become too crowded, so a separate high school for grades 10, 11, and 12 was built. The school built in 1912 then became known as the junior high. In 1983, the ninth grade also moved over to the high school, and the junior high became known as the middle school, as it is today. Two additional schools have also been built in Sidney to serve as elementary schools. The first school is known as the Central School and is located on Third Avenue SE. It houses the kindergarten classes as well as fourth and fifth grade. The second school is West Side Elementary, which is located at Fifth Street SW. It houses grades one through three, as well as preschool classes.

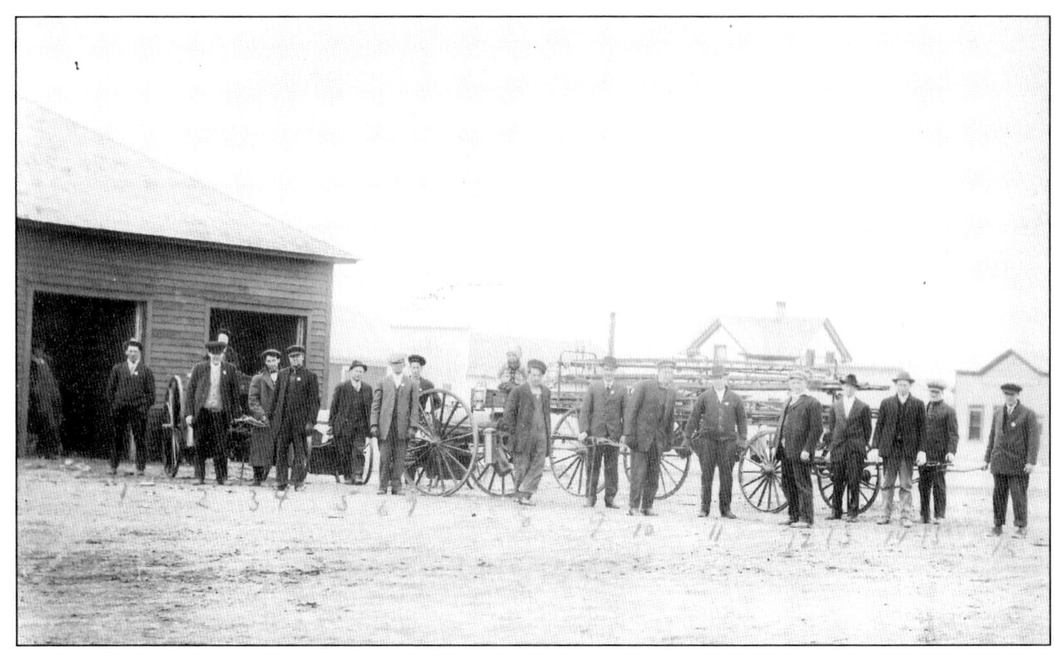

Just over a month after the school burned to the ground in 1912, the townspeople of Sidney were concerned about their ability to protect their homes from fire. A volunteer fire department was formed on January 24, 1913. There were 17 charter members. It was nearly a year before the members had a chance to test their efficiency and skill. On December 28, 1913, a fire started in the Richland Hotel basement at 4:00 in the morning. With the help of the fire department, everyone who had been in the hotel escaped without injury. Unfortunately, however, the hotel itself was a complete loss.

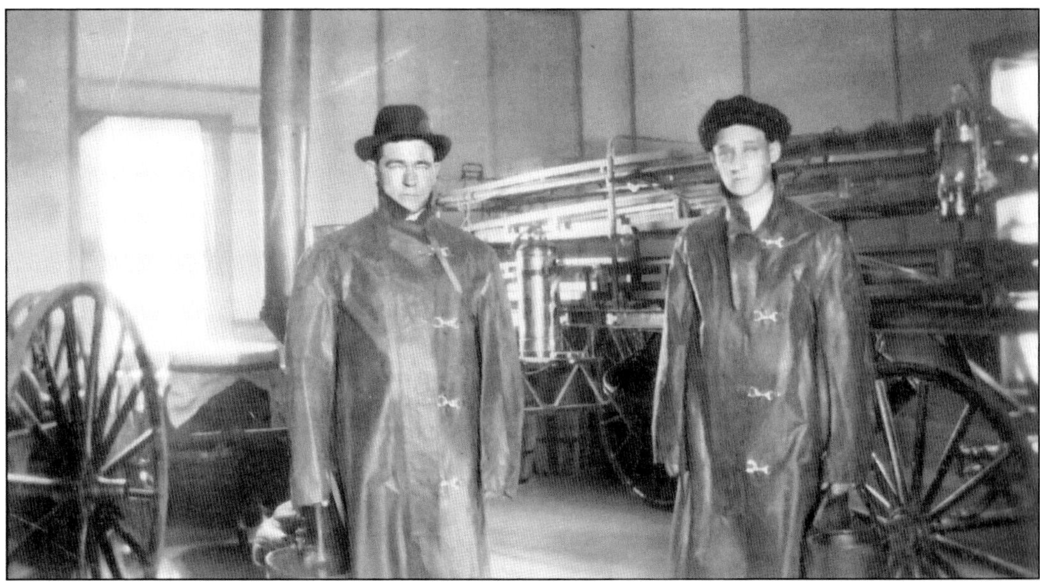

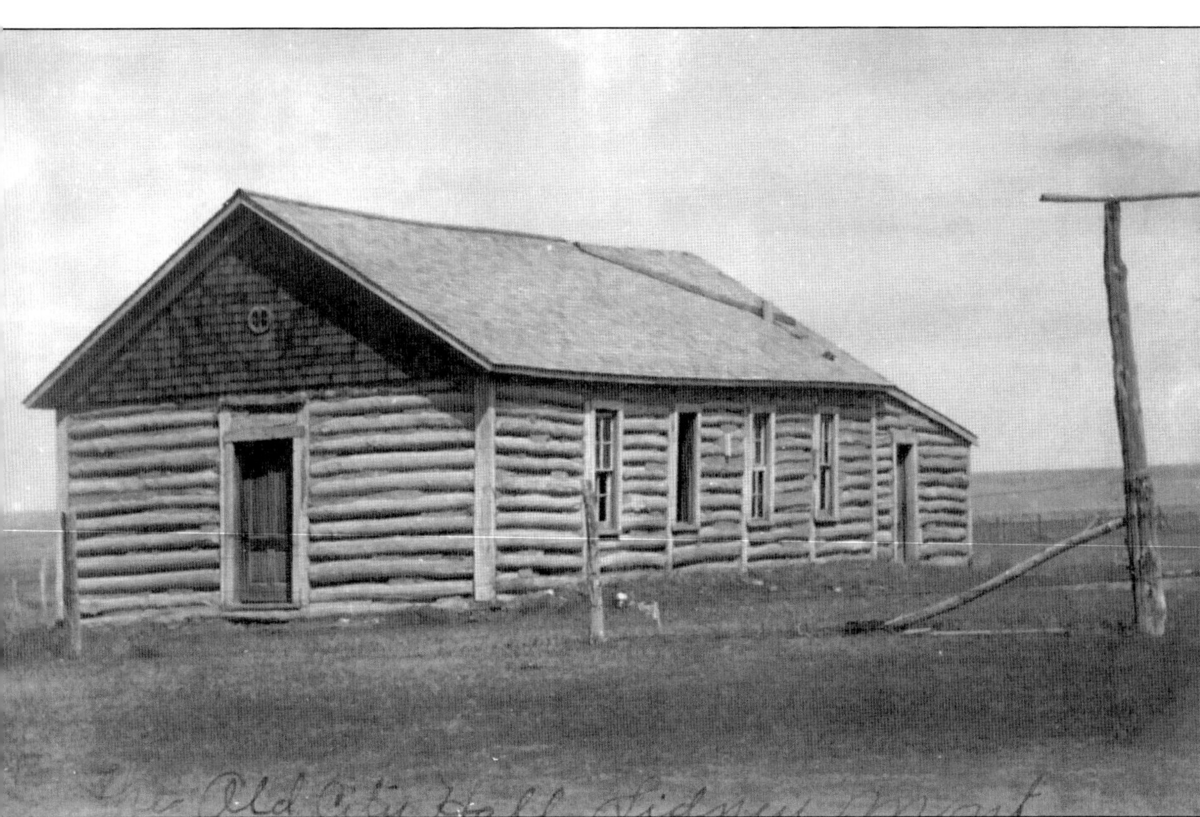

On January 27, 1911, a number of citizens met to discuss improving public services, including equipment purchases and city water. One citizen suggested that the city become incorporated so that it could provide better services to the community. A minimum of 50 signatures had to be obtained, and a census listing at least 300 residents had to be taken before a petition could be submitted to the Dawson County Commissioners for approval. Once the census was taken and the signatures were gathered, the commissioners approved the petition, pending a vote by the citizens of Sidney. On April 21, 1911, with a vote of 55 for and 1 against, the incorporation of Sidney was approved. In June 1911, local government was also approved, with Thomas Gardner voted in as the city's first mayor. Sidney's first city hall was located in a log building that also served as the Odd Fellows hall.

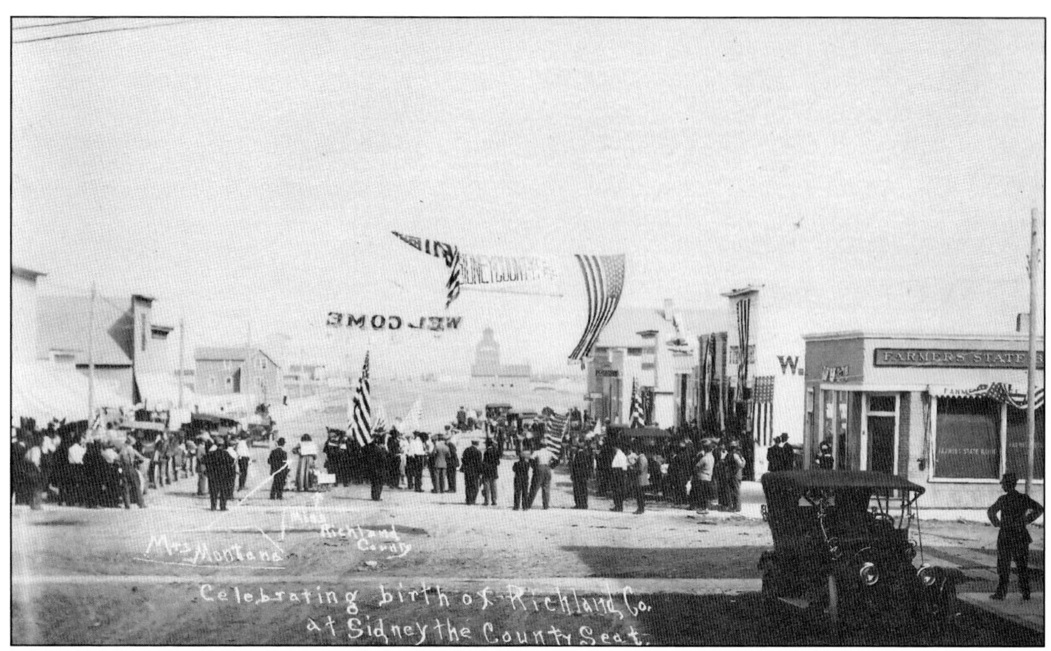

Now that Sidney was incorporated, it could take on its next challenge: becoming county seat. Sidney was originally part of Dawson County, whose county seat was in Glendive, about 50 miles south of the thriving Sidney. Dawson County had become very large, and there were worries about it being able to support itself. Many townsfolk were concerned about their tax money staying and helping their community, so after much deliberation and many meetings, Richland County was officially formed on May 16, 1914. At the same time, Sidney was named county seat. The townspeople, elated at the news, gathered to celebrate the birth of Richland County. (Below, courtesy of the *Sidney Herald*.)

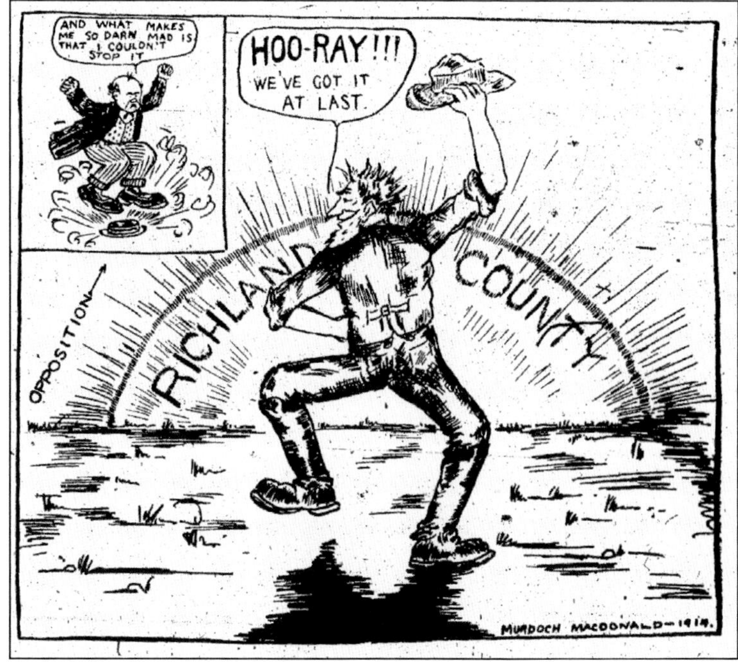

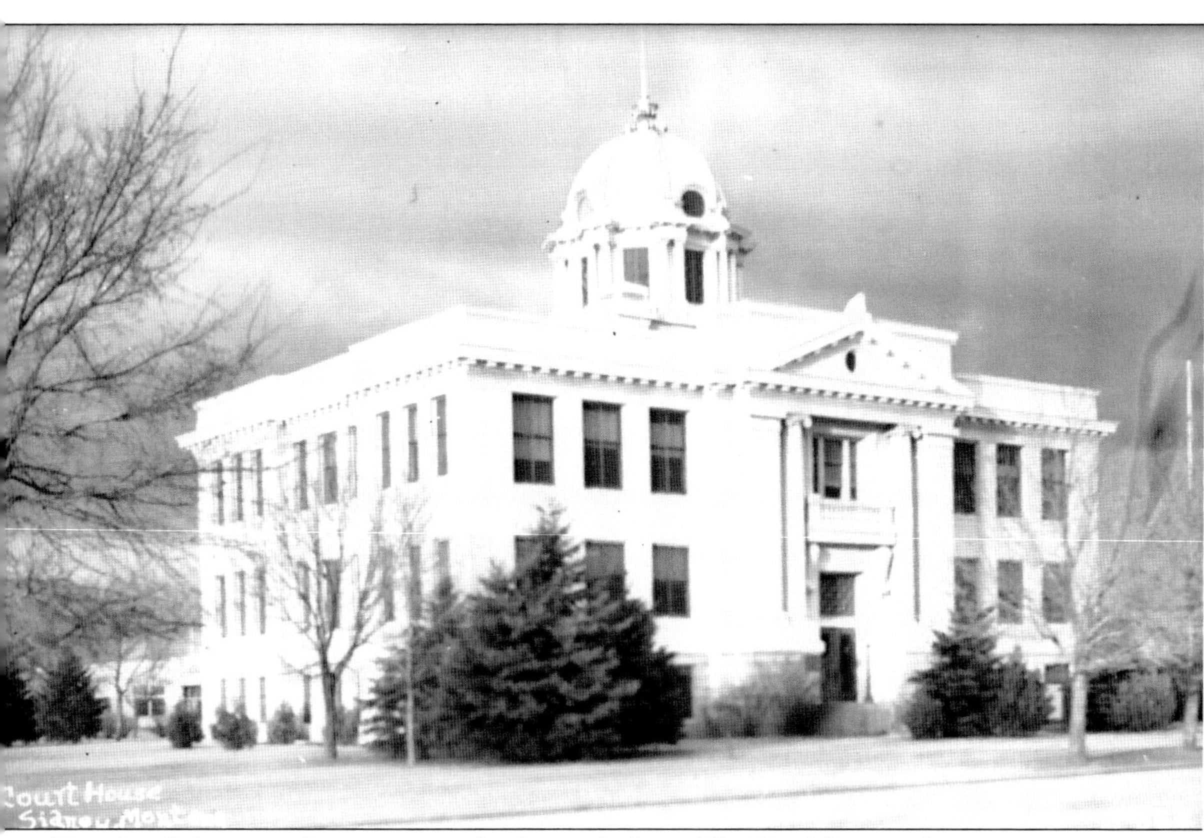

Now that Sidney was the county seat for the newly formed Richland County, the government needed a place to have its offices. Valley Mercantile and Lumber Company had recently been vacated, so the county leased the building and set up shop. By 1916, the small building was overflowing with the various county offices. The county commissioners asked the people of Richland County for a courthouse, which was staunchly opposed with a vote of 380 for, 1,339 against. In 1919, the commissioners tried again to get the funding approved for a new courthouse and were once again refused. Thinking it would never receive funding for a new building, the county purchased its leased building and began to make repairs and additions to it, including running water and a furnace for heat. Finally, in 1926, the citizens of Richland County took pity on their representatives and voted for a $85,000 bond for a new courthouse. Pictured here, it officially opened on May 4, 1928.

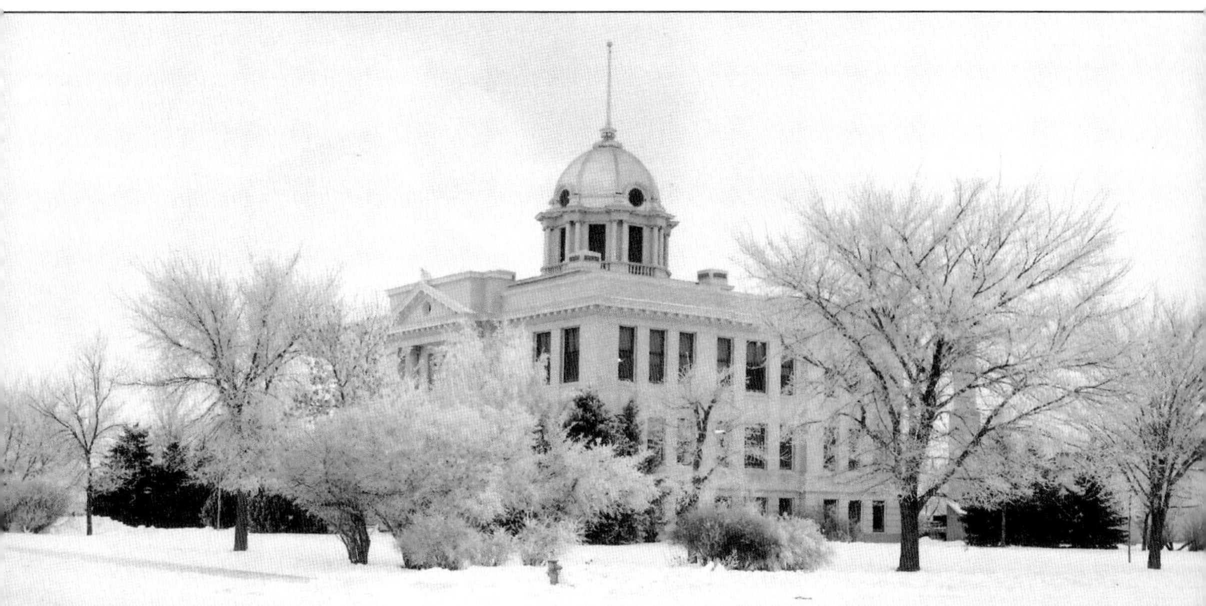

In this photograph taken by Osborn Studios in Sidney, the Richland County Courthouse is surrounded by freshly fallen snow on December 14, 1948. Built in the Neoclassical style, the courthouse certainly stands out compared to other buildings in Sidney. Just like the buildings used by the county for its original offices, the courthouse building became too small as both Sidney and the county grew. There are now several buildings around town that serve as county offices, including the Nutter Building, the Community Services Building, and the Law and Justice Center. The Richland County Courthouse, however, is still in use today, and county residents can visit the beautiful building to research the history of their home, purchase automobile license plates, procure a Montana driver's license or pay their property taxes, among other services. In 2013 and 2014, updates were made to the courthouse, just in time to celebrate the county centennial.

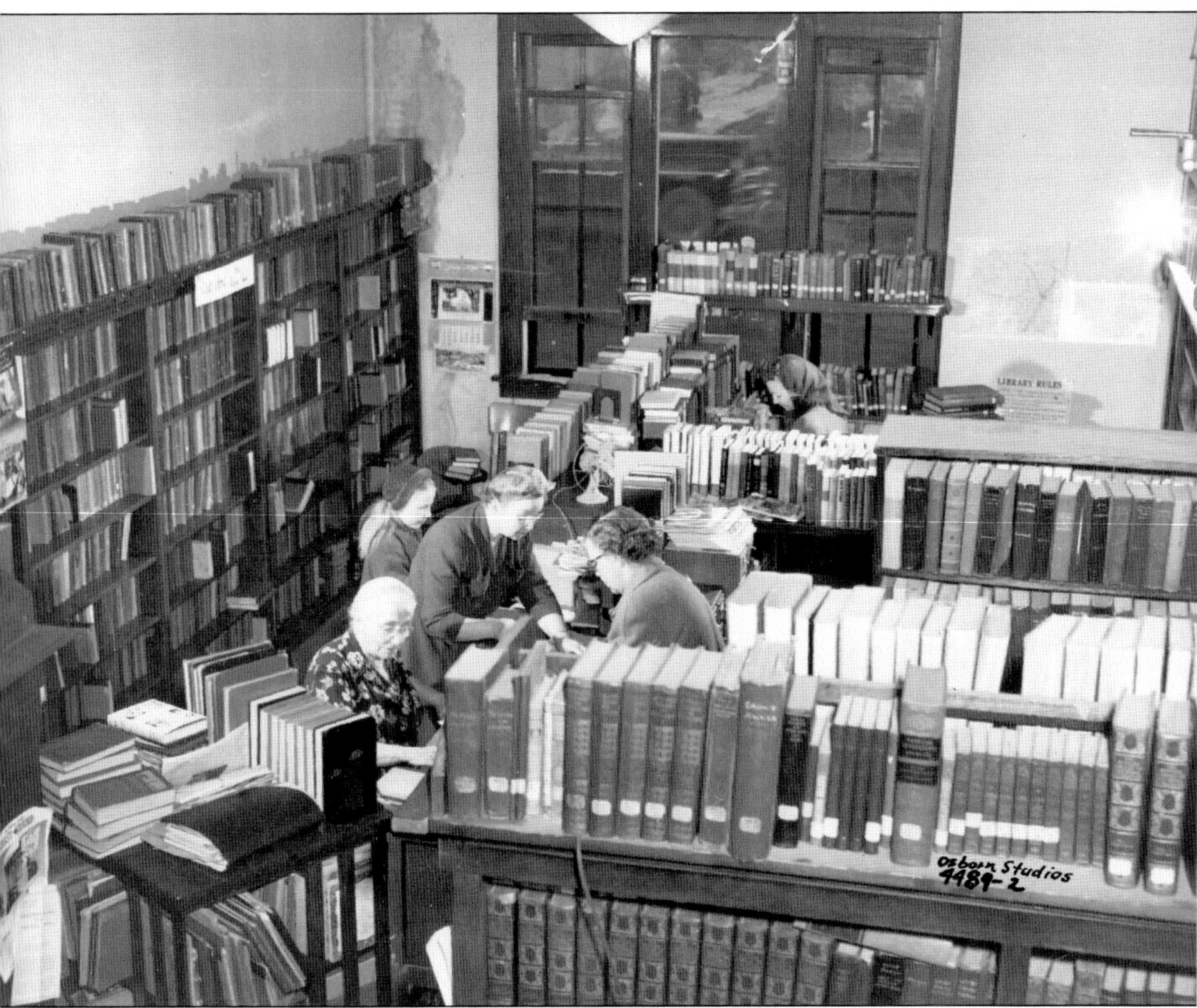

Beginning in 1914, the Sidney Women's Club had run a library for the community. Prior to that, the Methodist church and Turner Drug both had small libraries. None of them was able to accommodate the needs of the growing population. In 1918, the Women's Club asked the city council to take over the operation of the library, and on June 6, 1919, the council approved the club's request. In addition to the creation of a free public library, the city council also set aside funds for its maintenance and created a board of directors to manage it. Initially, the library was housed in an annex of the Richland National Bank, and then it was moved to a private home just west of the courthouse.

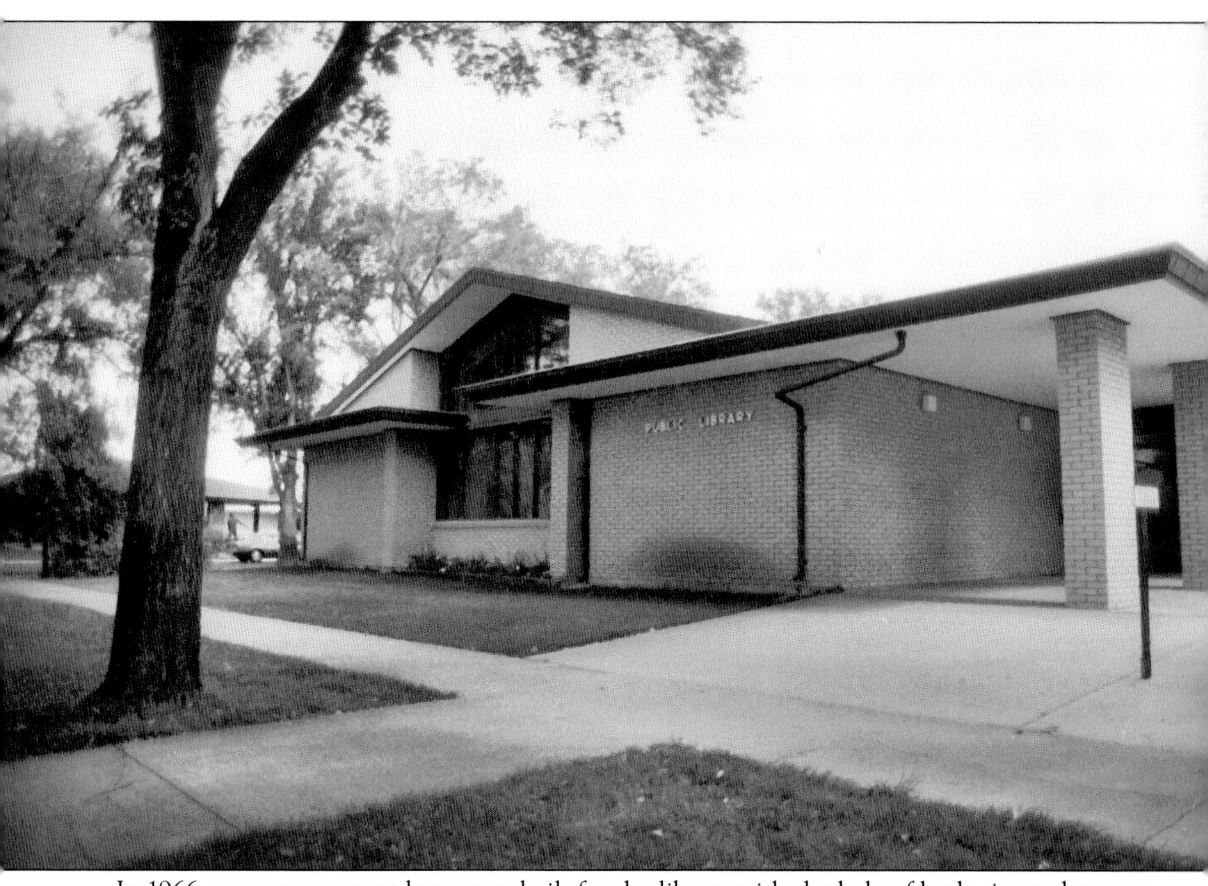

In 1966, a new permanent home was built for the library with the help of both city and county funds. Though the library building itself was new, it was built over an existing bomb shelter. The library also housed civil defense rooms, a meeting room, and several offices. In 1985, the library worked with the county, as well as with the Montana State Library, to apply for a Library Services and Construction Act building grant for $61,000. The grant was approved, and Richland County matched funds to build an addition to the structure that now serves as the front entry to the building. The library is still open to the public today, though the bomb shelter in the basement is no longer used due to the inability to make the area compliant with the Americans with Disabilities Act.

WATER SUPPLY TOWER, SIDNEY, MONTANA B-863

In addition to a new volunteer fire department, city waterworks plans were implemented. In 1916, trenches were dug around town in order to install mains with which water could be diverted directly to homes and business in Sidney. A system for sewage was installed at the same time, as was a street sprinkler, which cut down on the amount of dust created by traffic in town. The total cost of the upgrades came to $35,000. A water tower was built later in the northeast part of the city and still holds a clean supply of water for the town.

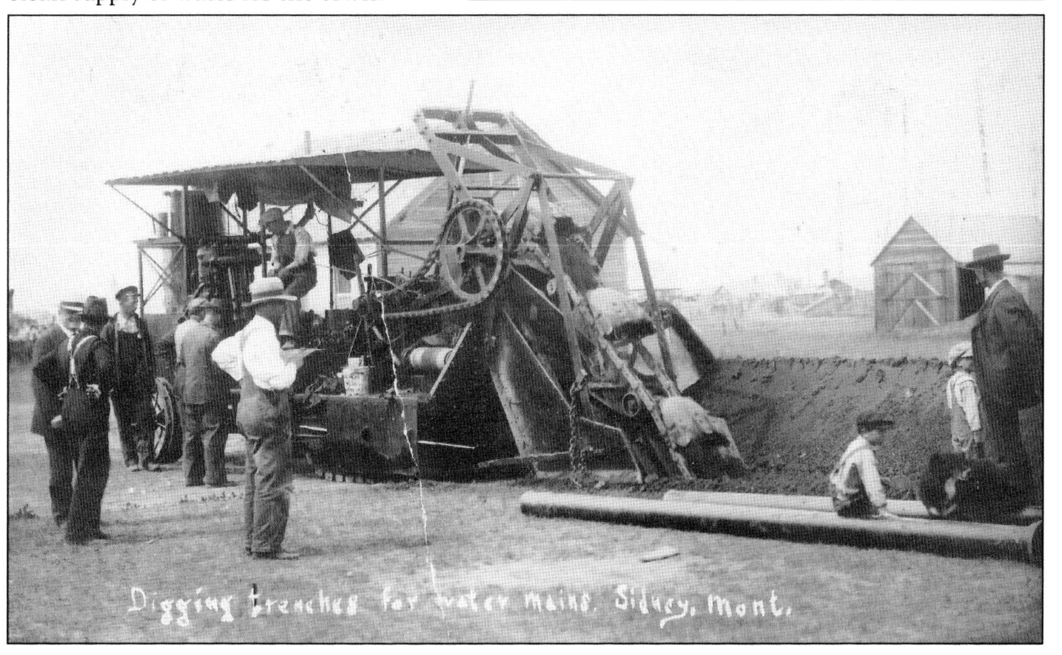

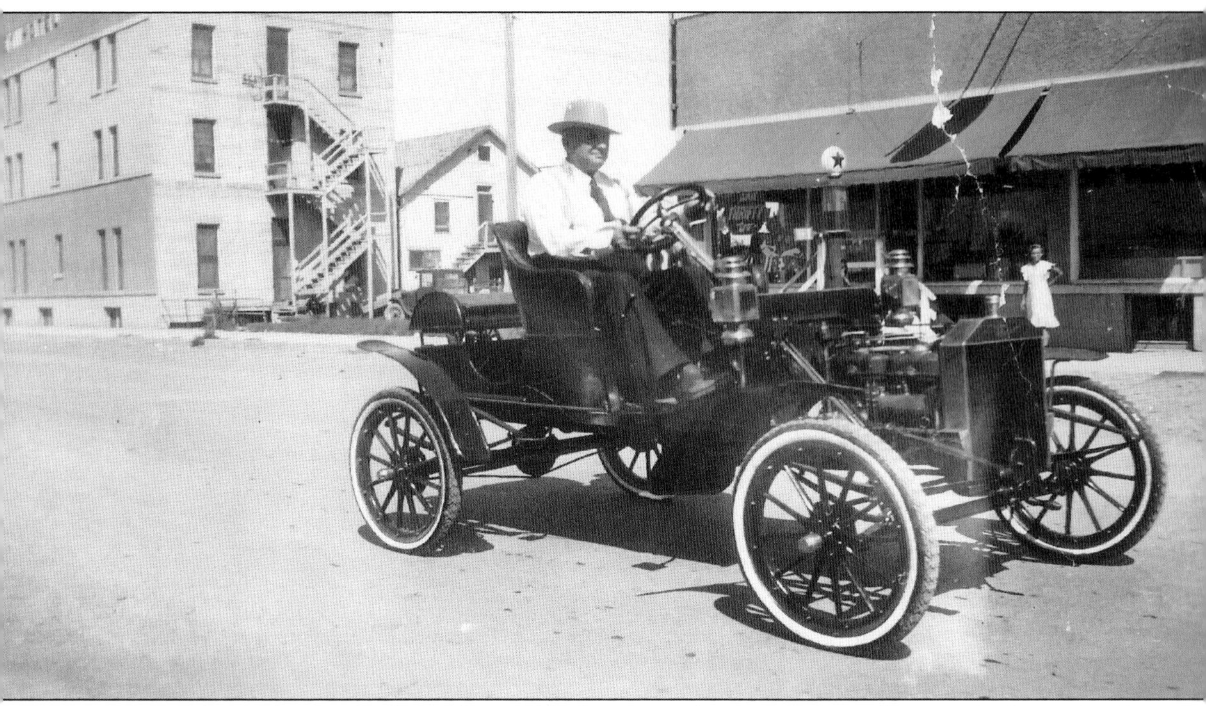

Having law enforcement the public could rely on was also important to the city. On June 11, 1911, just a few months after the town was incorporated, Jack Carberry was appointed the first city marshal of Sidney. Unfortunately, just a few months later, Carberry died of typhoid fever, and he was replaced by Roy Heiner. Once the city of Sidney was incorporated, Fred Hurst was appointed the first chief of police. Chief Hurst began his career in 1912 as deputy marshal, and he served in his position as chief of police for 26 years, from 1915 to 1941, while also serving as the chief of the fire department, street commissioner, garbage commissioner, and welfare commissioner. This photograph shows Chief Hurst in 1936 driving the first police car, a 1906 Ford Model N. On June 17, 1941, while on duty as chief of police during a bad storm, Hurst had a heart attack and died.

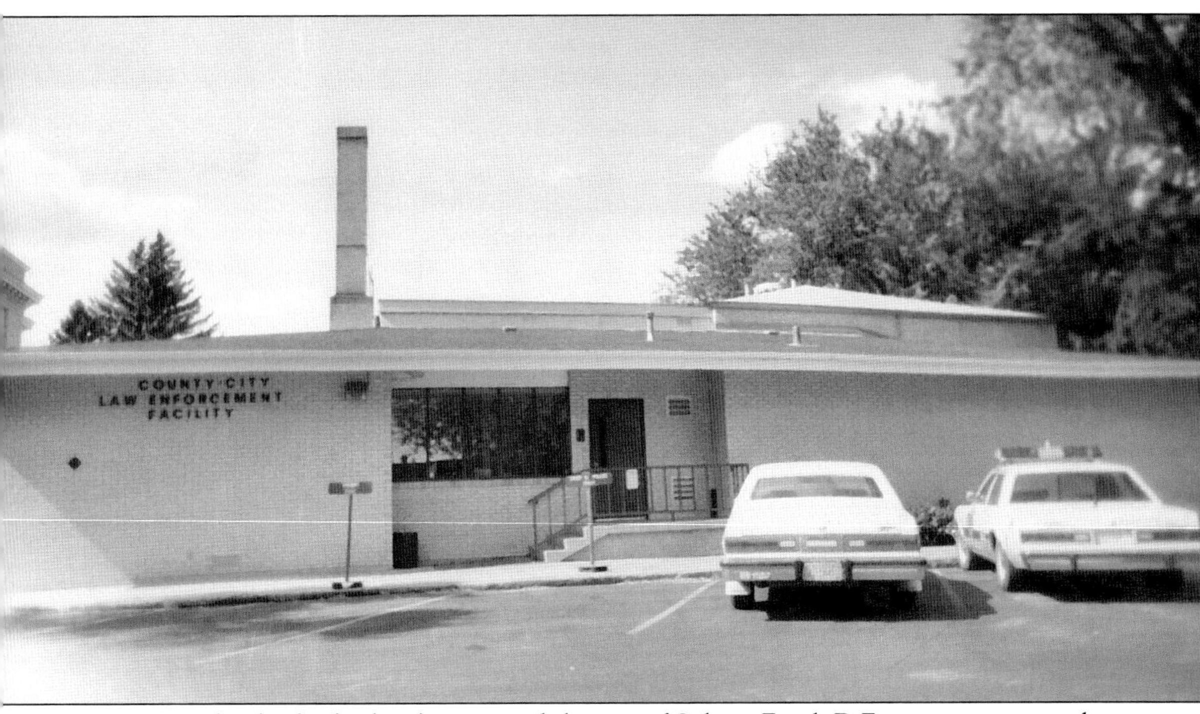

Since 1941, eight chiefs of police have served the city of Sidney. Frank DiFonzo was appointed chief of police in 1981 and continues to serve the citizens of Sidney today. The City of Sidney and Richland County both have jurisdiction in the city. Initially, they shared a small law enforcement facility just north of the county courthouse. As the population of Sidney grew, it became necessary to build a new law enforcement building. The Law and Justice Center was built in 2010, and both the Sidney Police Department and the Richland County Sheriff's Office moved in. The old law enforcement facility sat unused before it was torn down in 2014.

Three Big Da

RICHLAND CO

SIDNEY

SEPTEMBE

Something Doing All The Time

Come to your first annual county fair and help make it the biggest, best and most successful fair in eastern Montana. Help Richland County prove that it is the best Agricultural county in the state by taking a part in this Fair and making exhibits in accordance with the premium lists. Remember---the best exhibits will be sent to the Billings and Helena Fairs.

Come and See Animal Circus at the Grounds

Illu

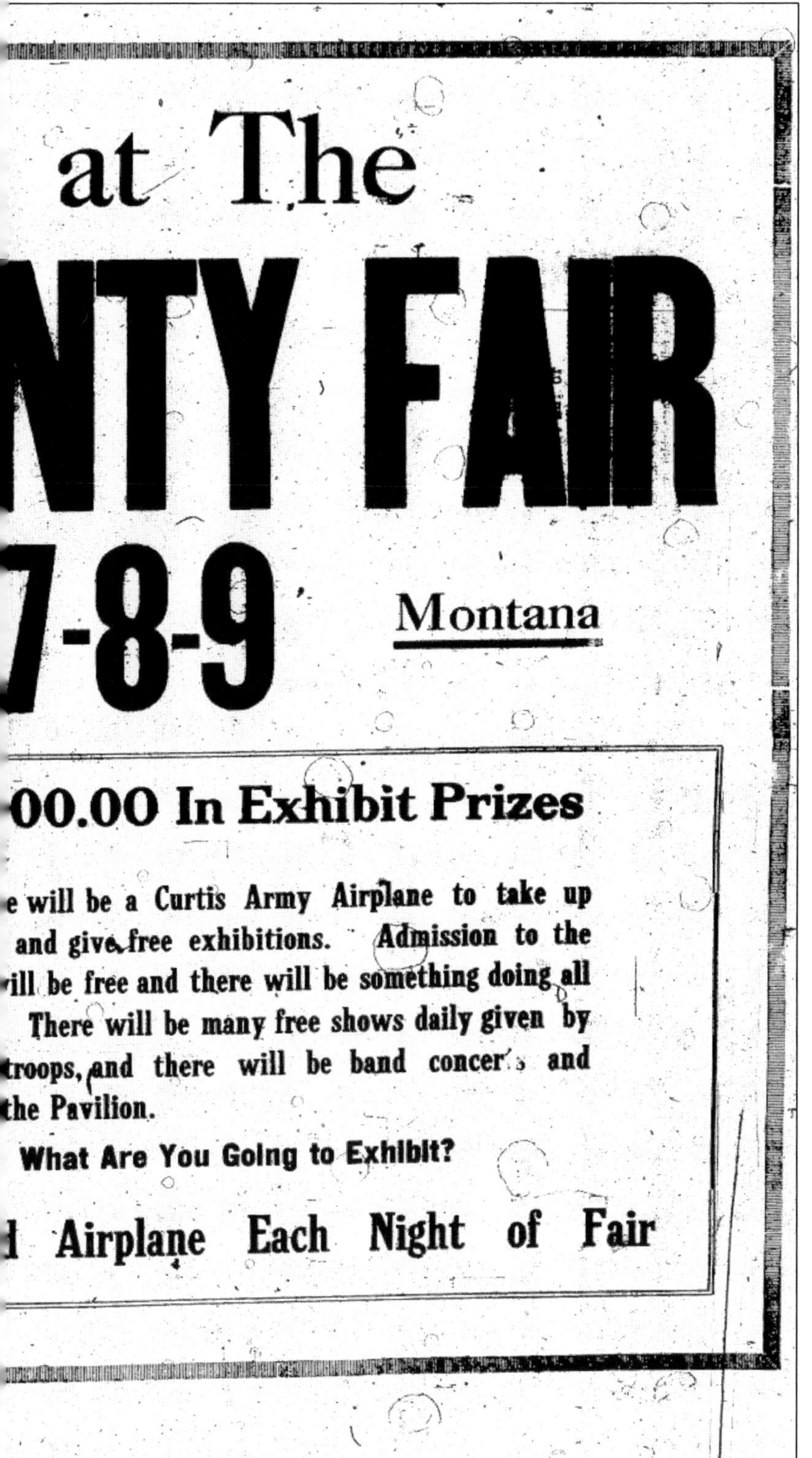
at The
NTY FAIR
7-8-9 Montana
00.00 In Exhibit Prizes
e will be a Curtis Army Airplane to take up
and give free exhibitions. Admission to the
ill be free and there will be something doing all
There will be many free shows daily given by
troops, and there will be band concerts and
the Pavilion.
What Are You Going to Exhibit?
l Airplane Each Night of Fair

Although street fairs had been held in Sidney, and even the Dawson County Fair, Richland County had never held a county fair in Sidney. In February 1920, the Richland County Fair Association started planning a fair to take place in the summer of that year. The event was advertised in the *Sidney Herald* the week before with a full-page ad that reads, "Come to your first annual county fair and help make the biggest, best and most successful fair in eastern Montana." The first fair was considered a great success, except for one minor snafu: the crash of a small plane. The pilot, who was flying the illuminated plane during a night landing, was unable to gain control of the plane after the engine misfired. About 400 yards from the landing field, the plane crashed and then burned, but left the pilot completely uninjured. (Courtesy of the *Sidney Herald*.)

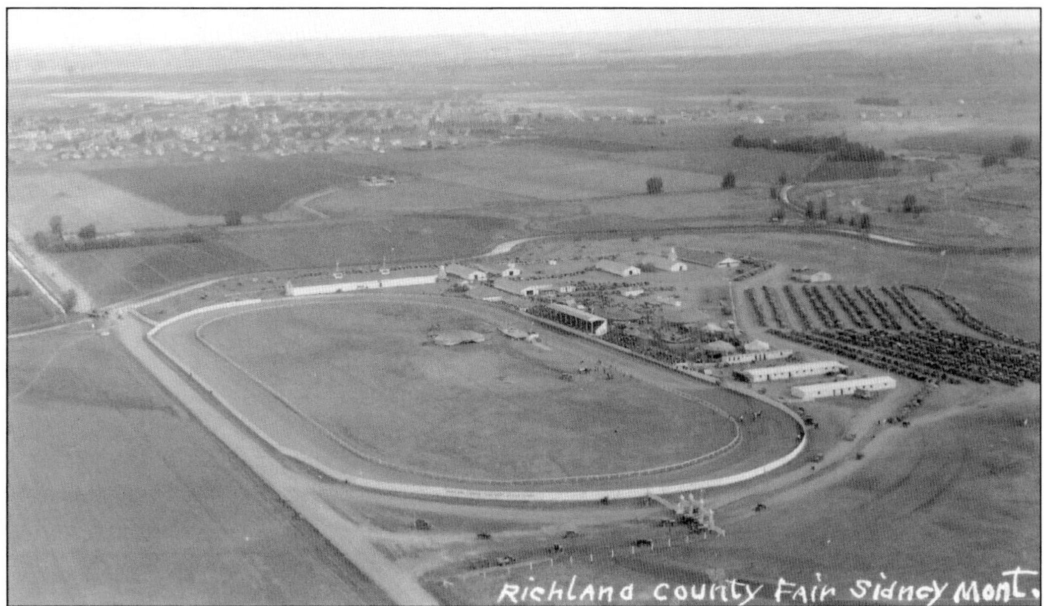

For two years during the Great Depression, in 1933 and 1934, the Richland County Fair in Sidney was put on hold. Fortunately, as the country was beginning to recover from the effects of the economic downturn, improvements were made to the fairgrounds, including adding buildings. Larger premiums were offered, which encouraged more communities to send exhibits in for judging. The fair was again cancelled for two years in 1943 and 1944 during the Second World War so that the townspeople could conserve resources for the war effort instead. The fair came back, however, bigger and better than ever before, and has not missed a year since.

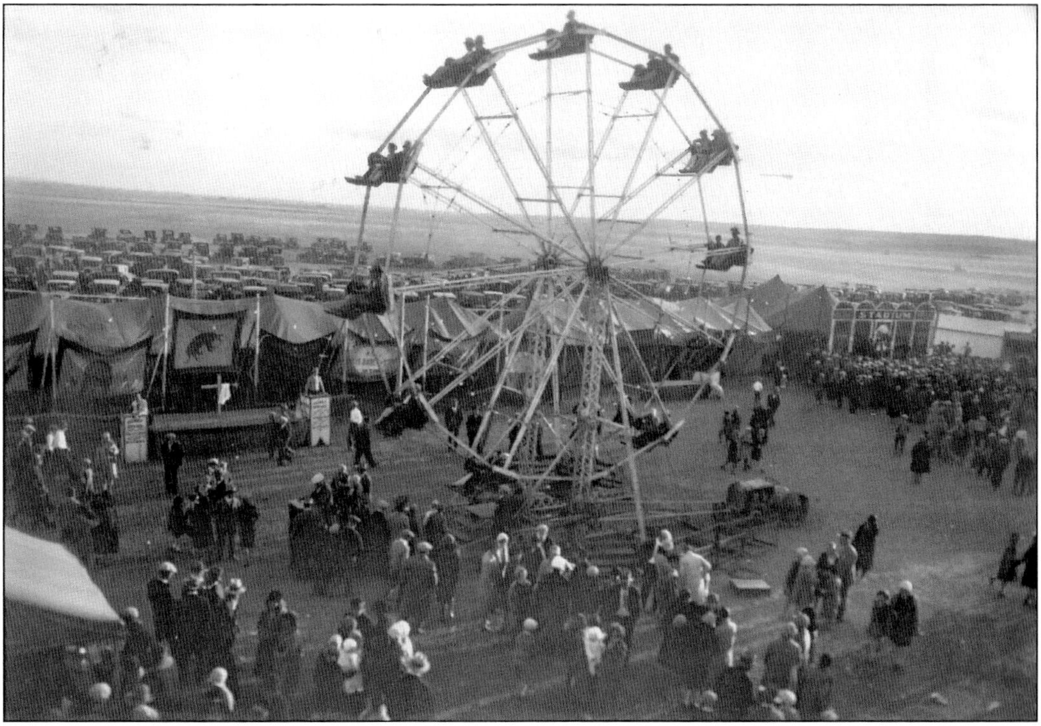

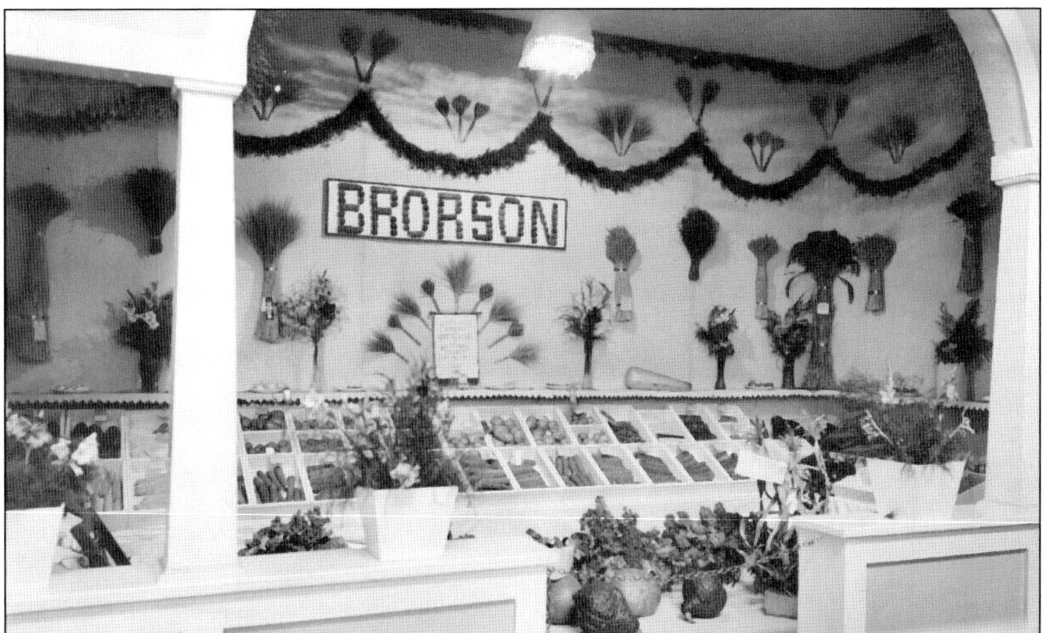

Vegetable and flower displays were some of the biggest draws for visitors to the Richland County Fair in Sidney. Cities and communities from all over the county would create elaborate exhibits out of agricultural materials and submit them for judging. Well-paying premiums attracted many of the entrants. Homegrown produce and flowers would also be submitted for individual prizes. Displays from nearby Brorson and Ridgelawn were among those submitted to the fair each year. The Brorson sign hanging on the back wall was made from halved corncobs, and its third-place award is surrounded by grain shocks. Boxes of produce can be seen in each photograph.

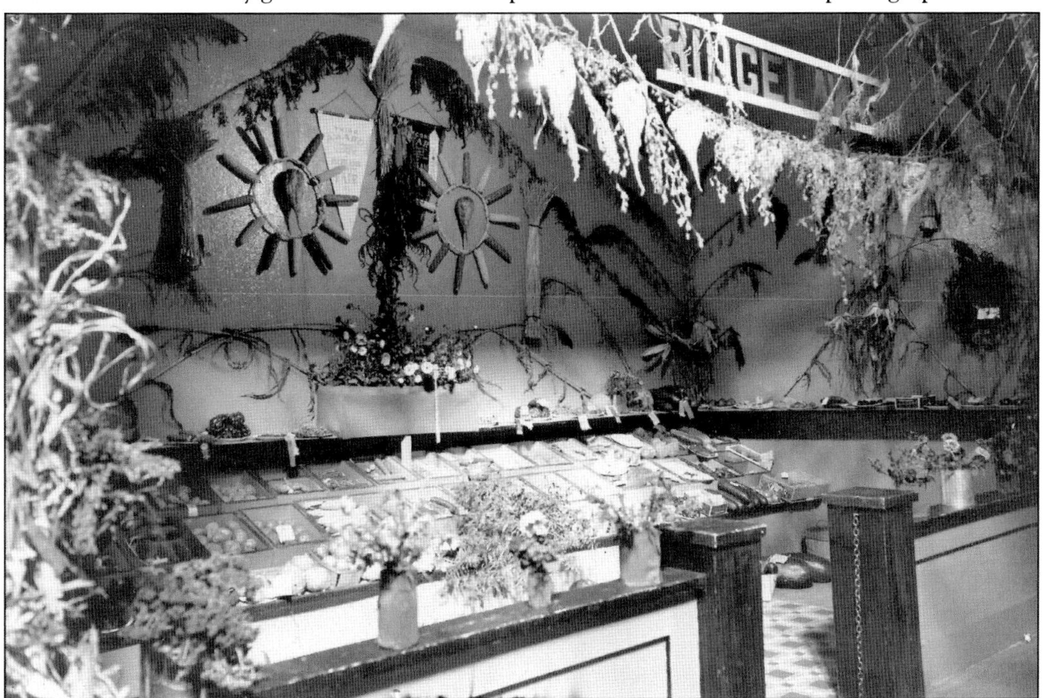

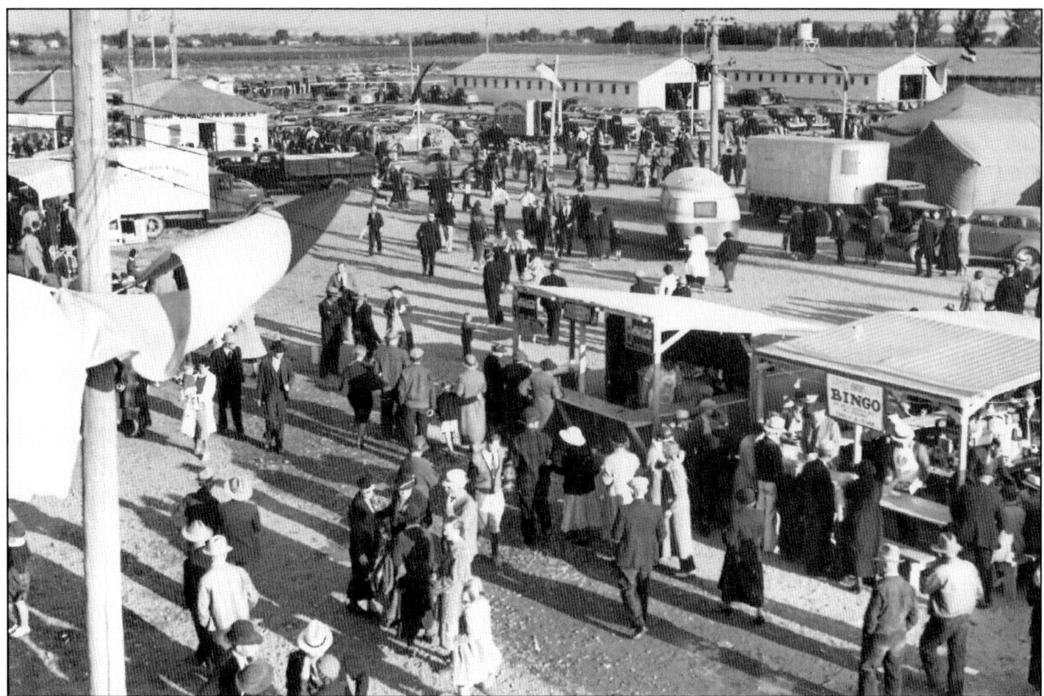

The Richland County Fair and Rodeo was always well attended by the public because it offered the opportunity for socializing as well as a break from the early harvest season in Montana. The bingo booth, seen in the photograph above, was a popular booth to visit, as was the grandstand, which can be seen on the left in the photograph below. Live entertainment was frequently booked in the grandstand, including weddings that fair attendees could enjoy. Those who got married at the fair were offered cash prizes as well as savings accounts and credit at local stores. Tents with food, buildings filled with exhibits, and barns brimming with prizewinning livestock all offered additional fun at the fair.

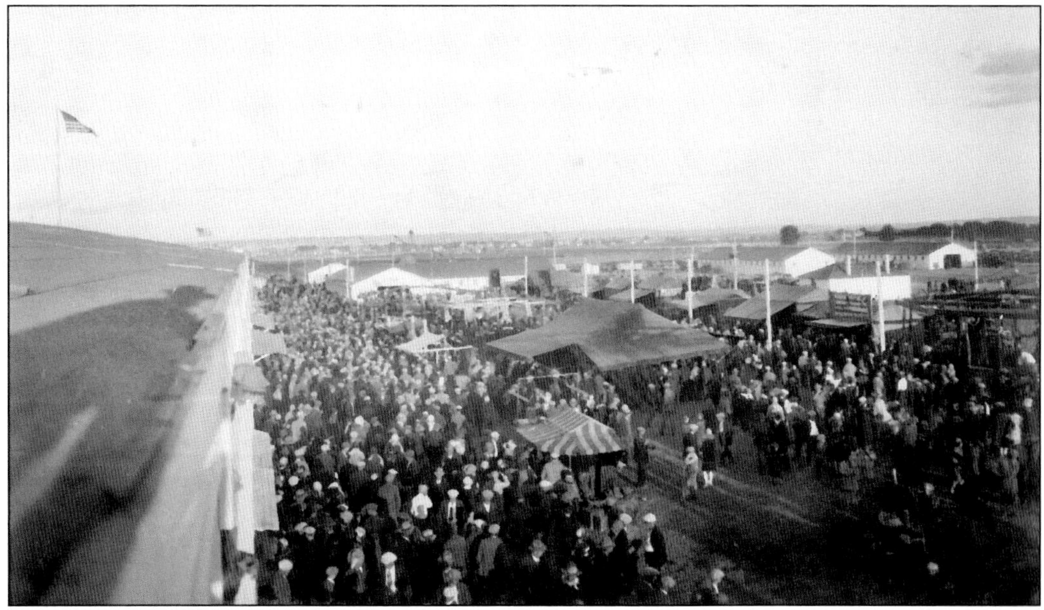

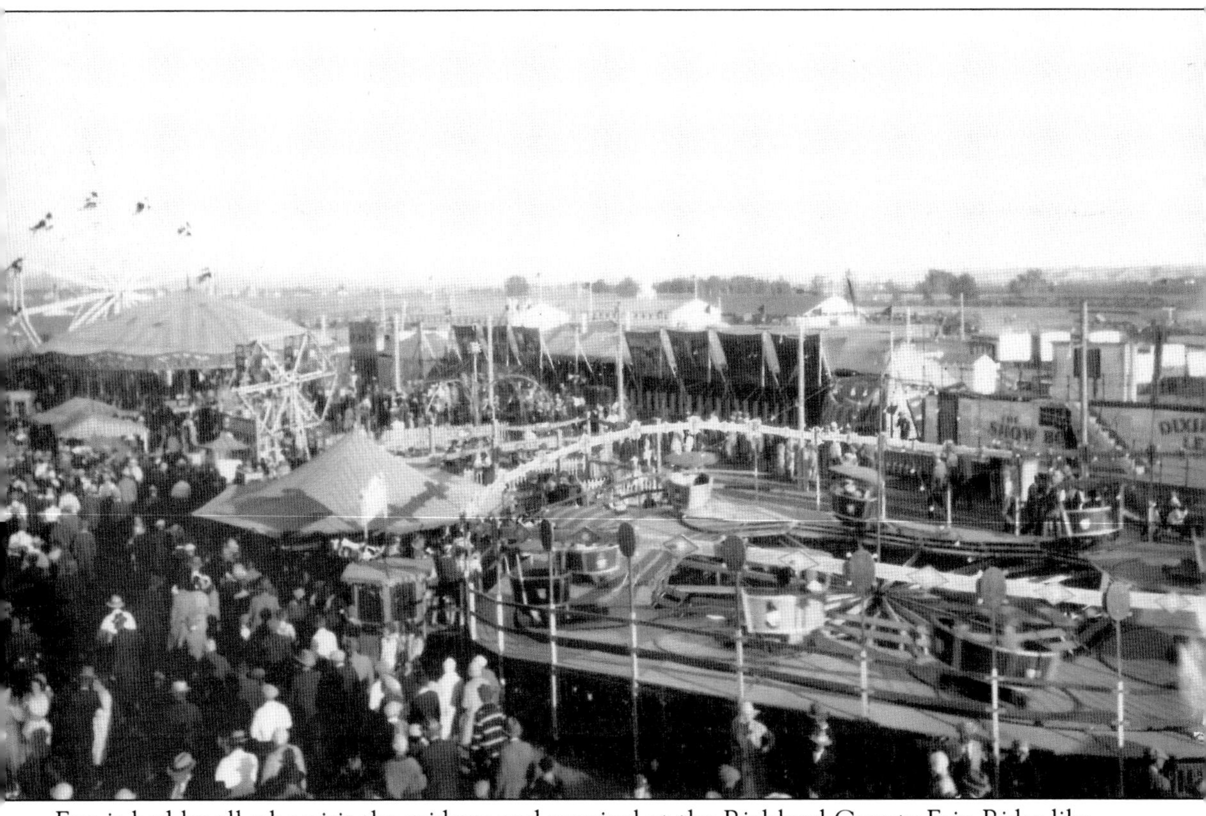

Fun is had by all who visit the midway and carnival at the Richland County Fair. Rides like the Ferris wheel, which can be seen in the background of this photograph, the Tilt-A-Whirl in the foreground, and the carousel were very popular with visitors to the annual event. The midway was contracted out to Zeiger's United Shows before the two-year break during World War II. After the war, Northern Exposition Shows took it over and featured around eight rides and approximately seven additional features, like a sideshow and a showboat. Having rides and other entertainment was surely an improvement over the early days of the fair, when amusements included tug-of-war, footraces, sack races, and a greased pig contest. Today, the carnival is put on by North Star Amusements.

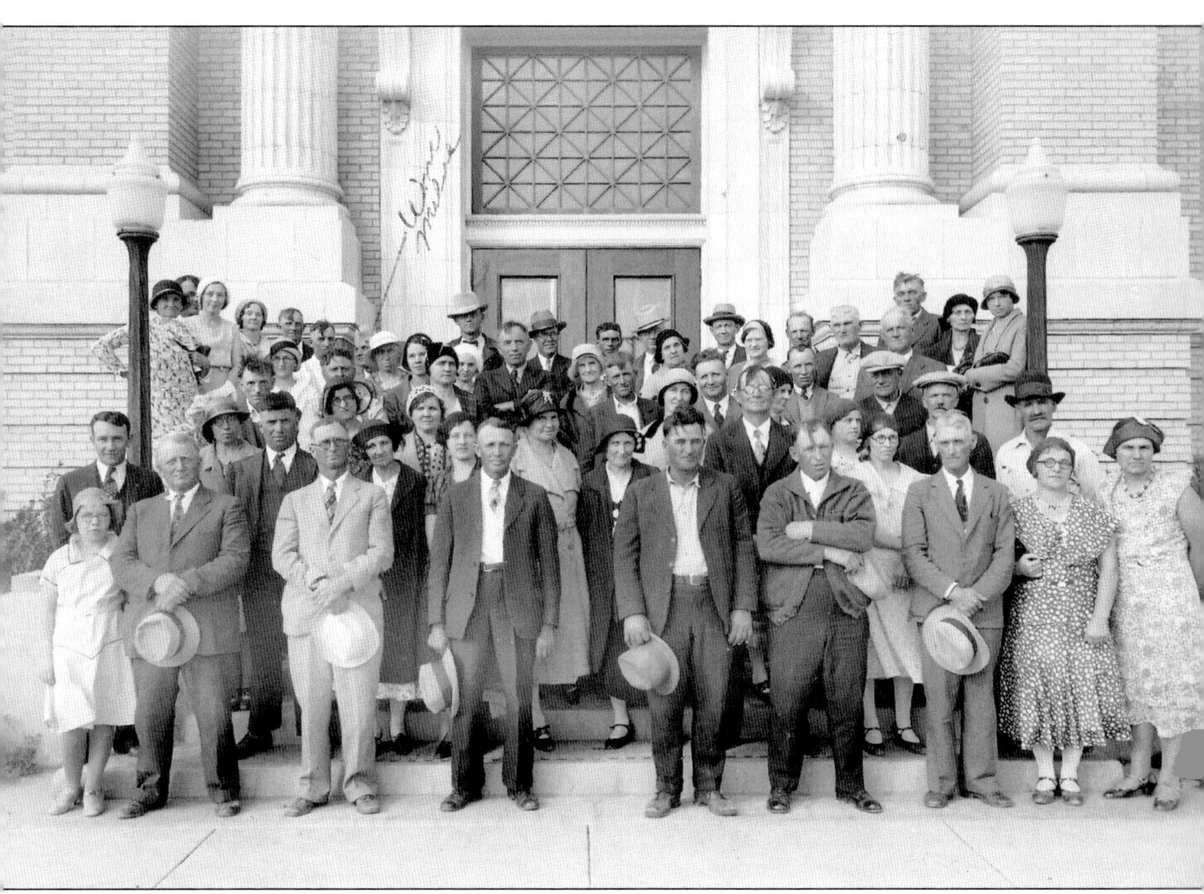

The fair board worked hard year-round to make sure that each year's fair was successful and that the community would continue to return. This photograph shows the Richland County Fair Board standing on the courthouse steps in the 1930s. There were a few instances when the fair board had to make tough decisions in regards to the event, like closing it during the Great Depression and World War II and cutting back on entertainment and other events at the fair due to disasters. In 1925, attendance at the fair was dwindling, especially from the farm community. With the help of the county extension office, the fair was given more of an agricultural feel, hoping to entice more farmers to show their crops and livestock at the fair and to provide opportunities for education on how to improve their farms. With the changes in place, attendance increased dramatically that year, and it was decided that agricultural exhibits should grow each year.

Two

Agriculture in Sidney

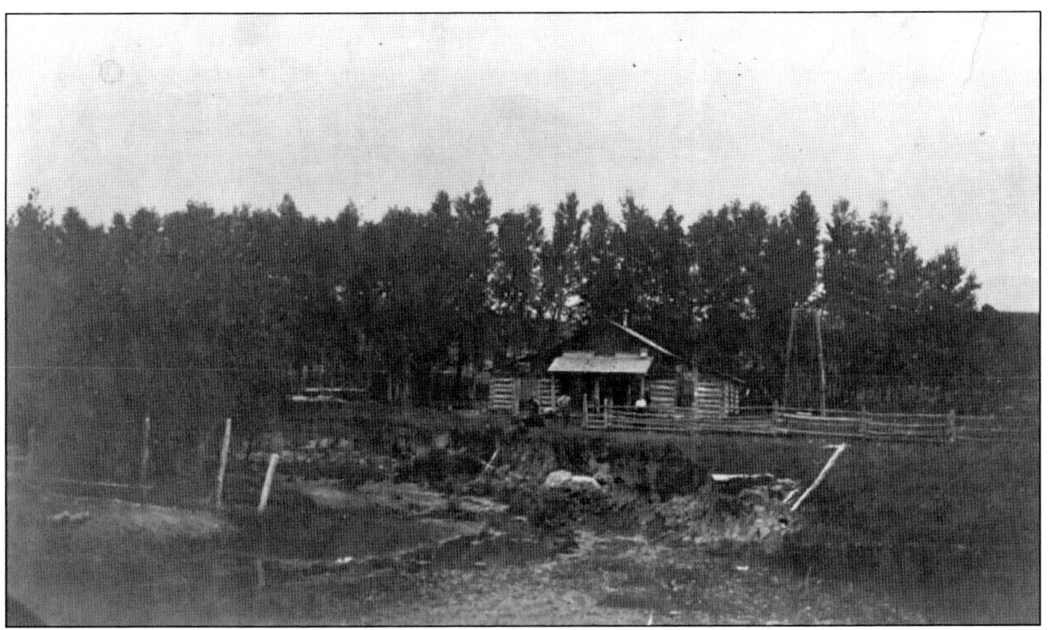

Probably the single most important step for the improvement of agriculture in Sidney was the Lower Yellowstone Irrigation Project, which allowed farms and ranches in the area to expand not only their crops but also their herds of livestock. Before the project began, farmers had to dig laborious irrigation ditches on their property to water their crops, like Emmet Dunlap did on his farm, shown in this picture.

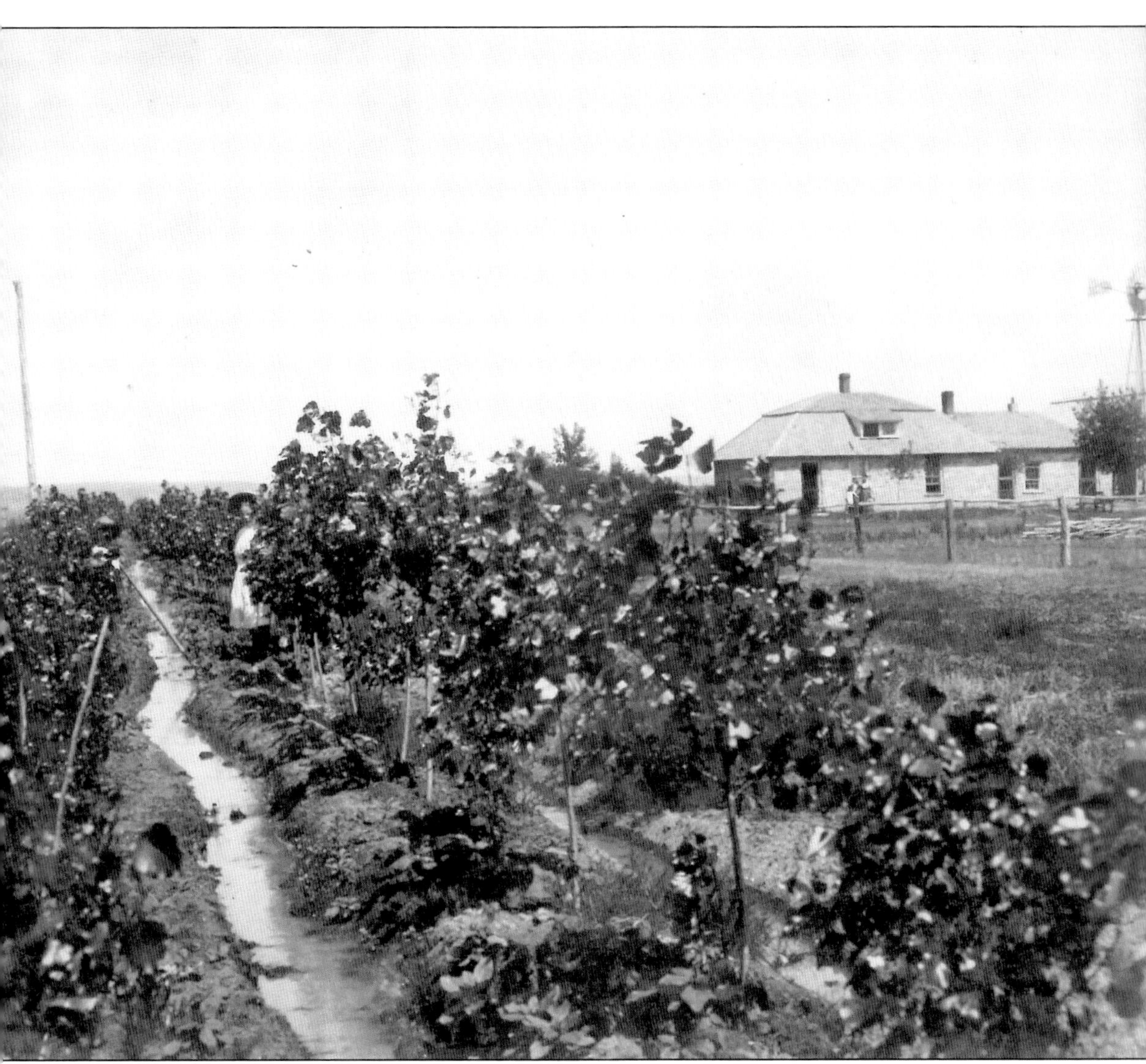

Praying for rain did not always work for farmers who were trying to keep their crops watered. Like Emmet Dunlap, Lossie Dawe dug an irrigation ditch in 1909 on his farm. Dawe had purchased the farm from dentist Charles Stockwell in 1904, who had also been using his home as a post office. Dawe purchased the farm so that his children could attend the Sidney School. The trees were planted along the irrigation ditch to serve as shade for the property. A woman can just be seen taking advantage of the shade near the ditch. The Dawe family lived on the farm until 1920, when it was sold to the Cooleys. The Stockwell-Dawe-Cooley home is considered the oldest house in Sidney. It was built in 1895, and because it was made of limestone, it is still solid as a rock today.

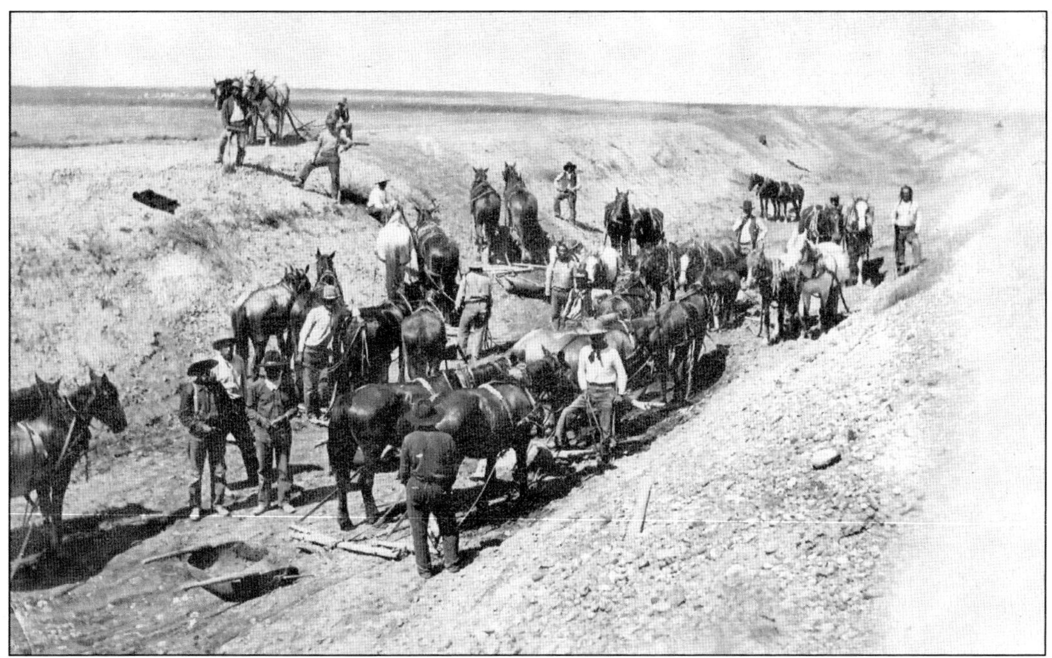

Although there had been talk in the late 1800s of building an irrigation ditch along the Yellowstone River, it was not until the Newlands Reclamation Act of 1902 that farmers really got excited about making the project happen. An engineer was hired to create a preliminary plan for the irrigation canal, and it was approved by the secretary of the interior on May 10, 1904. Work on the Lower Yellowstone Irrigation Project began in 1905. Steam shovels did some of the heavy lifting as dirt was pulled out of what would become the canal, but men and horses completed a lot of the work as well. The "big ditch" was an enormous project that tried the souls of the men working on it. Workers on the project rotated regularly due to the extremely hot or extremely cold weather conditions in northeast Montana.

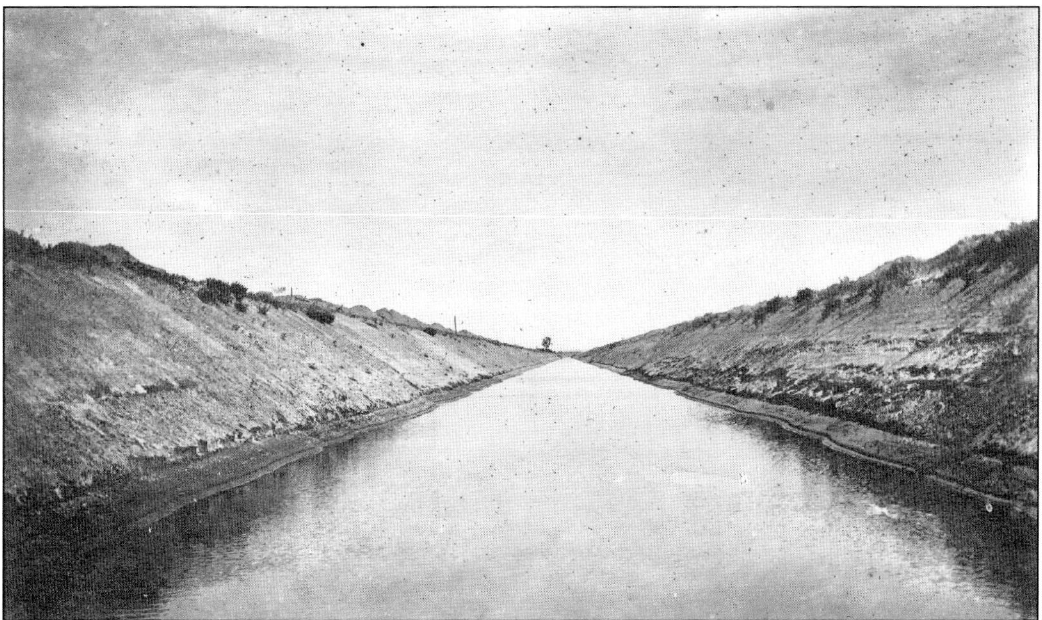

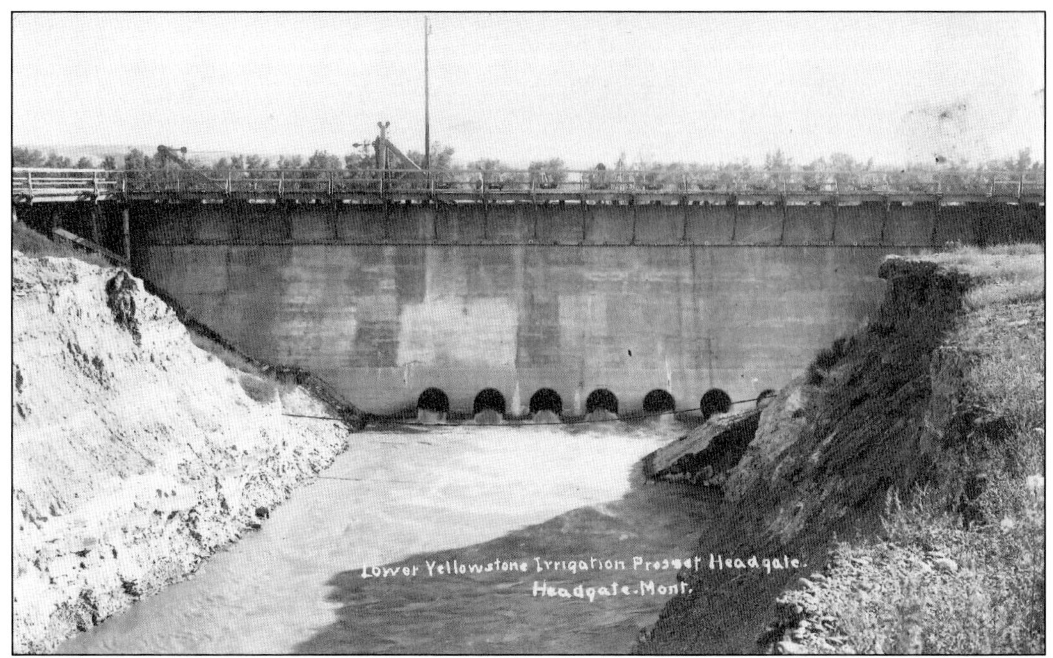

Over the course of four years, workers built enough canals to carry water for farmers to irrigate 40,000 acres of crops. In addition to canals and spillways, a 12-foot-high wood and stone diversion dam was built to create a reservoir for the Lower Yellowstone Irrigation Project. The dam was called the Intake Diversion Dam or the Yellowstone Diversion Dam. The photograph above shows the dam at low flow, while some construction work can still be seen in the background. Another view can be seen in the photograph below, where a young child plays near the canal.

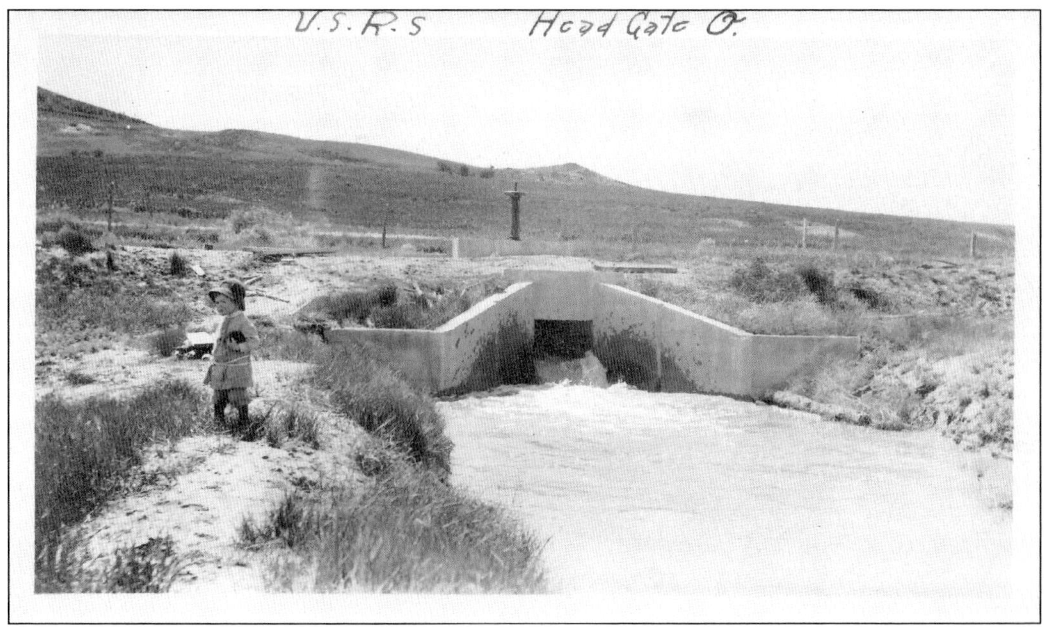

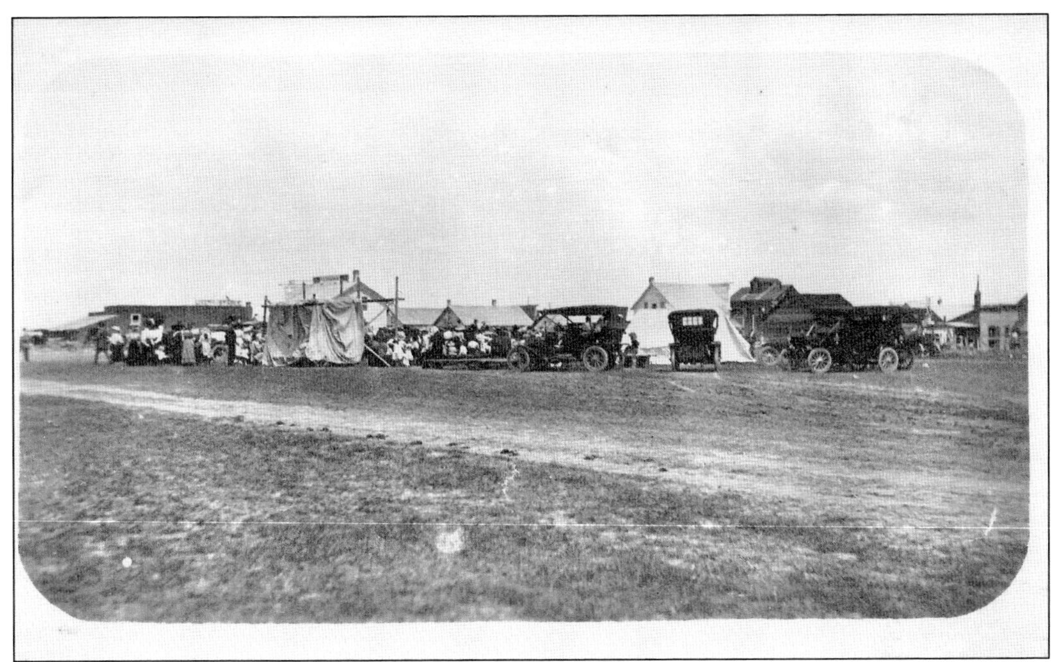

Locals celebrated the first delivery of water along the canal on June 24, 1909. Tents were set up and a large gathering took place to honor the occasion of 64 miles' worth of water being carried along the canal. By the time the Lower Yellowstone Irrigation Project was finished in 1931, the main canal was 100 miles long and was crossed over by 225 miles of lateral canals that allowed farmers to water their crops. The dam across the headgates formed a reservoir that could store water to be used in the project.

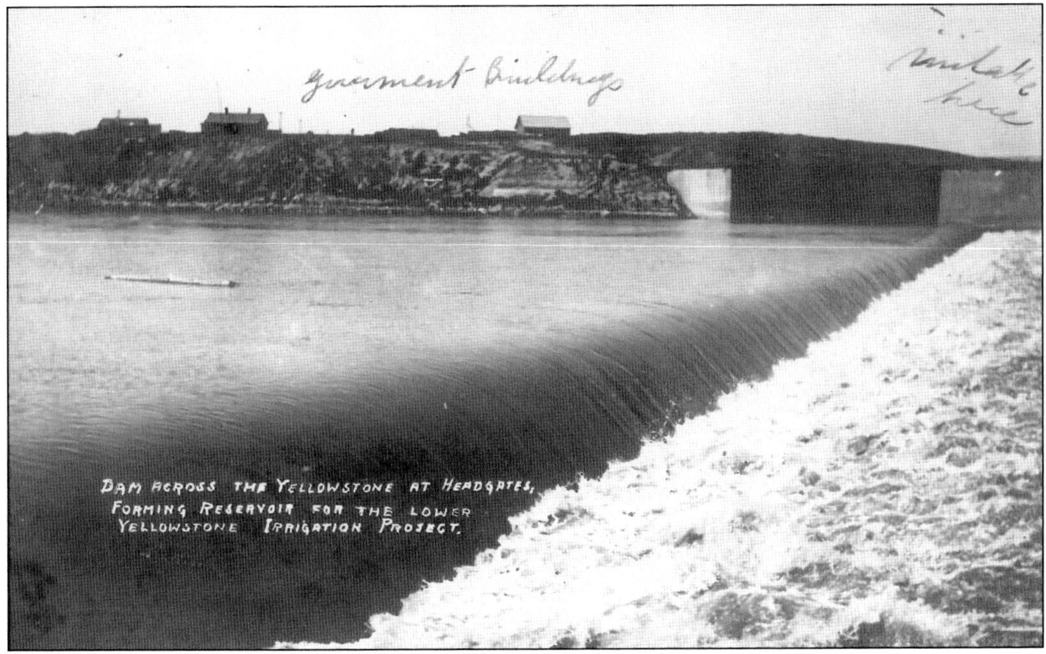

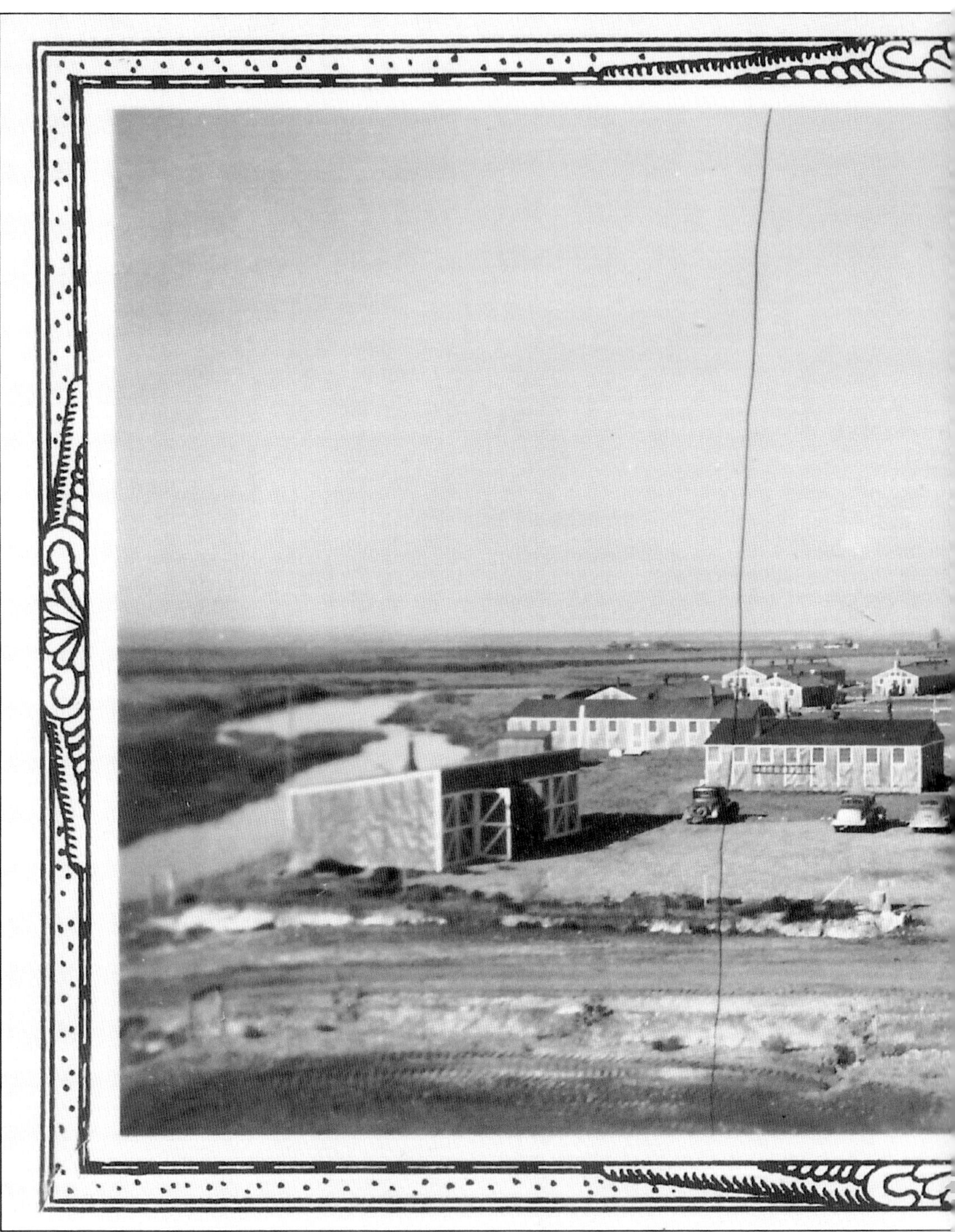

Construction of additional drains along the Lower Yellowstone Irrigation Project was made possible through the hard work of the members of the Civilian Conservation Corps, which set up camp just north of Sidney. The CCC was formed in 1933 as part of Pres. Franklin Roosevelt's New Deal that created jobs for unmarried, unemployed men between the ages of 18 and 23. The requirements were eventually expanded to include men between the ages of 17 and 28. The CCC

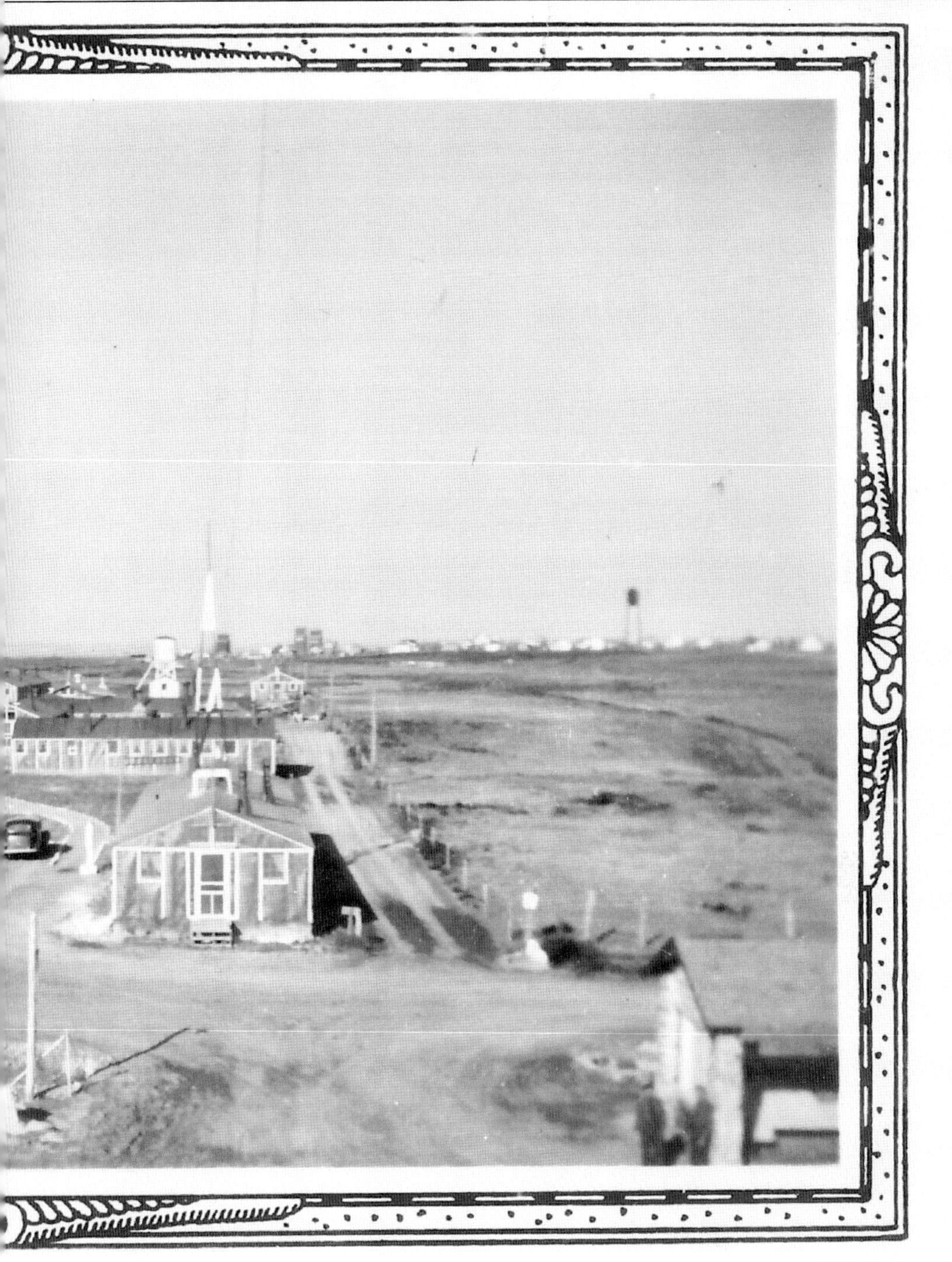

stayed at the camp for nine years, assisting with other jobs like the prevention of soil erosion. While it was started as a tent camp, eventually barracks and other buildings were constructed to allow for more creature comforts for the workers. A library was added, as were areas to participate in physical fitness and sports. This photograph shows the CCC camp with Sidney's water tower visible along the skyline.

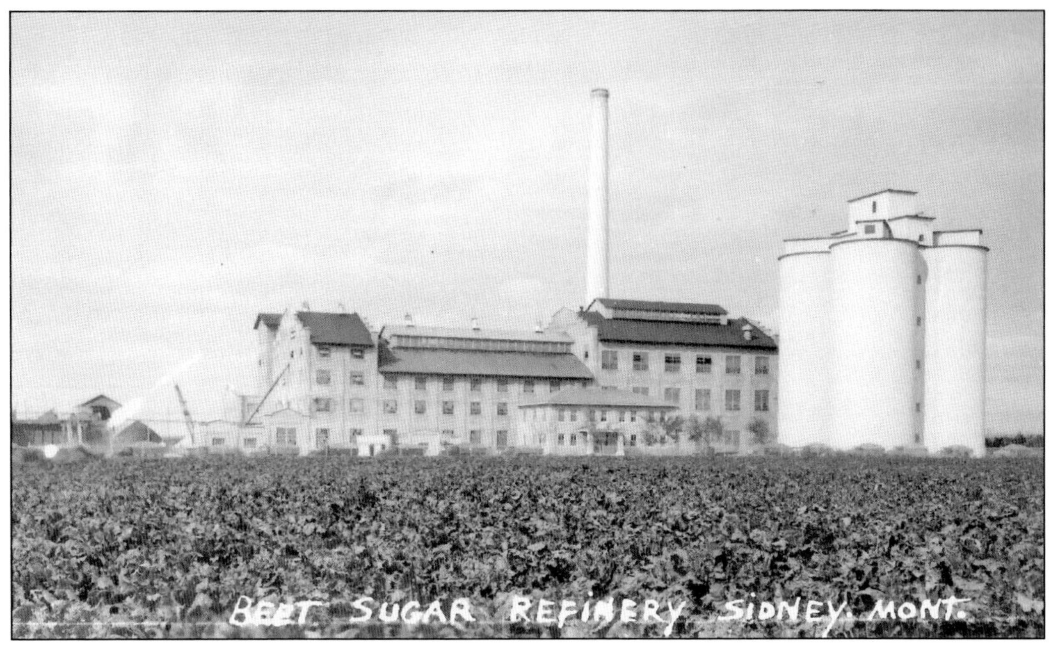

Sugar beets have long been grown in Sidney and the surrounding area. Once harvested, they would make the journey to Billings, nearly 300 miles away, to be processed. In 1924, Midland Sugar Company told beet growers that it would build a factory in Sidney if the sugar beet farmers would devote 10,000 acres to produce the 120,000 tons of beets the company would need to warrant the building of a factory. The farmers agreed, and in December 1924, construction began on the facility. Ten months later, the factory was ready for the harvest. The name of the company was later changed to Holly Sugar. These photographs show two views of the factory site.

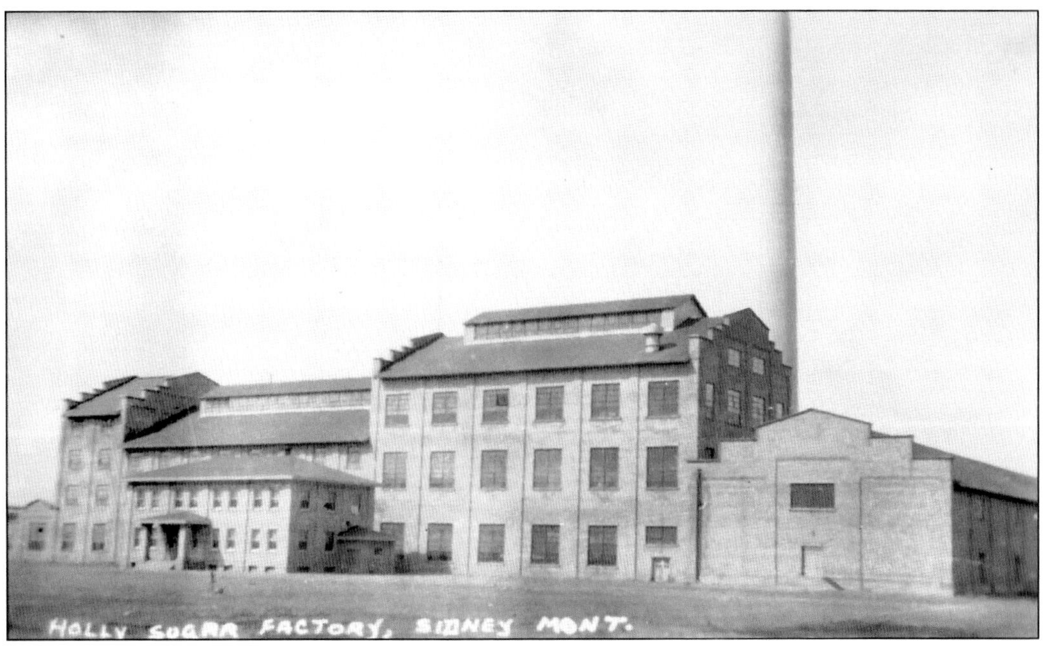

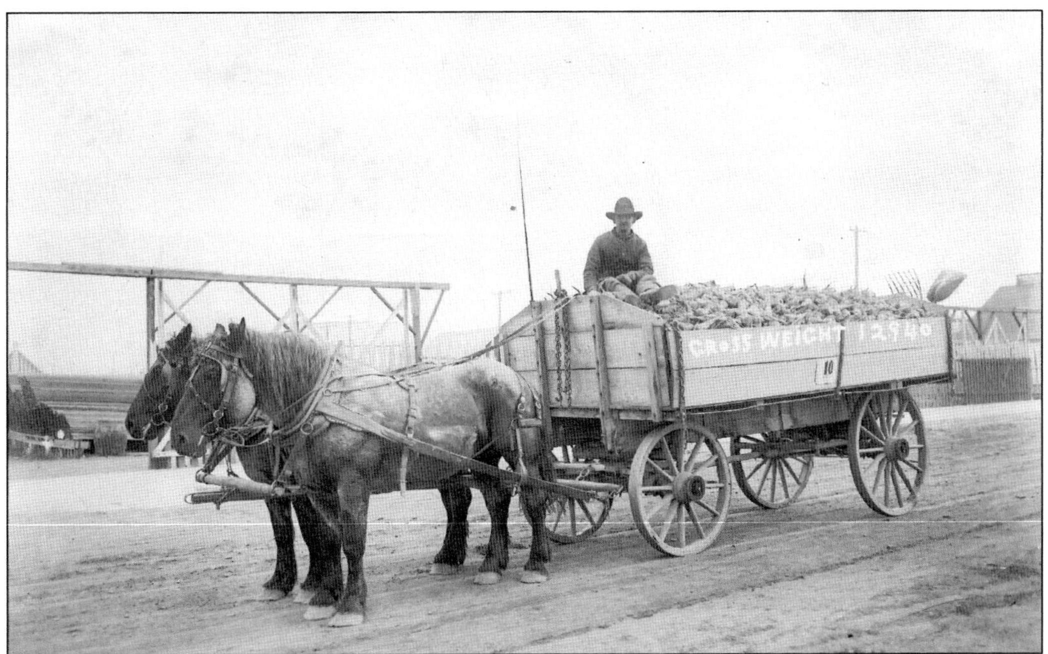

A sugar beet refinery in Sidney meant the nearby farmers no longer had to make the 600-mile round-trip to drop off their annual harvest. Farmers could simply haul their beets into town, have them weighed, and drop them off. Here, a farmer poses in his wagon filled with sugar beets. The gross weight is listed at 12,940 pounds.

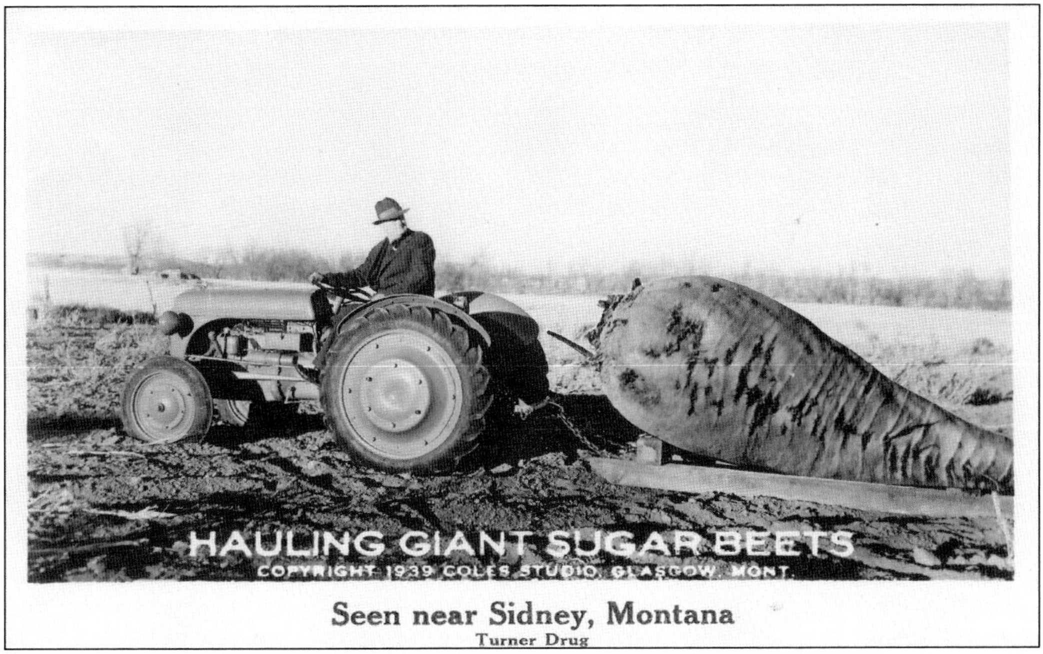

Turner Drug, a local store in Sidney, sold a series of comical postcards to capitalize on the success of the sugar beet crop in the area. Postcards featuring giant sugar beets and other produce were popular in the first half of the century and were a great way for towns to advertise their agricultural business.

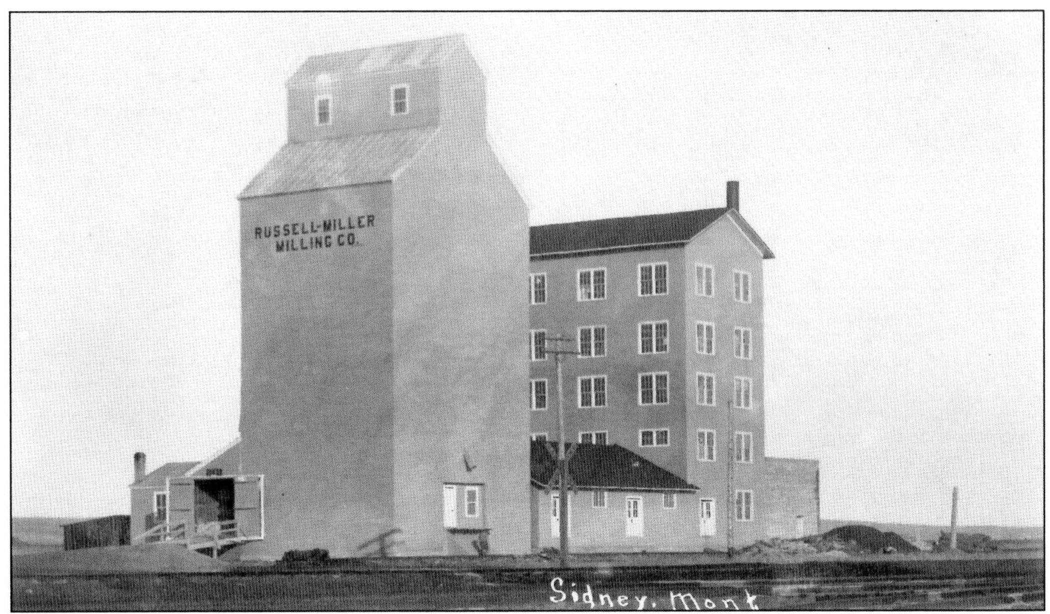

The Lower Yellowstone Irrigation Project not only allowed sugar beet farming in Sidney to prosper, it also allowed for wheat milling to flourish. In July 1913, the Russell-Miller Milling Company of Minneapolis announced that it was to begin work on a mill in Sidney. Among the plans for the new mill were a 50,000-bushel grain elevator and a 300-barrel mill that would eventually be increased in capacity to 400 barrels with improvements. The milling company promised to use local contractors and workmen to complete the construction on the buildings and was proud to announce that it would be the most up-to-date flour mill in the Northwest. The mill was finished and up and running before January 1, 1914.

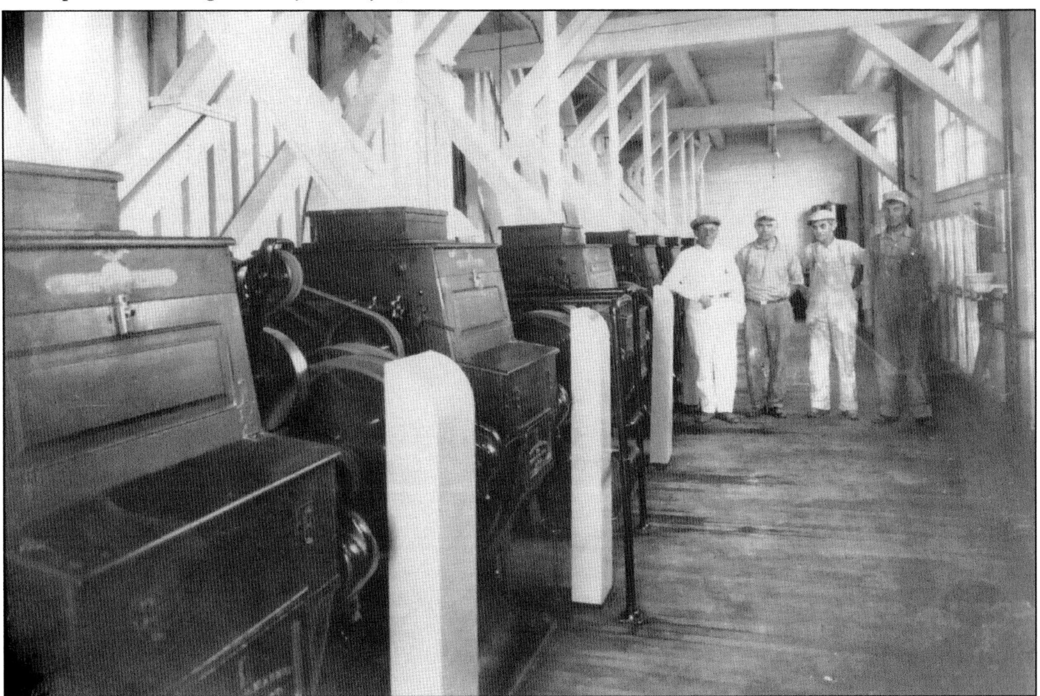

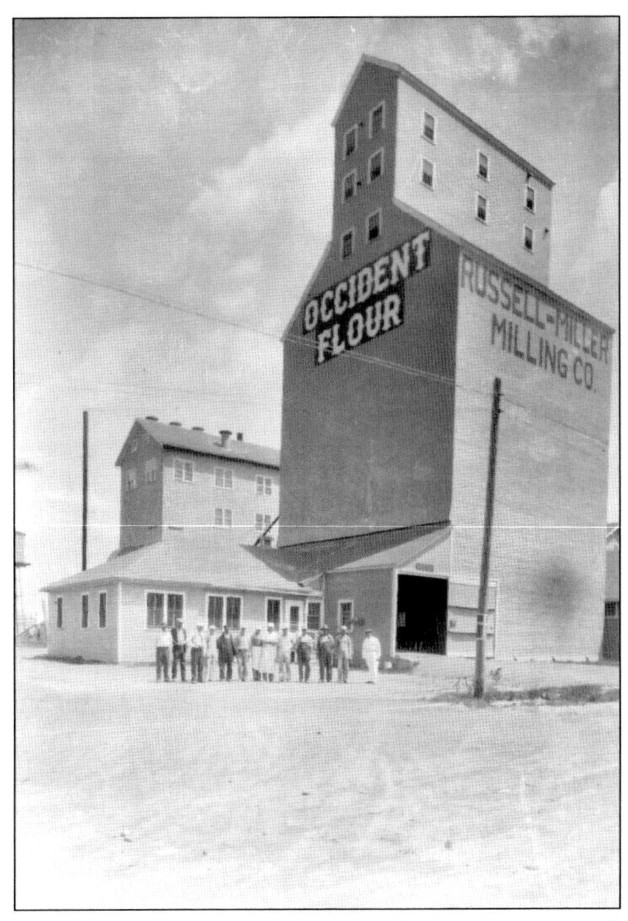

In addition to the grain elevator and mill, the Russell-Miller Milling Company also built three flour storehouses that had the capacity for 300 barrels apiece. The storage space would allow the mill to run full-time. There was also a storage area for wheat to insure against a shortage and to give wheat farmers another option when looking for purchasers of their product. The flour milled in Sidney was called Occident Flour, or flour "out of the west." The mill operated until 1921, when it burned down. It was soon rebuilt and was a mainstay of the community until 1943.

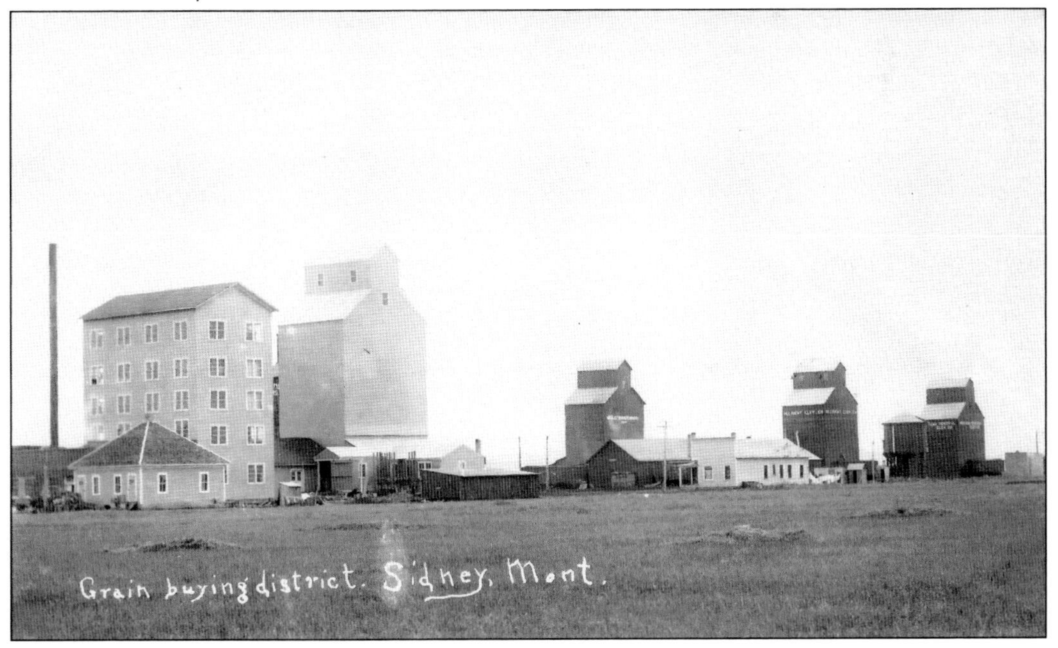

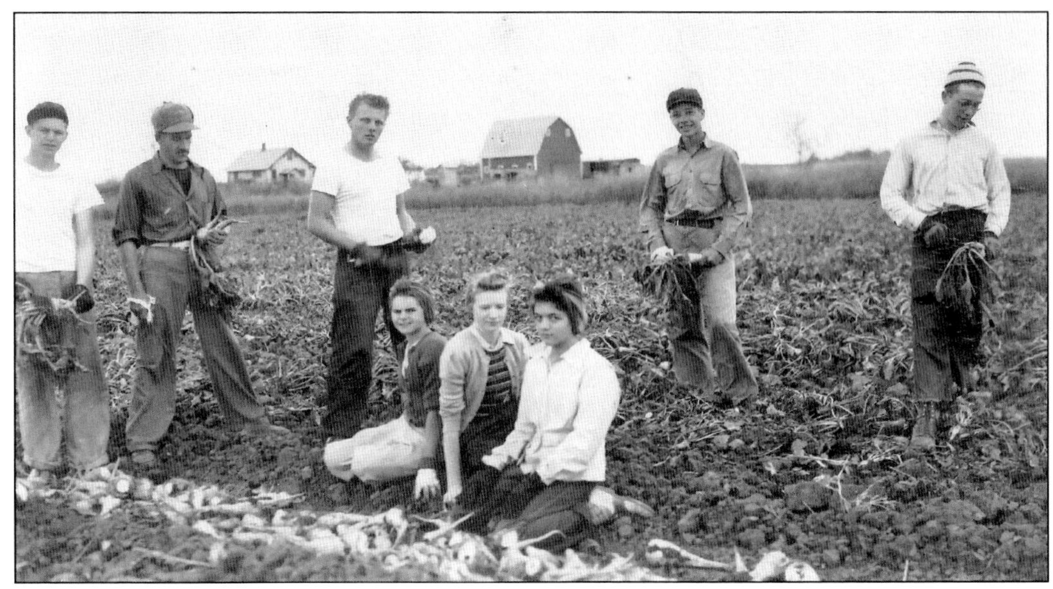

Farmers in and around Sidney have long needed help harvesting their crops in the fall. Newspapers frequently put out the call for harvest help, especially during times of war, when many of the local young men were overseas. At some points, the schools in Sidney closed so that all hands could be on deck to help with the harvest. The pictures here show students and businessmen helping out with the harvest. During World War II, many of the Japanese American citizens who were interned in Wyoming were bussed up to Sidney to assist with the sugar beet harvest. While in Montana, they utilized the Civilian Conservation Corps camp just north of town.

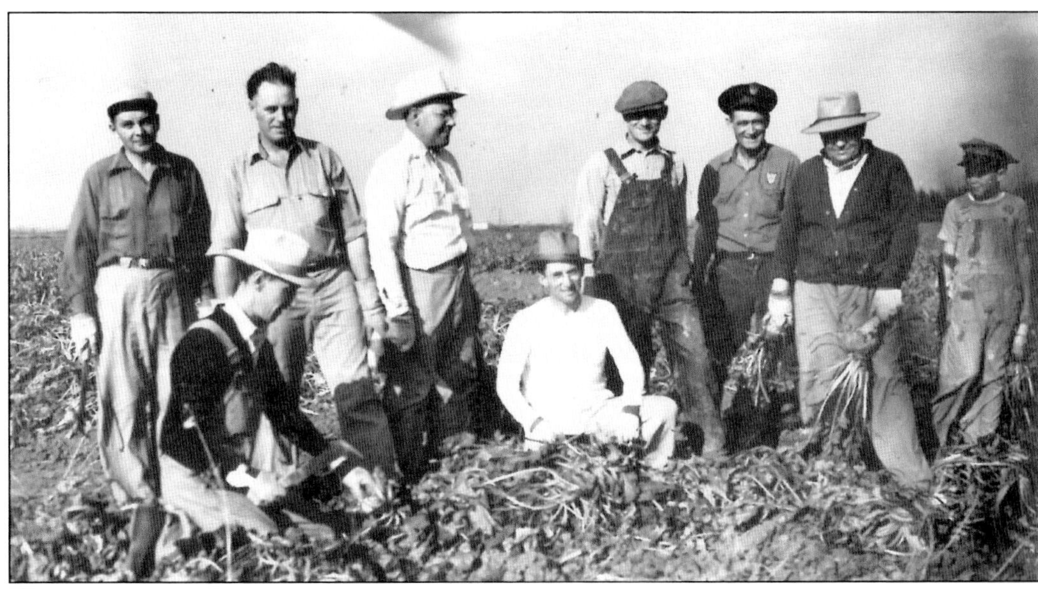

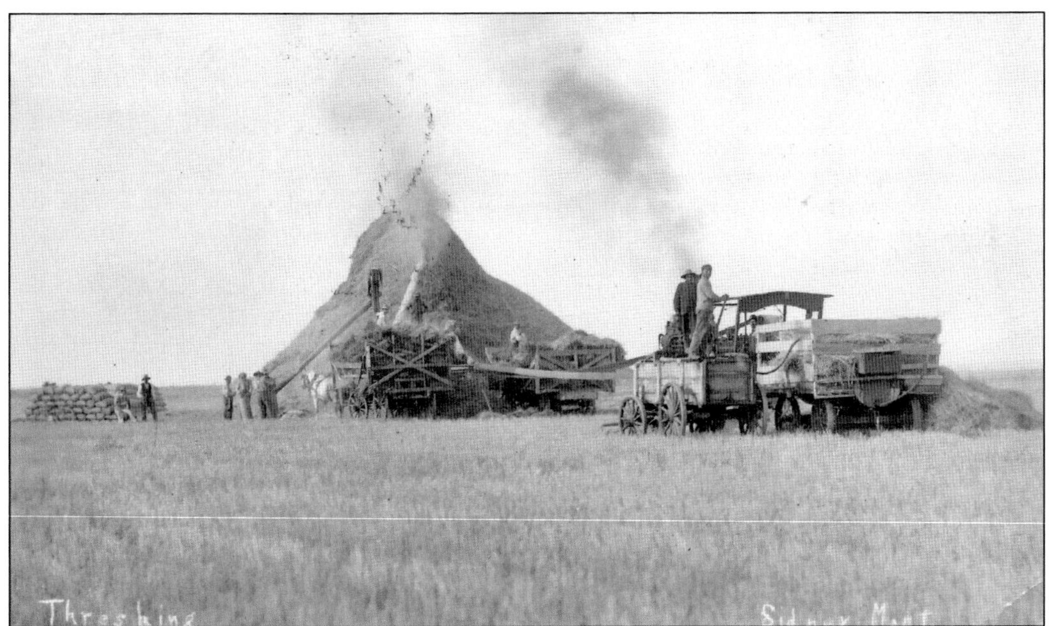

This photograph shows threshing in Sidney in 1911. The threshing machine was used to separate grain from stalks and husks, a job that had originally been done by hand using a flail. The thresher allowed for quick separation, which meant that the grain could be milled and turned into flour much faster.

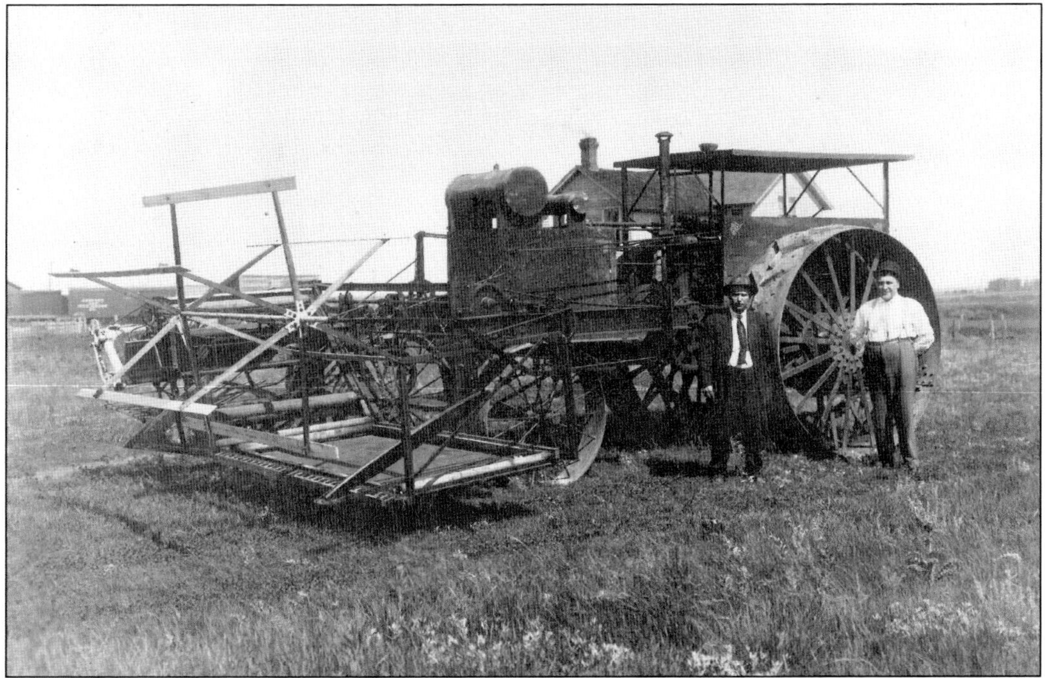

Next to this Sidney farmer sits a binder. The binder would reap, or cut, small grain crops and tie them into small bundles. Those bundles would then be stood up, resembling a cone, to allow them to dry before they were placed into the threshing machine. The binder and the threshing machine have now been replaced by the combine harvester.

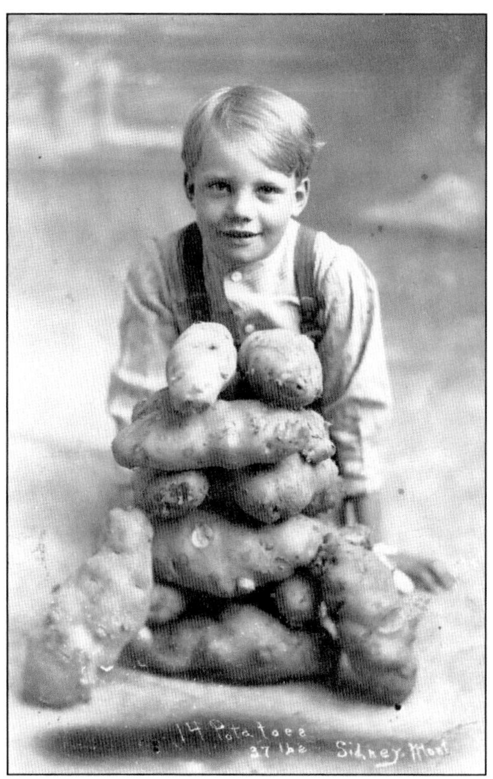

Wheat and sugar beets were not the only crops grown in Sidney. Potatoes were also very popular because of their longevity. If placed in a dark, cool, well-ventilated storage area, potatoes could be stored for 10 to 12 months. This photograph shows a young boy posing with enormous potatoes. According to the caption, there are 14 potatoes weighing a total of 37 pounds.

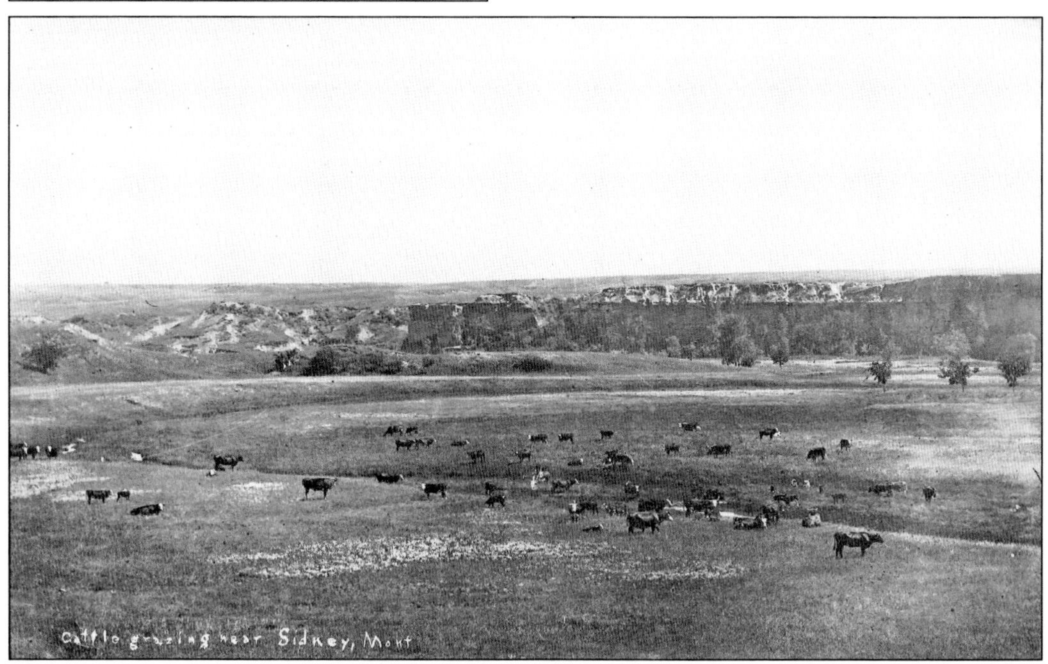

Cattle ranching was successful in Sidney before the Lower Yellowstone Irrigation Project, but became even more successful once it was finished. Irrigation allowed farms to grow and expand, which meant purchasing and raising more livestock, including cows, sheep, and hogs. Thousands of cattle were marketed annually from farms and ranches adjoining the irrigation project.

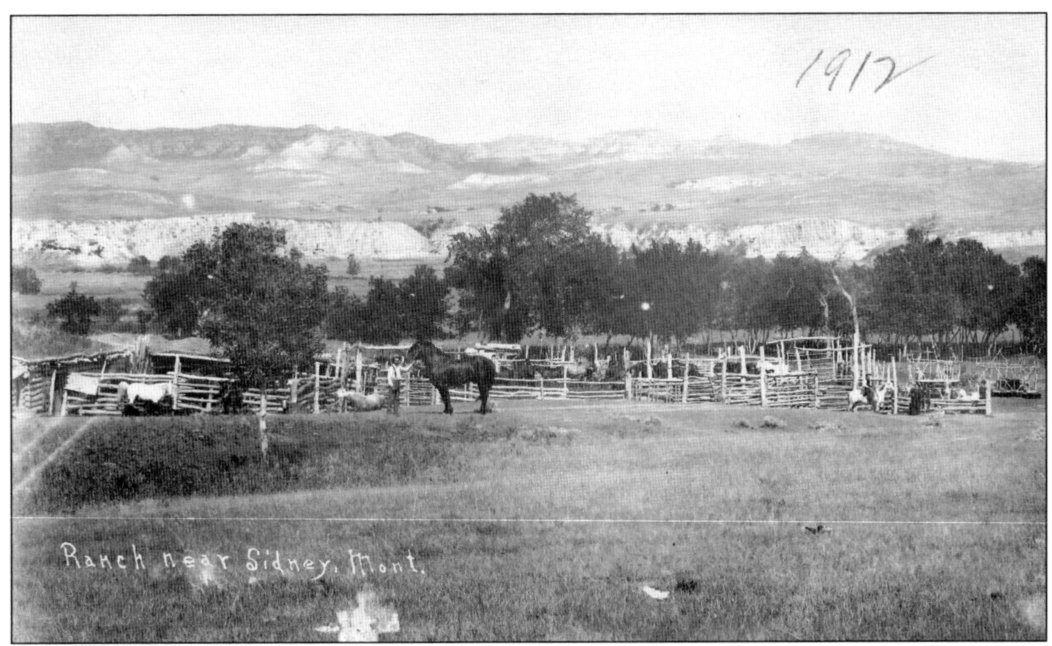

Large, sprawling ranches were popular in the Lower Yellowstone River Valley as it was being settled. This was especially true of land that was not near readily available irrigation channels. Ranchers would use horses to guide their cattle around their grazing lands across their property. Because they could not watch their livestock at all times, the ranchers would brand their horses and cattle with specially made marks, making it easy for them to recognize their property. There are over 300 different brands in the area that have been identified. Once the Lower Yellowstone Irrigation Project was finished, some of the ranchers converted their ranchlands to farmland.

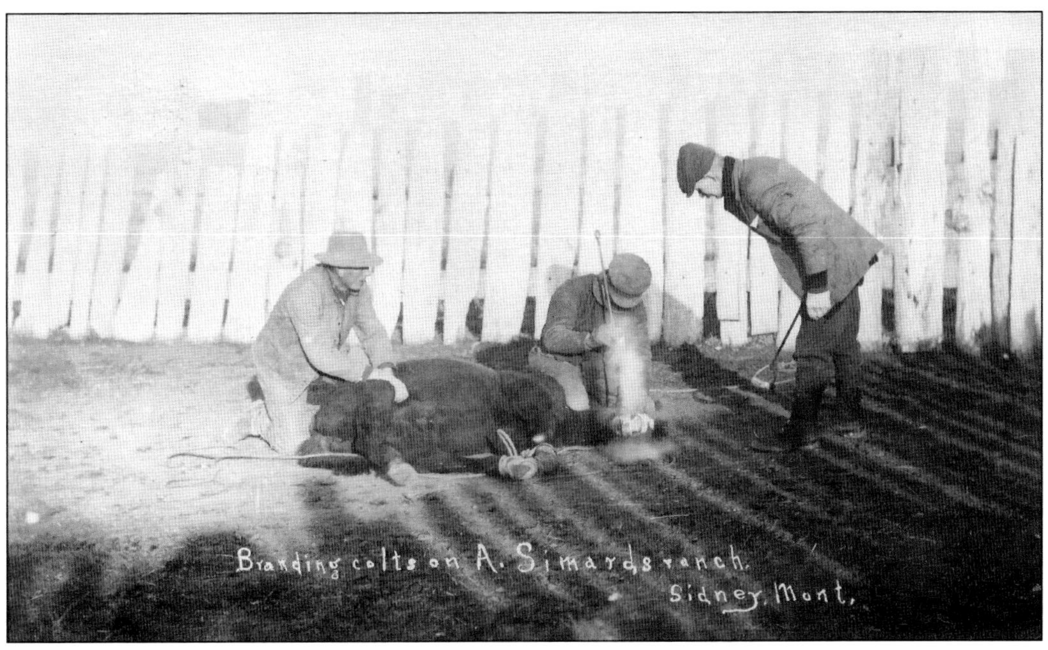

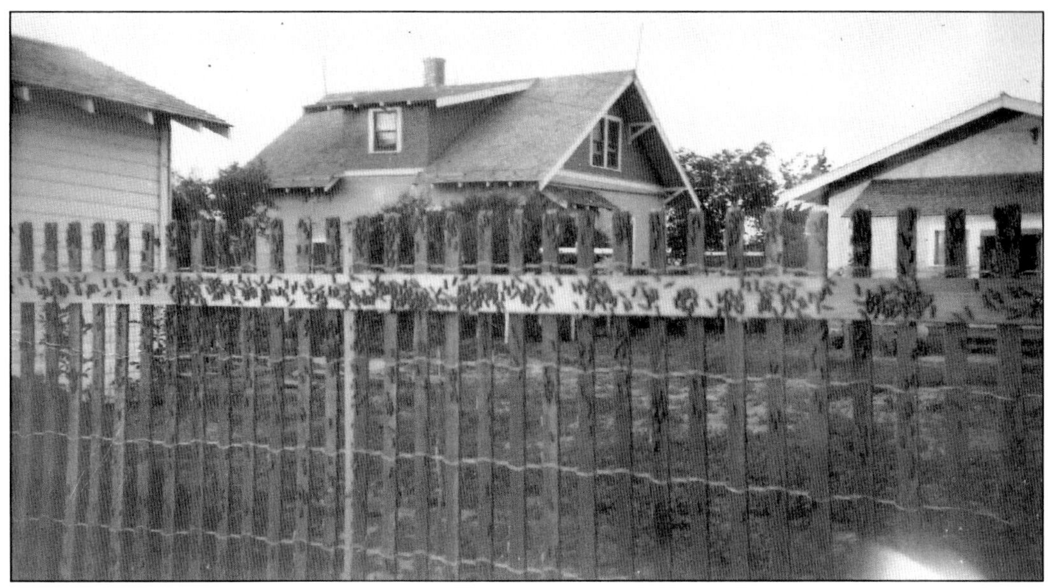

Grasshoppers have been a problem for farmers since biblical times. They are plant-eaters and as such can become serious pests for farmers and the crops they are attempting to grow. Grasshoppers thrive in sunny, dry conditions, making northeastern Montana a great place for them. In 1938, a grasshopper scourge overtook Sidney. The backyards of Sidney's townsfolk were carpeted with the pests, and farmers desperately tried to harvest their crops in an attempt to salvage what they could. Unfortunately, most of the crops were a total loss, and the farmers abandoned the task of cutting their grain. These photographs show grasshoppers covering an outside wall and fence in Sidney.

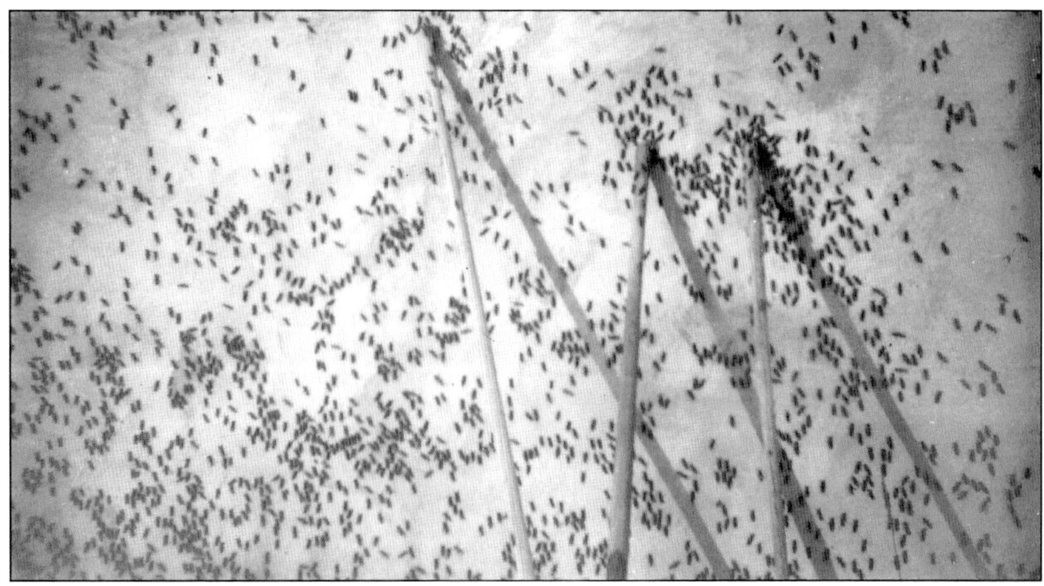

Three

Businesses in Sidney

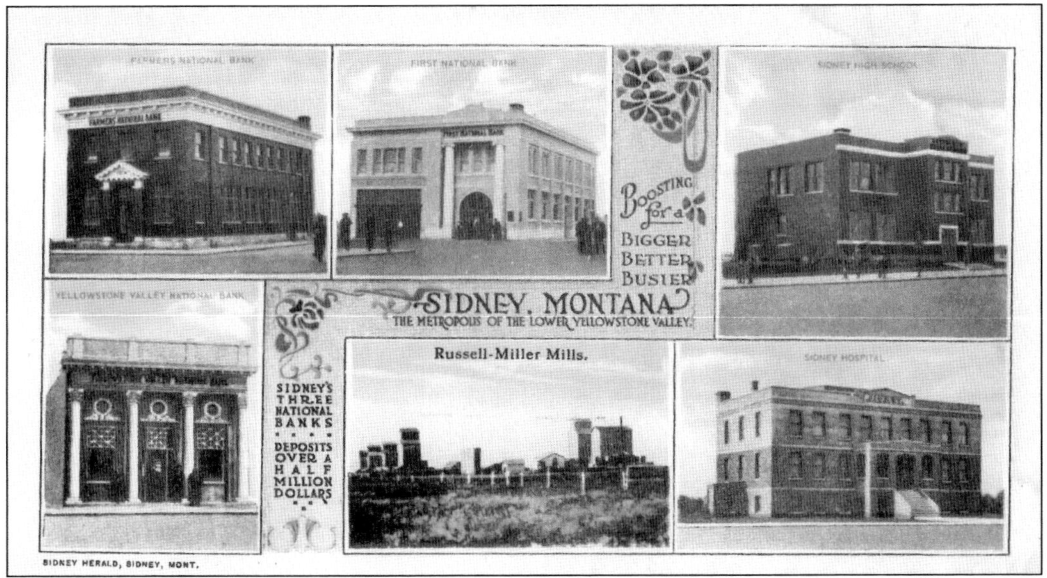

Featured on this brightly colored envelope are a few of the prosperous businesses in Sidney, Montana. Heralded as "The Metropolis of the Lower Yellowstone Valley," Sidney was trying to boost its reputation by showcasing the three national banks in town. Farmers National Bank, First National Bank, and the Yellowstone Valley National Bank, as well as Sidney's high school, hospital, and the Russell-Miller Milling Company, are all featured in the advertisement.

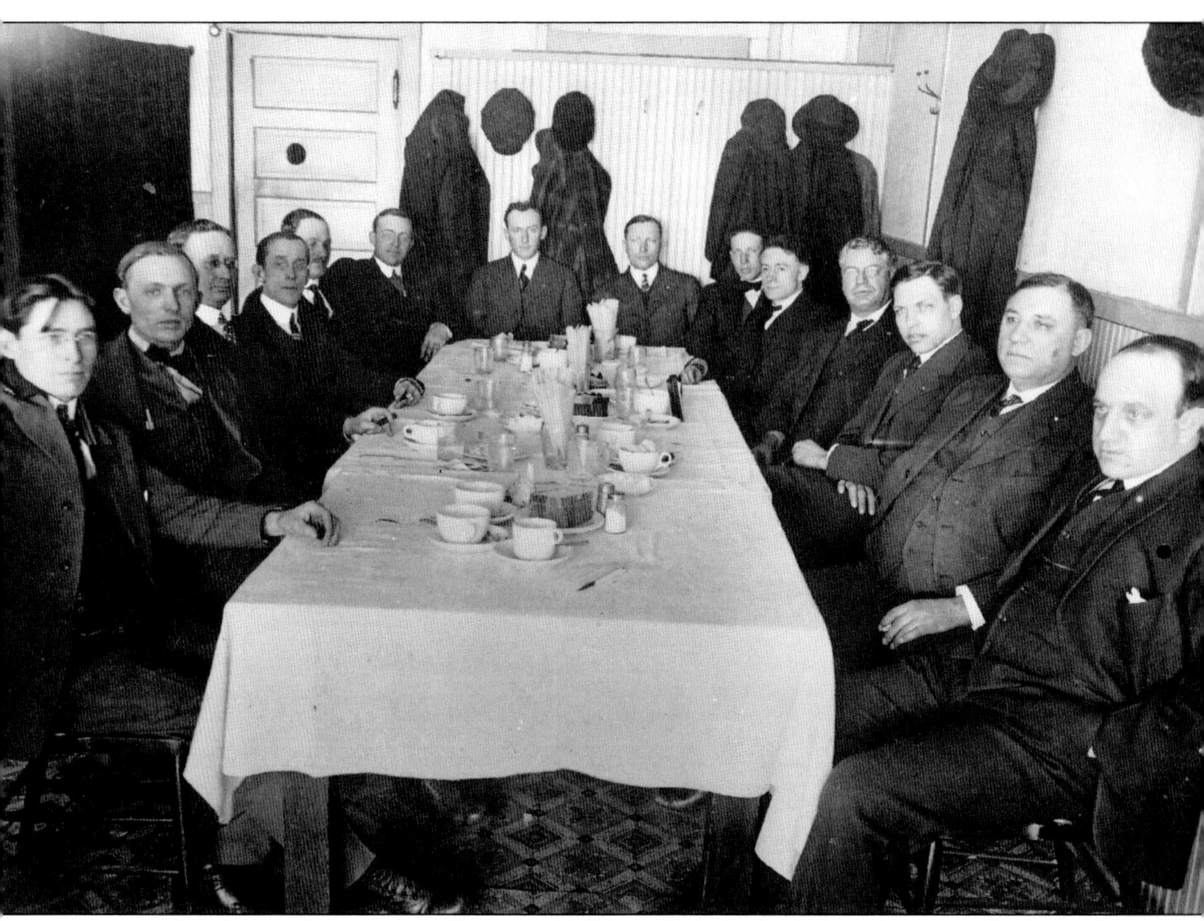

In 1908, what would eventually become the Sidney Chamber of Commerce and Agriculture was formed. It was originally known as the Sidney Commercial Club, and membership was made up of active businessmen from the community. The men worked tirelessly to help incorporate Sidney and to help provide city services to the residents. The Sidney Commercial Club also worked to bring the railroad to town, to add more mail routes, and to establish Richland County. The first board of directors meeting for the Sidney Chamber of Commerce took place in 1916. Members of the board included Harry Ketcham of the *Sidney Herald*, Dr. J.S. Beagle, and W.K. Adams of First National Bank in Sidney. In 1923, the growing organization decided that the position of secretary should be a paid one, and the salary started out at $10 per month. In 1926, it was raised to $25 per month. In 1946, a full-time manager was hired. The organization is still in existence today and is a mainstay of the business community in Sidney.

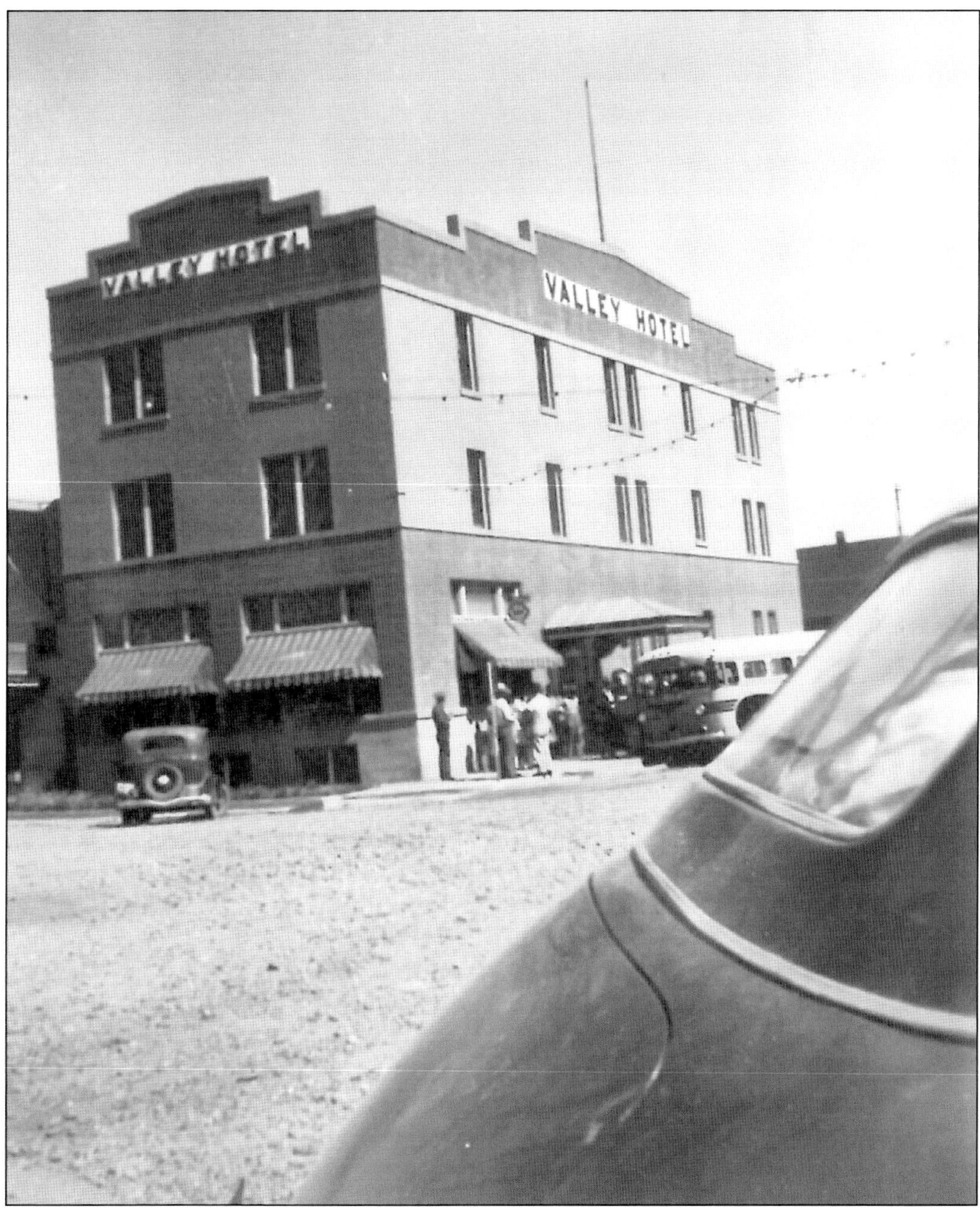

On May 17, 1905, William and May Ball purchased Glendenning's Livery Stable at the corner of Second Avenue NE and East Main Street. On that site, they built and operated the Valley Hotel until 1944. The pair ran a swift trade at the hotel, keeping busy during the influx of irrigation construction and homesteading from 1908 to 1914. The hotel even operated its own light and water systems until the city built municipal facilities. In addition to running a successful hotel, the Balls built a home on the site. In all, there were four buildings constructed in the area of the hotel to stay on top of the steady restaurant and hotel business in Sidney. The building that held the Valley Hotel remained until 1977, when it was torn down and replaced by a Kentucky Fried Chicken franchise.

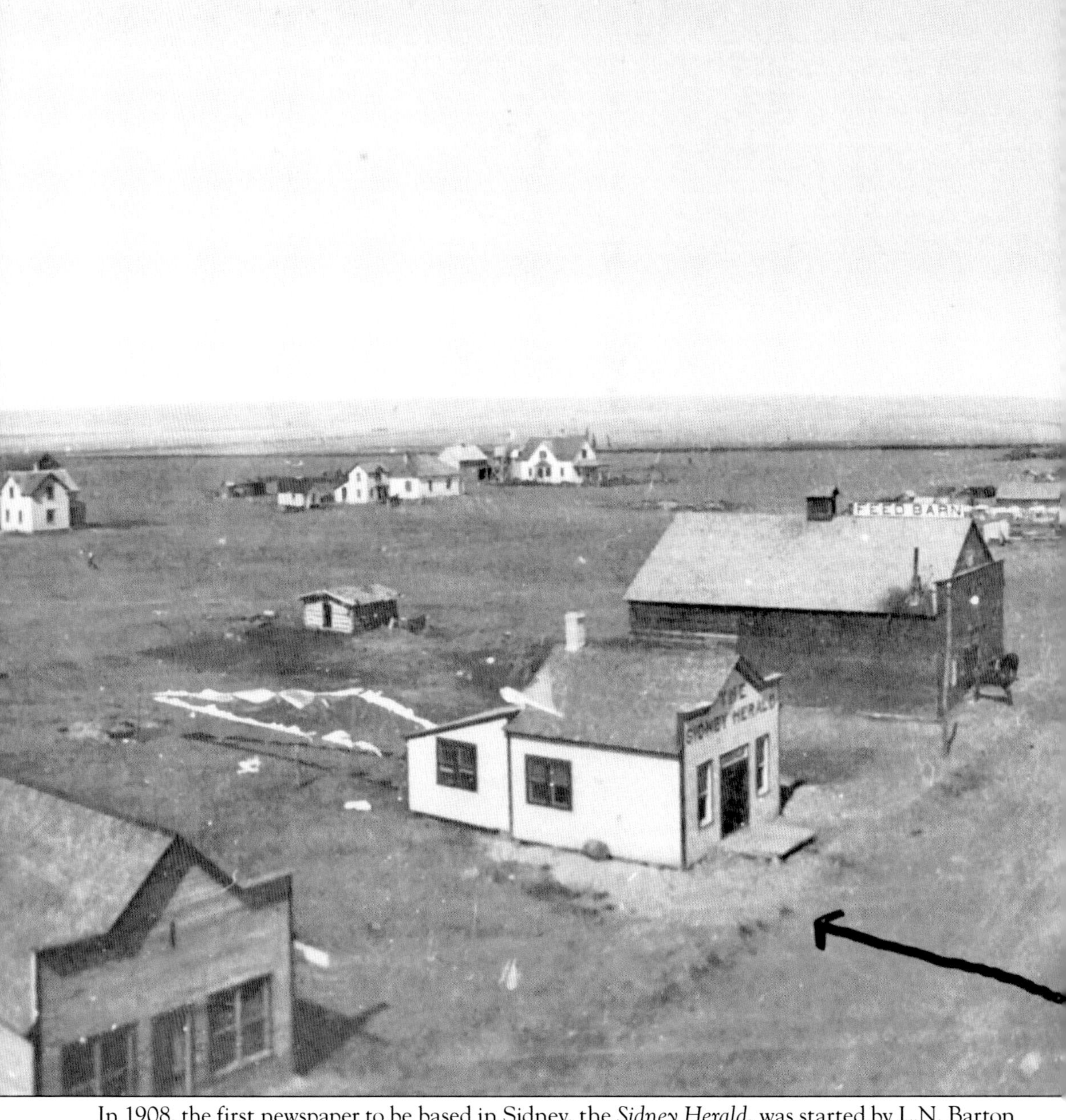

In 1908, the first newspaper to be based in Sidney, the *Sidney Herald*, was started by L.N. Barton and F.J. Matoushek. Their newspaper office was in the back of Mercer's Pool Hall before it was moved to a building on South Central Avenue near where the Lalonde Hotel stood from 1949 to 1999. In 1909, the paper was sold to William H. Ketcham, who in turn sold it to his son, Harry,

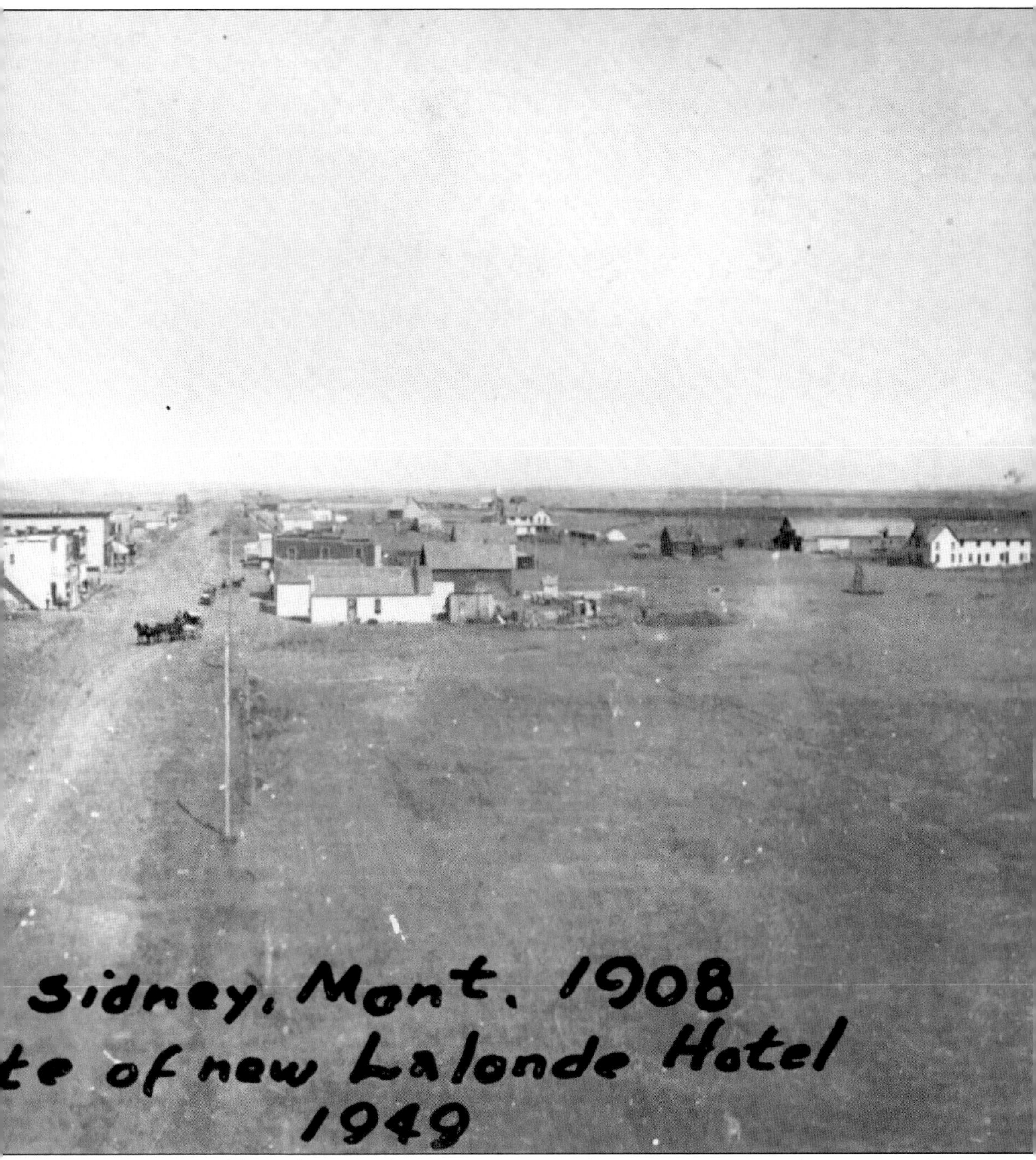

in 1912. Harry would run the paper for 14 years, moving the operation to a new location at 119 North Central Avenue, where it would remain for the next 74 years. The paper changed hands once more when the Wick Newspaper Group took over in 1958. Wick, a family-owned business, still owns and operates the *Sidney Herald* today.

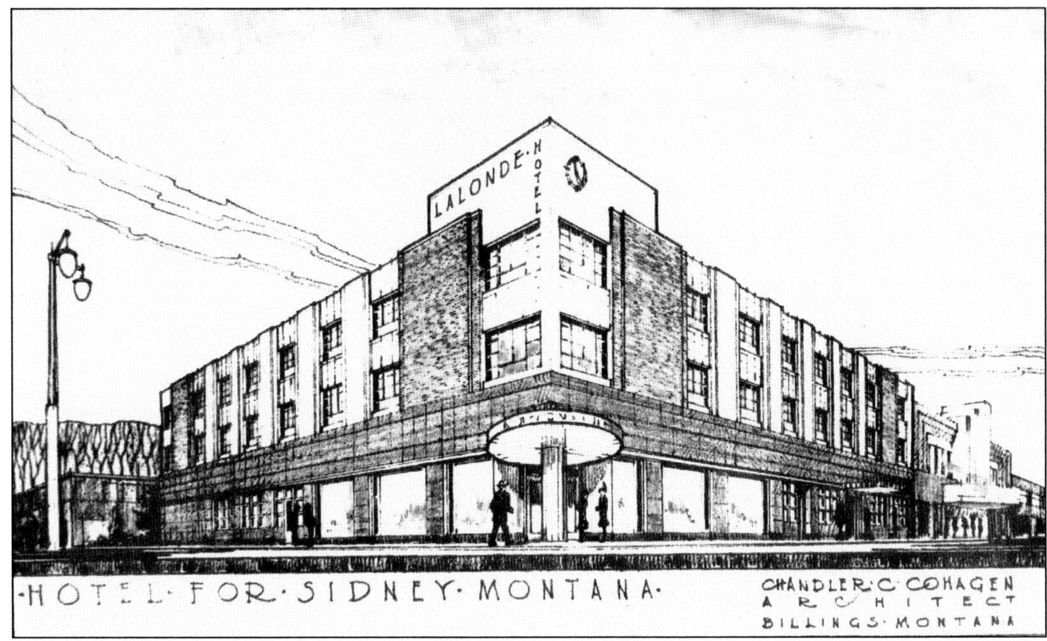

The Lalonde Hotel was advertised as "New as Tomorrow." Built in 1949, the hotel was "one of the most modern in America." The grand opening was attended by 3,000 people. With 80 beds and 80 baths, the hotel was air-conditioned and included a coffee shop, a dining room, a cocktail lounge called the Yellowstone Lounge, and a banquet room big enough to seat 300 people. There was also an attached drugstore on the main level called Turner Drug. In addition to all of the amenities that the Lalonde Hotel offered, the Sidney Hotel Group also claimed that the hotel was fireproof.

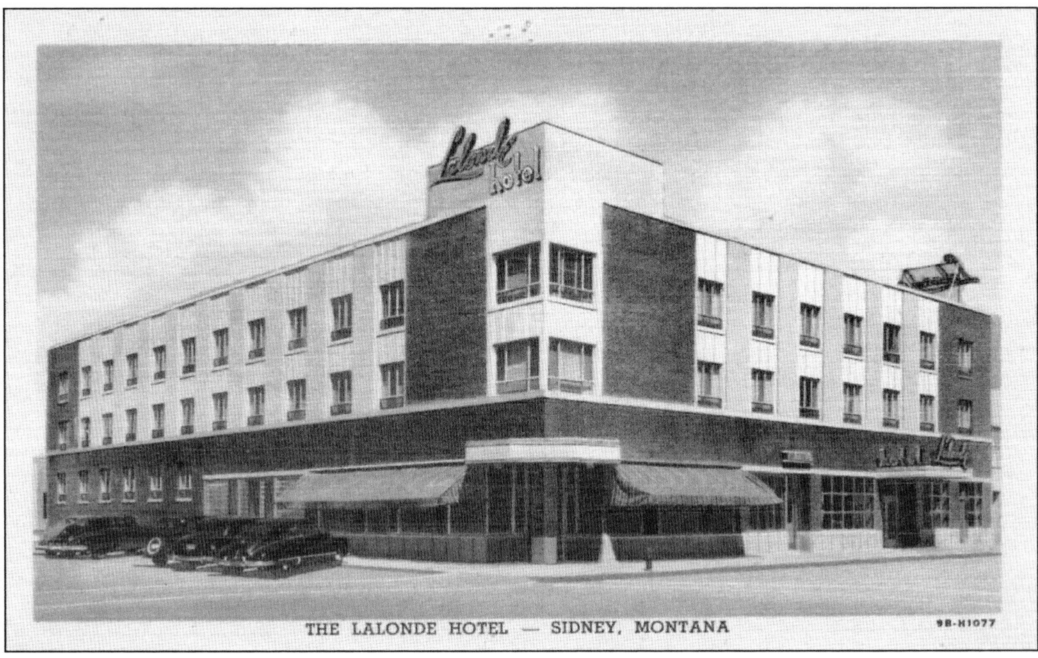

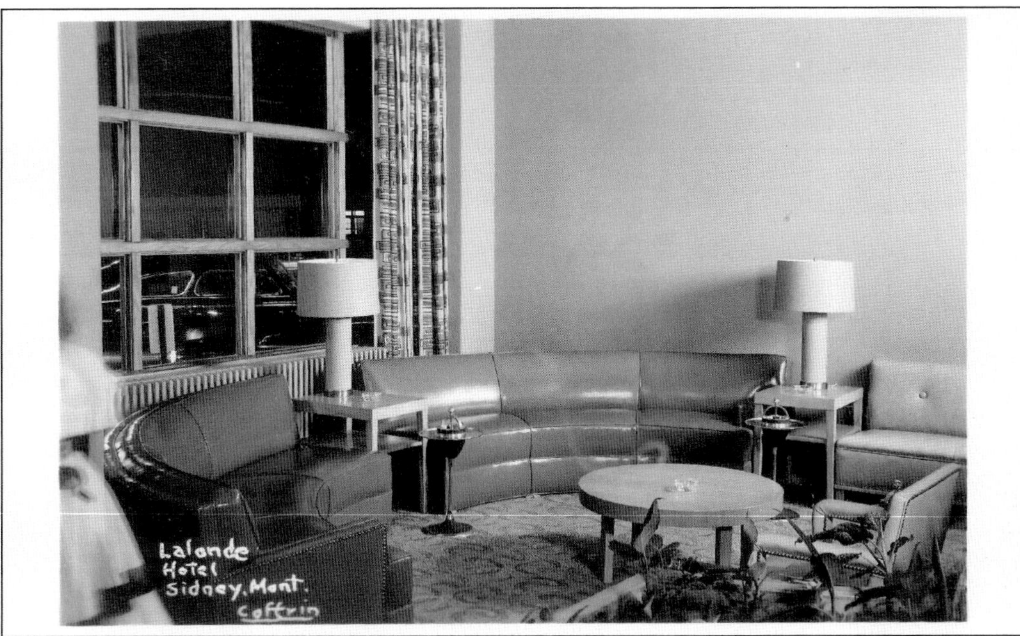

The color scheme for Lalonde's furniture and interior design featured blush mahogany, very modern for the time it was built. Carpeting for each of the hotel rooms, as well as the lobby, and other furnishings were purchased from Marshall Field Company in Chicago, according to the *Sidney Herald*. Venetian blinds covered the windows, along with "blending drapes." By all accounts, Lalonde Hotel was a huge draw for visitors and residents of Sidney alike. Fifty years after it was built, however, the Sidney Hotel Group was proved wrong when an electrical fire burned the hotel down in 1999.

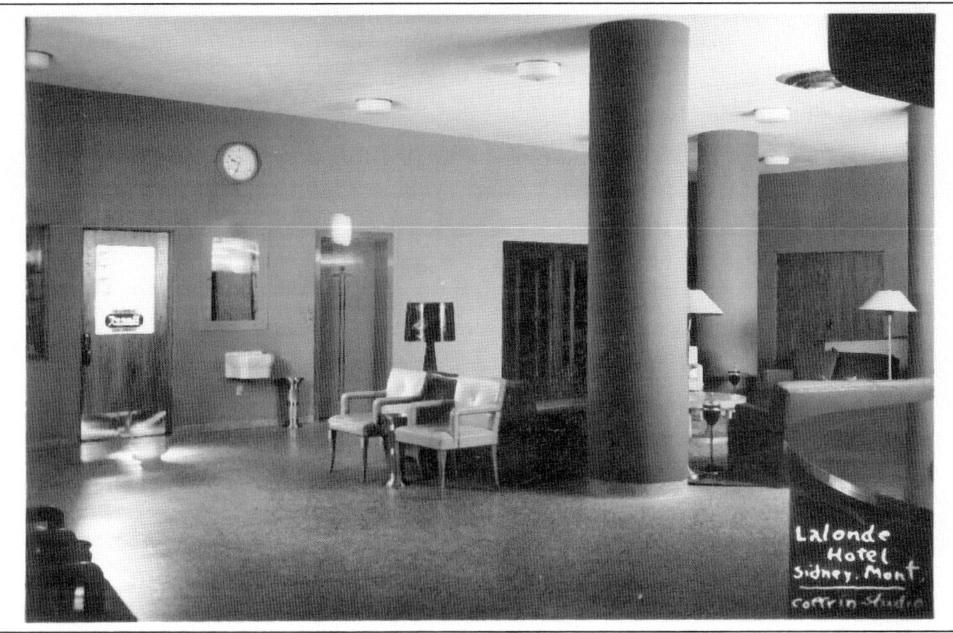

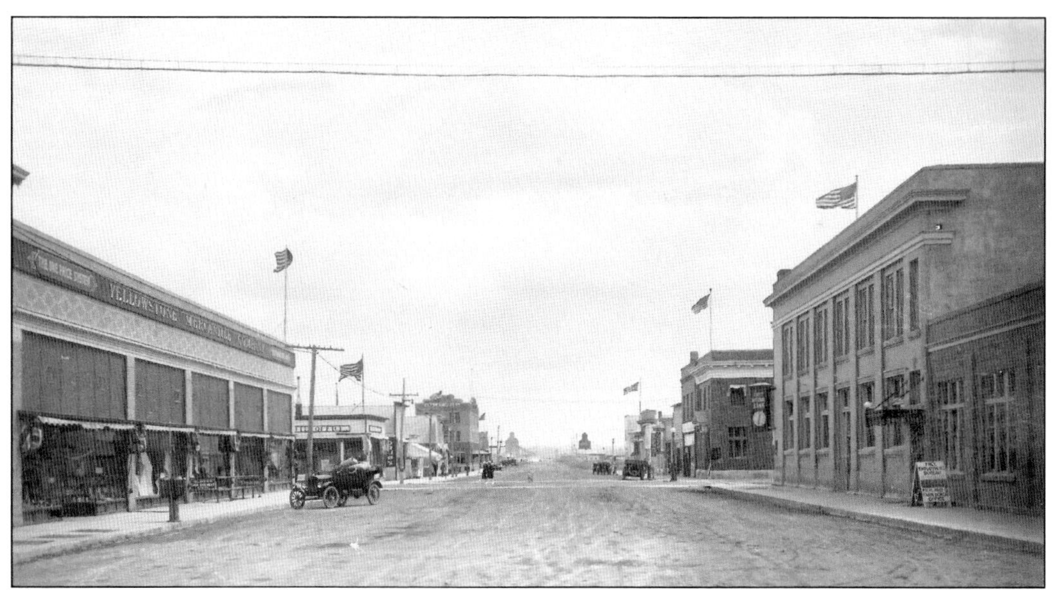

Yellowstone Mercantile, seen above on the left, began business in Sidney in 1906. Charles Earl Varco, originally of Rose Creek, Minnesota, had erected a frame building in which to sell his wares. In 1916, construction was completed on the brick building, and the original store was used as the grocery department. Yellowstone Merc, as the company was commonly known, was in business until 2007. A unique aspect of the Yellowstone Mercantile was its money exchange method. The cash rail system was a series of pulleys with a cup that had a clip attached. When customers paid for their wares, coins would go into the cup and the receipt and paper money would be clipped to the bottom. The money would travel up into the cash office, where the bill would be posted. The building is now known as the Yellowstone Marketplace.

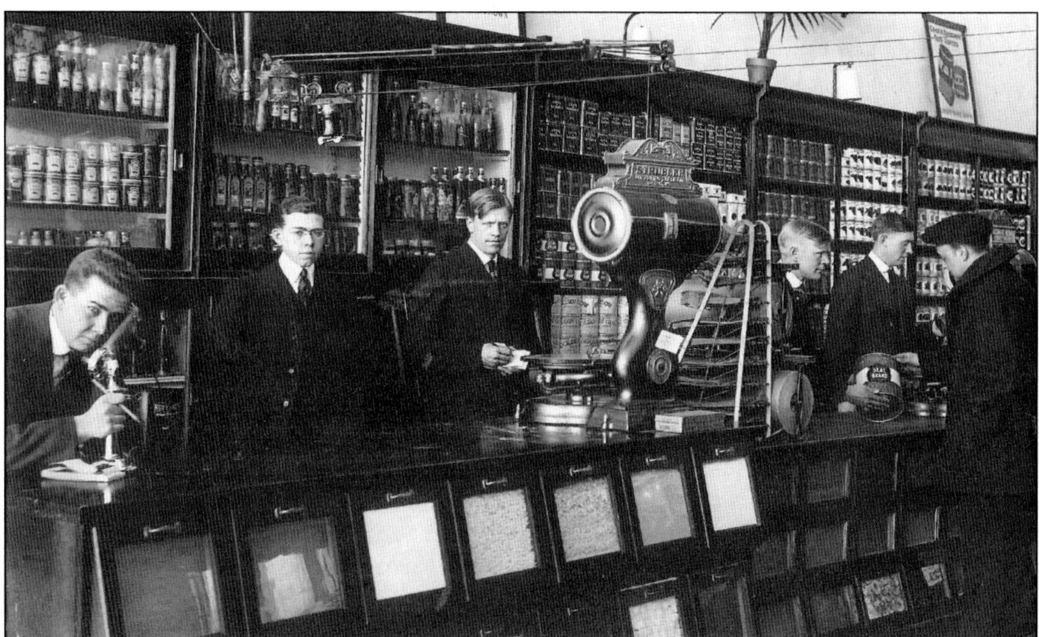

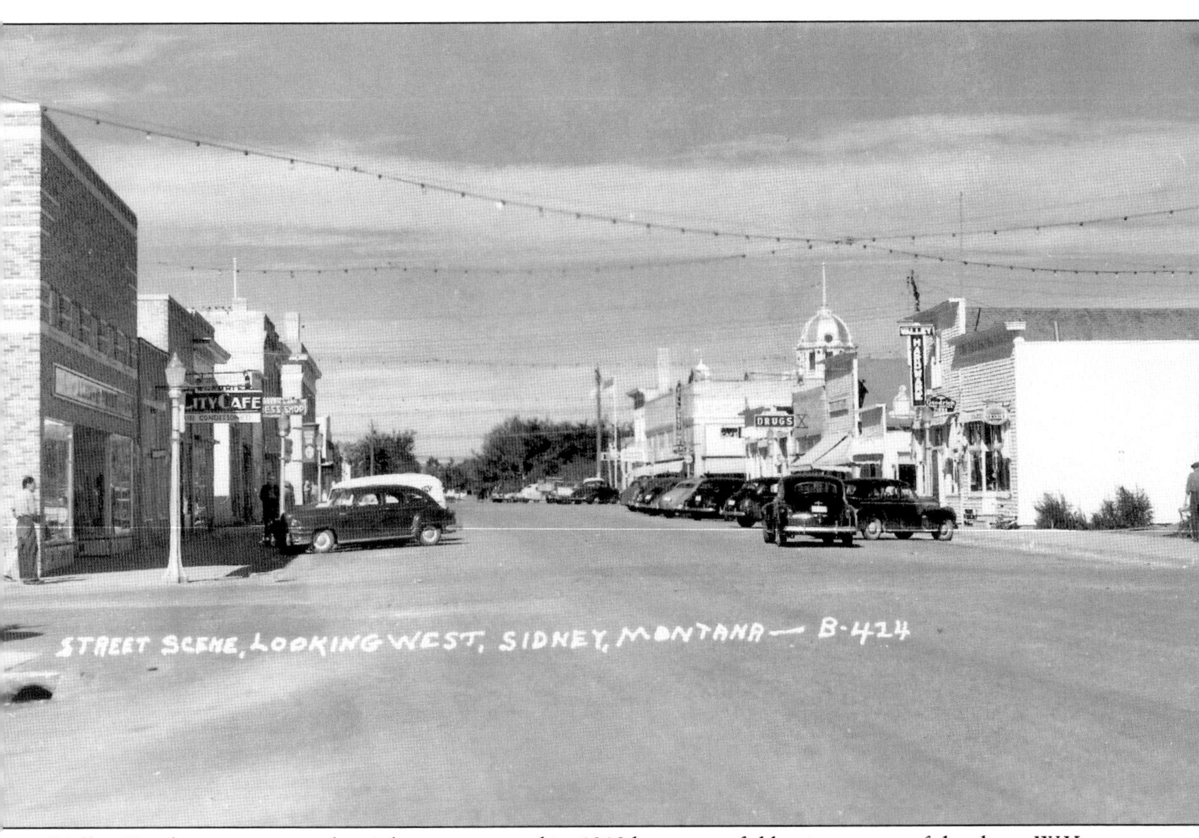

Valley Hardware, seen on the right, was created in 1910 by successful businessmen of the day—W.K. Adams, Arthur Nelson, Augustus Vaux, Dr. J.S. Beagle, and Charles Earl Varco. The Yellowstone Mercantile and Valley Lumber had handled hardware and farm implement sales up to that point. Valley Hardware took over the sale of farm implements from International and John Deere and also offered a variety of hardware and other household and farm supplies. According to Art Nelson, who served as the store's secretary, treasurer, and manager, the first item to be sold by the Valley Hardware Company was an axe that Pete Quilling picked out. The business grew steadily until 1951, when the original building was torn down; a new building was completed in 1952. Also visible in the photograph along East Main Street are J.C. Penney, City Café, Sidney Drug, and the dome of the courthouse.

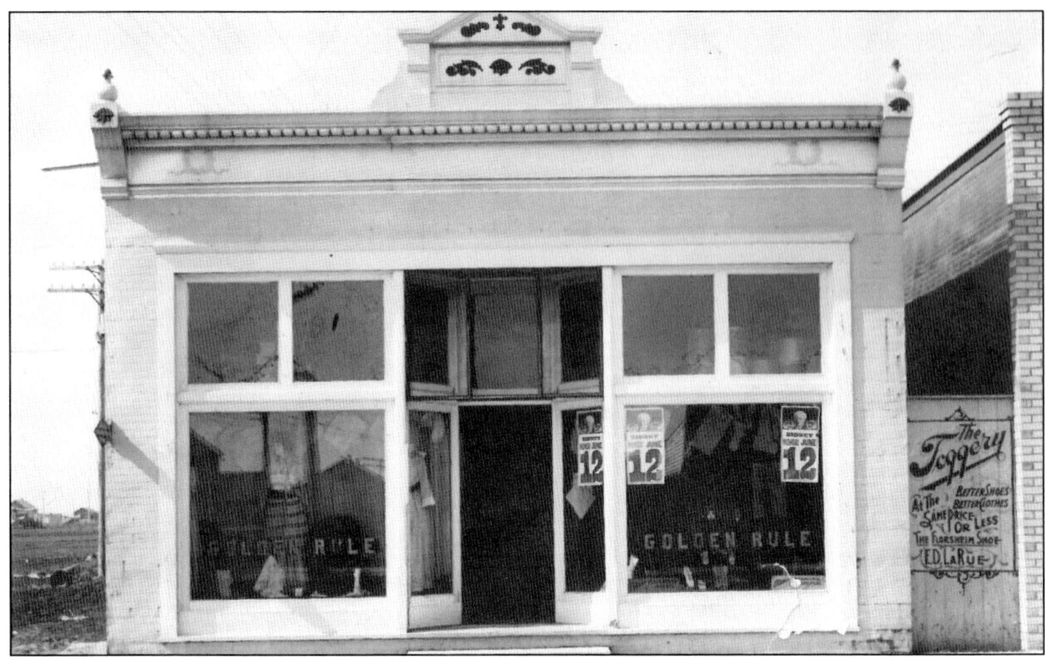

A cousin of the J.C. Penney department stores, Golden Rule stores provided dry goods to the communities in which they operated. J.C. Penney initially had a non-compete clause in Montana. This 1914 photograph shows Sidney's Golden Rule store, owned by Lottie and John Roscoe Shaver. J.C. Penney eventually opened a banner store in Sidney in 1941. It is now the oldest active J.C. Penney in Montana.

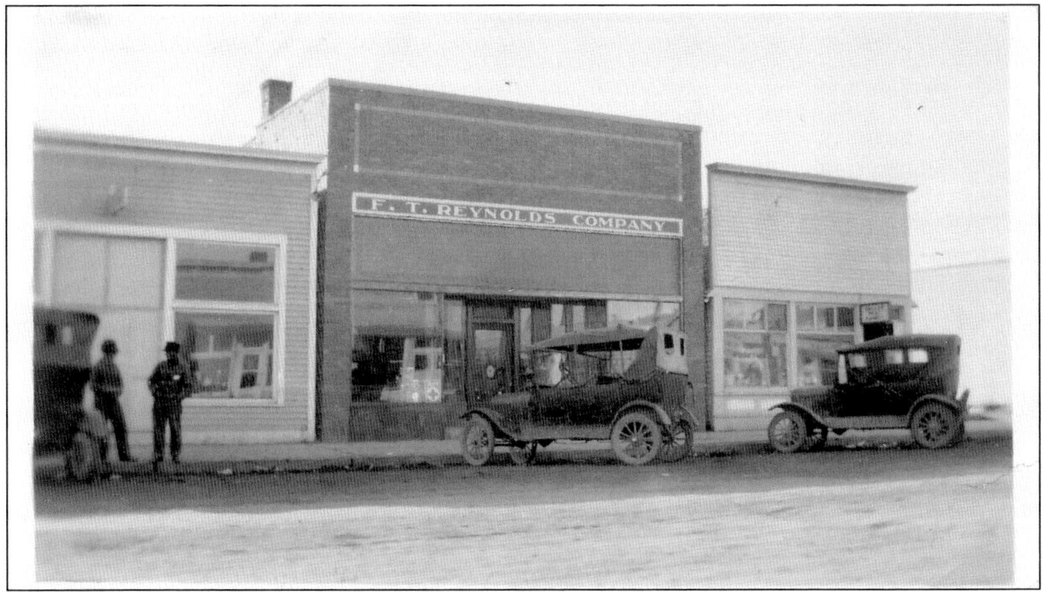

F.T. Reynolds Company, a grocery chain, was created by Frank Reynolds in 1925. His first store was established in Glendive, and a second store opened in August 1925 in Sidney. Reynolds's stores were touted to be "Where your dollar buys most." As Sidney grew and the demand for groceries increased, Reynolds changed locations several times. Reynolds is still in operation 90 years later, with a location in north Sidney.

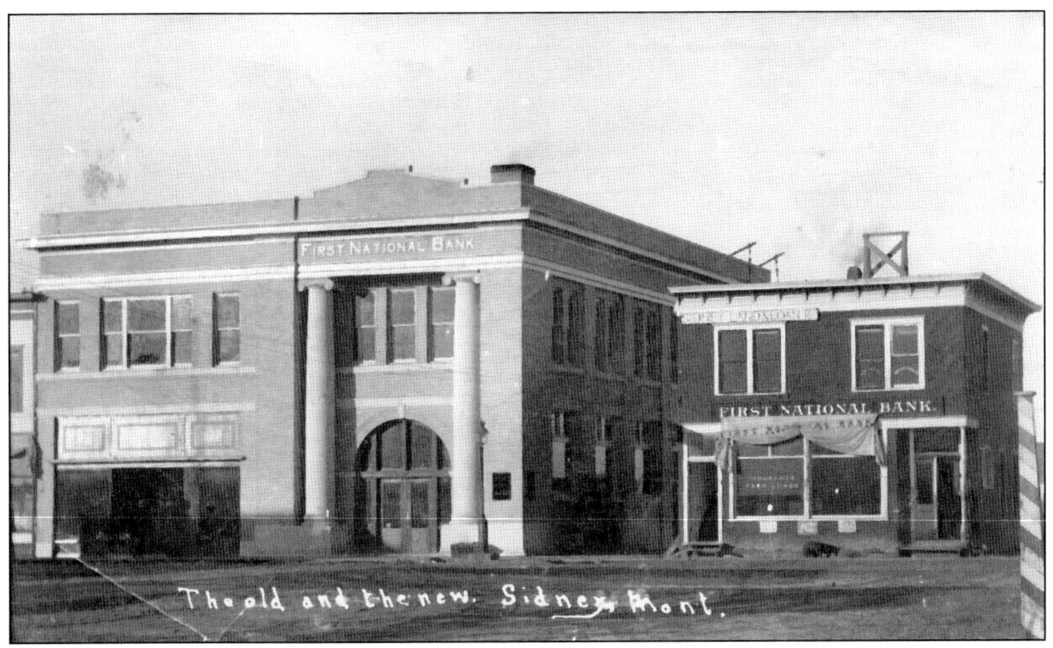

In 1913, architect B. Riveness designed a fine new replacement building for the First National Bank in Sidney. The old First National Bank was moved into the street so that the new building could be constructed. Coming in at a cost of $30,000, the bank had two stories and a full basement. The north half of the first floor was to be used by the bank, and the south half was designed to be used by the Turner brothers for their drugstore. The bank featured hot and cold running water, heat, and a fireproof vault and was built using reinforced concrete with gray Hebron pressed brick on the sides of the building. Handsome marble pillars were added to the front of the building as well.

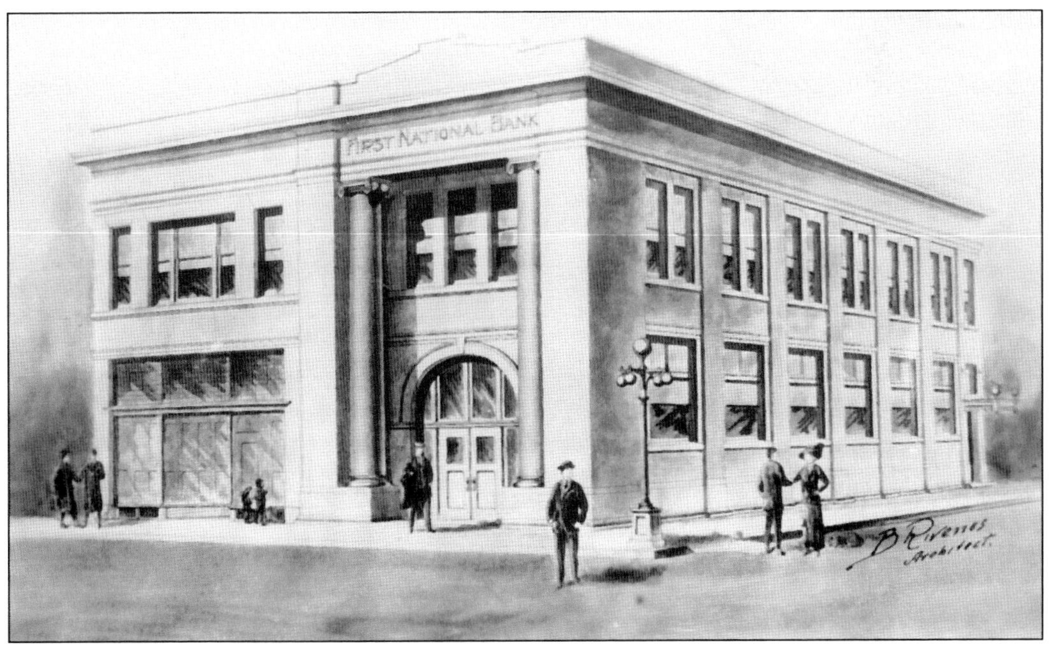

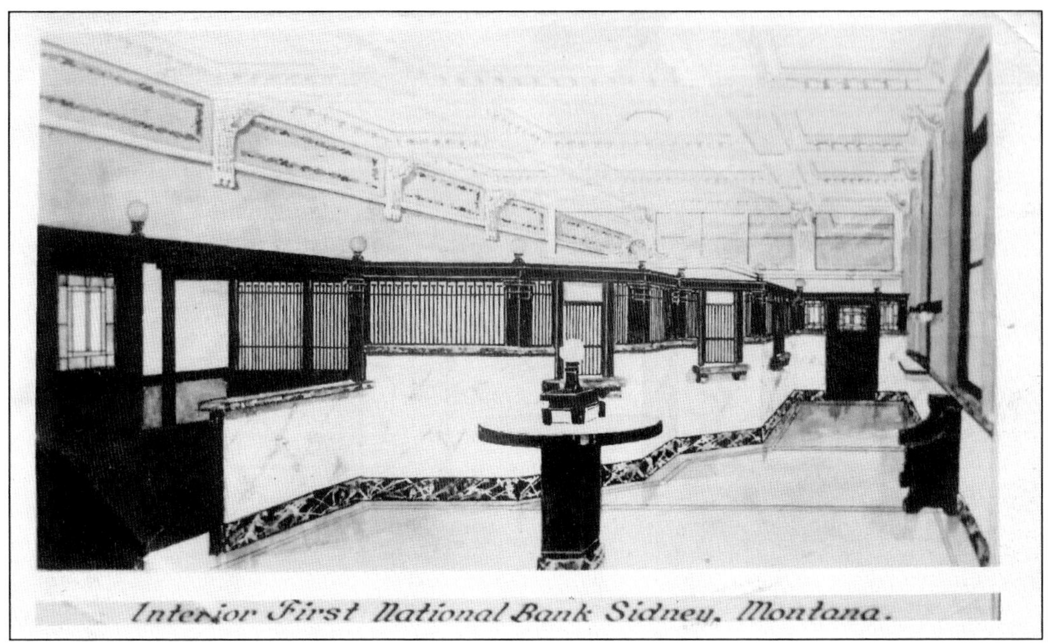
Interior First National Bank Sidney, Montana.

The interior of the new First National Bank was admirable as well. The floor of the banking room was laid with beautiful, glossy tile, and the design of the floors flowed in harmony through the rest of the bank. Art nouveau–style glass windows were fitted on the doors within the lobby, and friezes were installed at the top of the walls near the ceiling. The teller cages were also beautifully outfitted. Turner Brothers Pharmacy installed its business in the space south of the bank, and additional office space was rented out to doctors, lawyers, and to organizations like the Masons to hold their meetings.

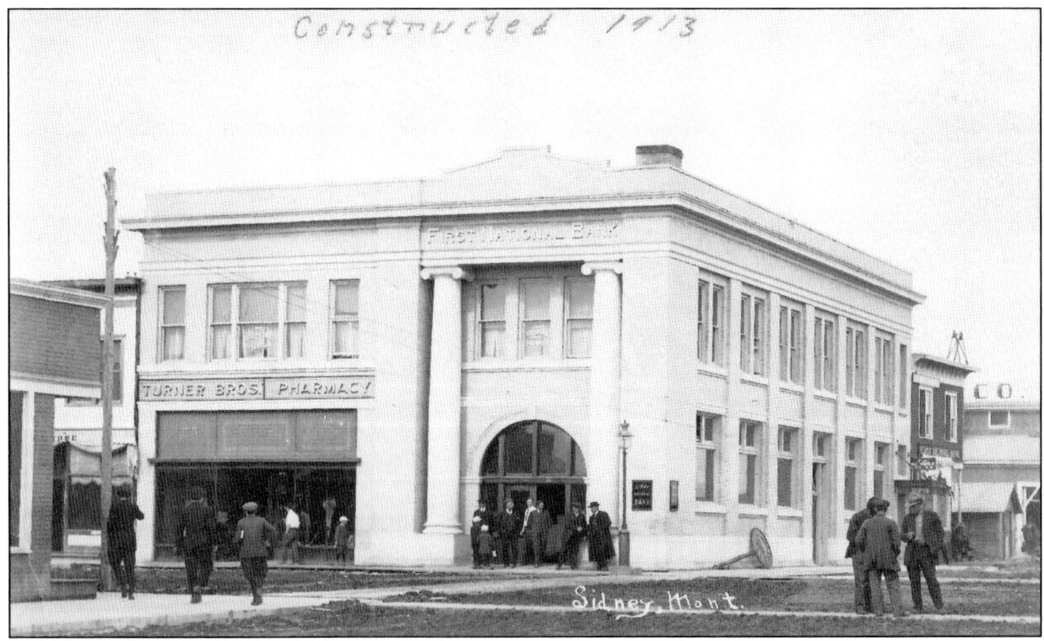

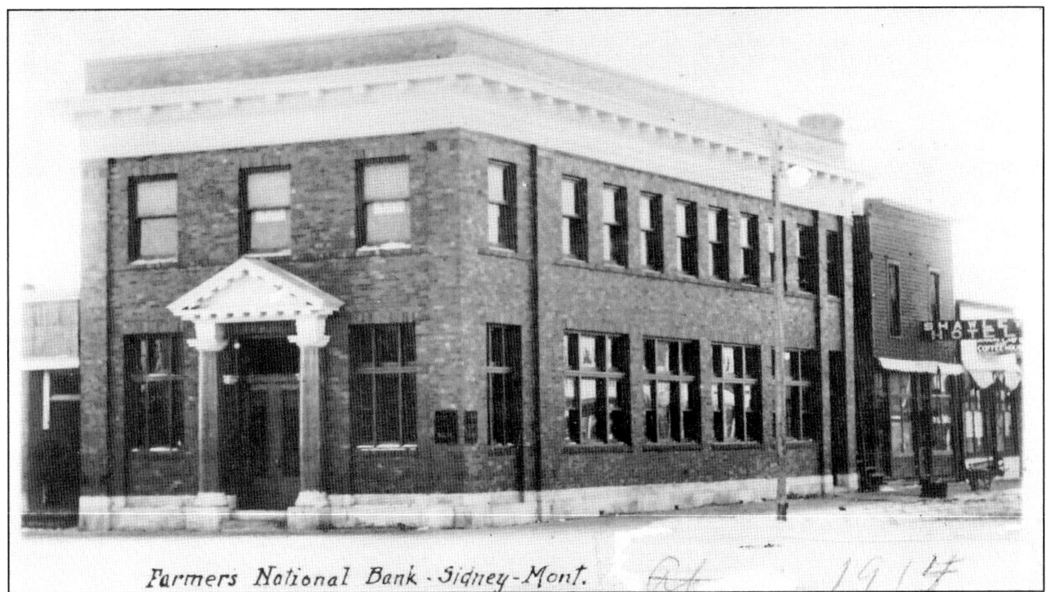

Farmers National Bank replaced Nutt Farmers State Bank in 1914. Farmers National Bank was much admired for its handsome facade, which included granite pillars and a raised vestibule. Additionally, it featured a fireproof vault, a workroom, a customer room, a director's room, and steam heat. Eventually the Farmers National Bank became Yellowstone Valley Bank and Trust Company and finally Sidney National Bank in 1925. The cashier counter and many of the items used by the cashiers shown in the photograph of Sidney National Bank are now on display in the MonDak Heritage Center, and the Cheerio Lounge took over the building in 1958.

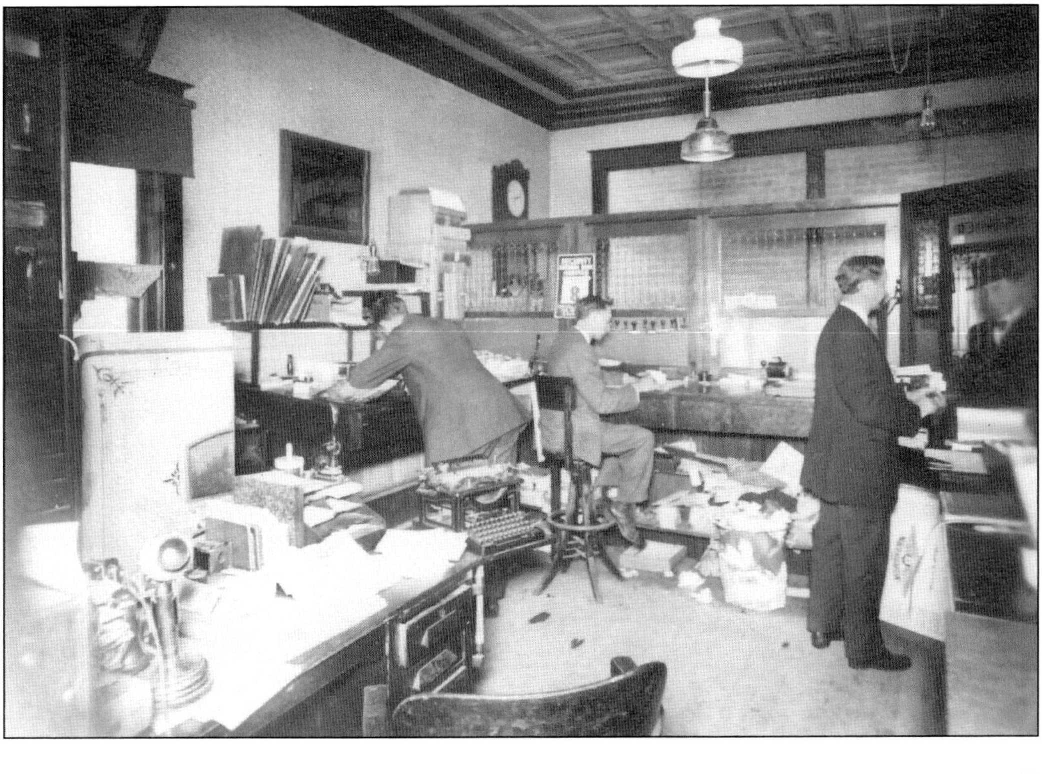

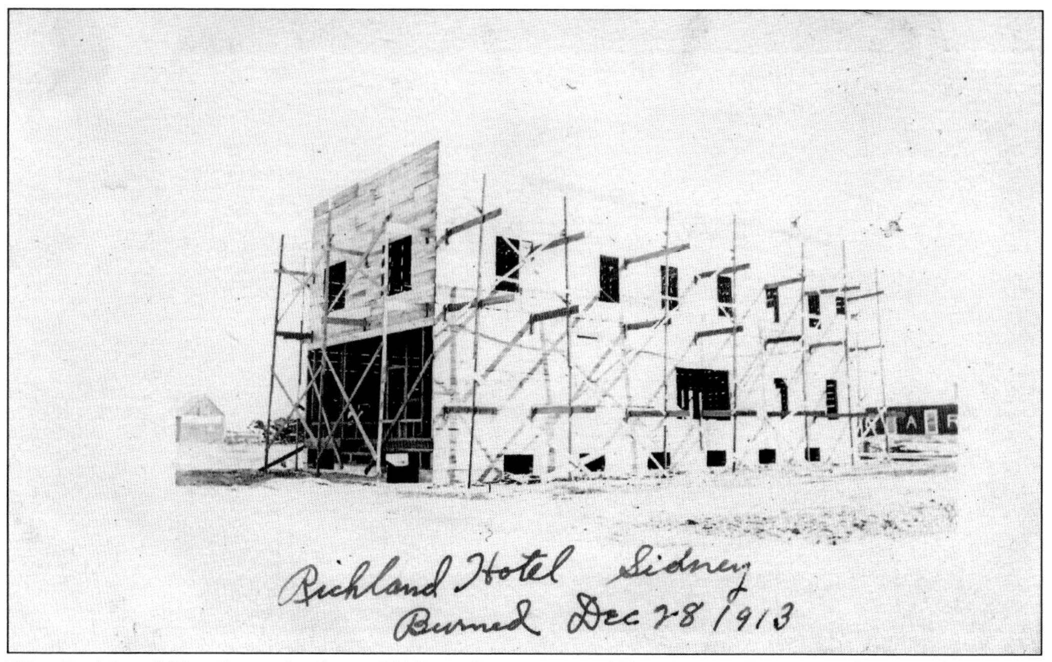

The Richland Hotel was built in 1913 at the corner of East Main Street and Second Avenue SE in Sidney. Unfortunately, the hotel did not last long. On December 28, 1913, at 4:00 a.m., a fire was discovered in the hotel basement by the chef. The alarm was sounded, and with the help of the newly formed Sidney Volunteer Fire Department, all of the hotel's occupants escaped grave injury.

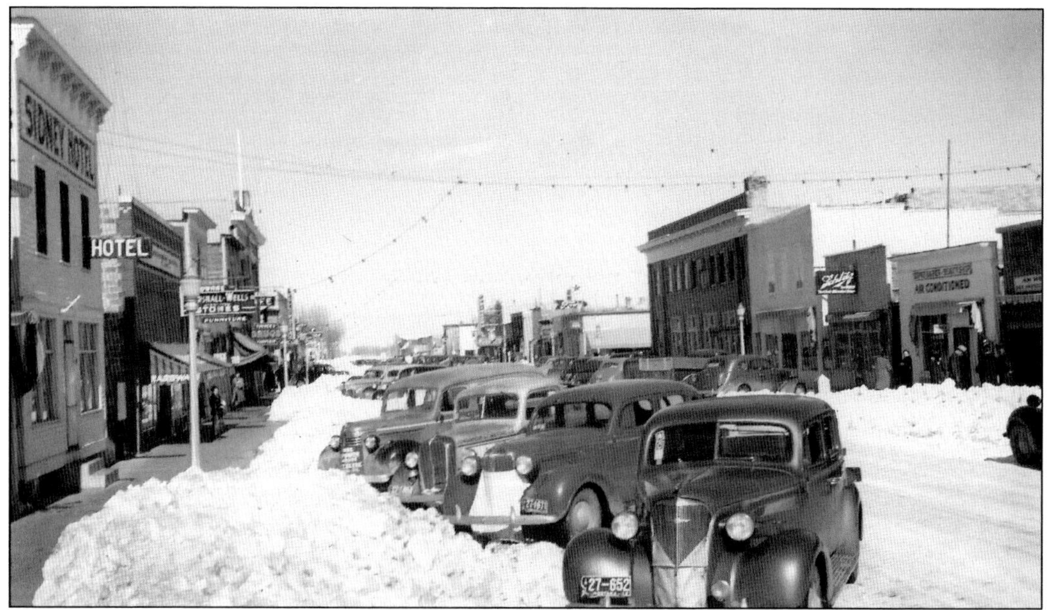

The Sidney Hotel, which can be seen on the left in this picture, was yet another of the early hotels in the area that ran a swift trade in the first half of the century. This photograph shows Central Avenue in Sidney, and Johnson Hardware is now located on this site.

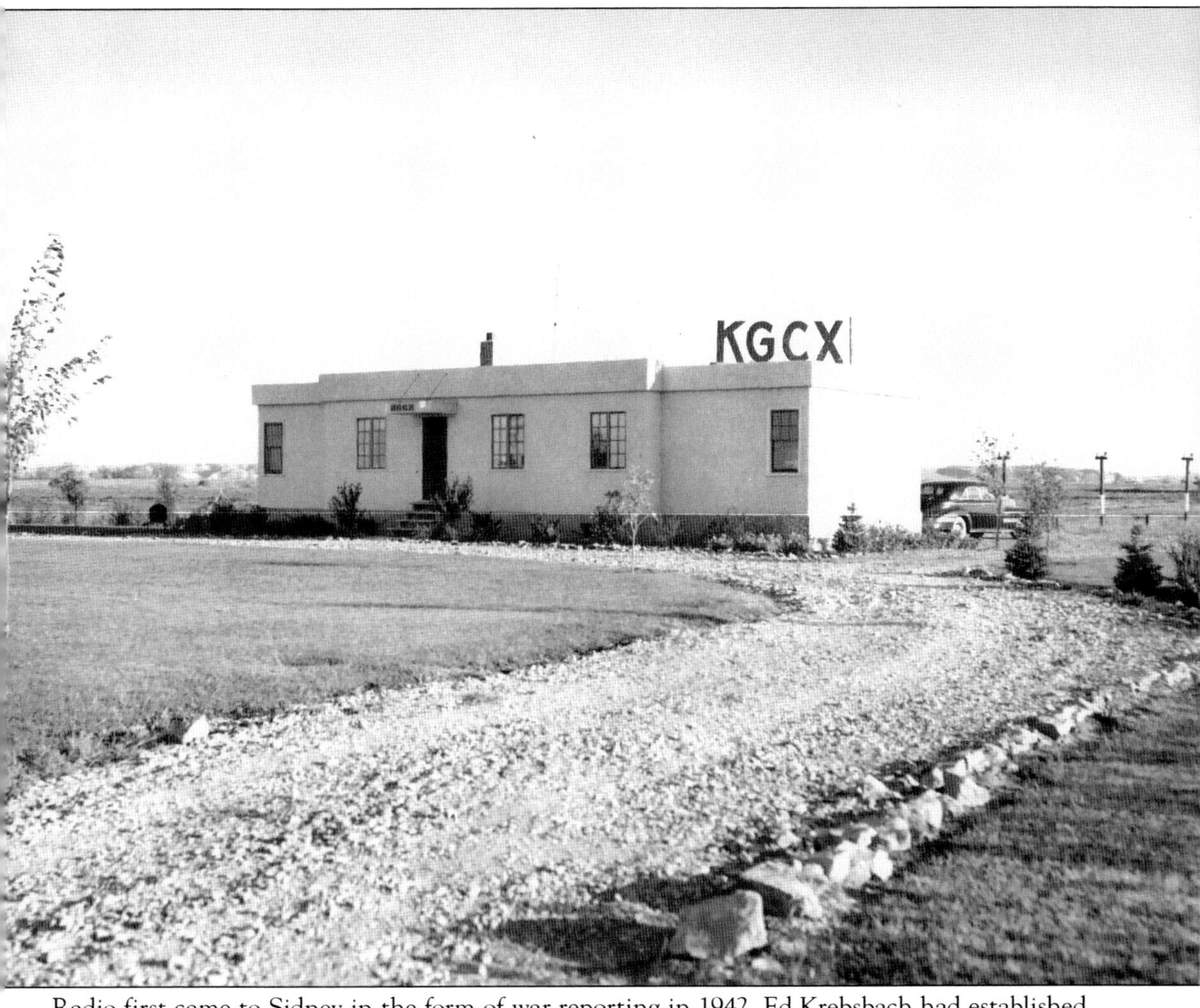

Radio first came to Sidney in the form of war reporting in 1942. Ed Krebsbach had established KGCX in 1926 from behind the First State Bank of Vida, Montana, operating at just 7.5 watts. The schedule included one hour of programming every day at noon and a talent show on Sunday afternoons. In 1929, the station moved to Wolf Point, where a new transmitter was added with an output of 250 watts. The schedule then increased to nine hours daily, with three-hour shows at breakfast, lunch, and dinner. In 1942, the station was moved to Sidney, and six years later, a 5,000-watt transmitter was installed. Later, a new building was constructed to house the transmitter, which was radio controlled from the studios. In 1976, KGCX celebrated 50 years on air with an open house, offering listeners the chance "to come in for a visit anytime." KGCX still operates out of Sidney 39 years later under Marks Group Broadcasting.

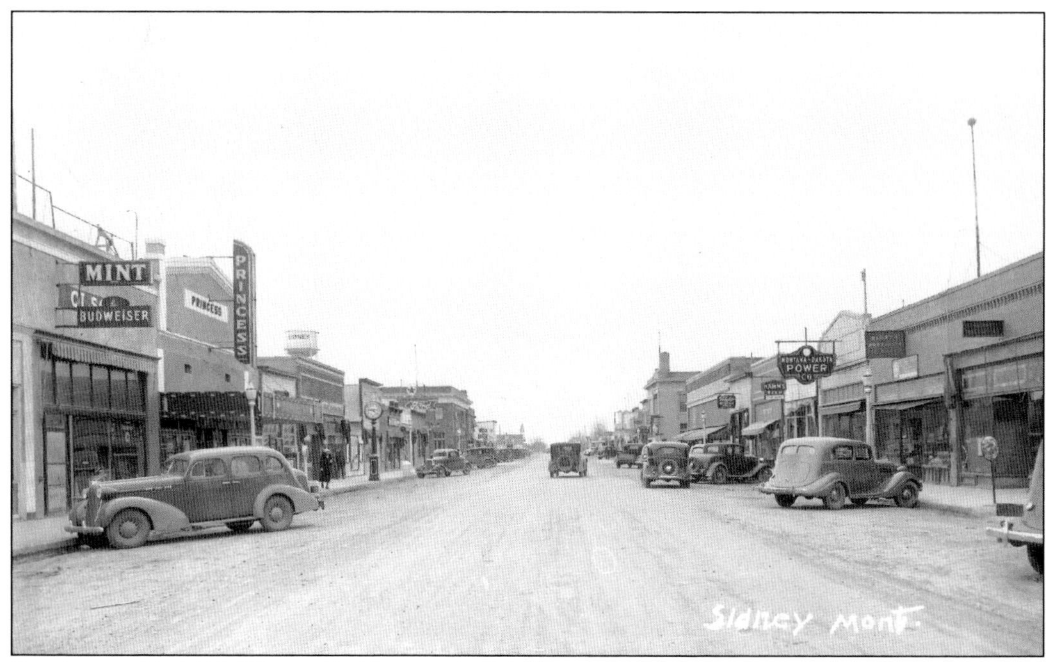

On August 30, 1915, Edman Redding and a Mr. Fox opened the Princess Theatre to the public in Sidney. The "amusement house" featured second-run movies, as well as musical and theatrical performances. The theater remained open until 1951, when it was replaced by the Centre Theatre. The Princess Theatre can be seen along Central Avenue on the left.

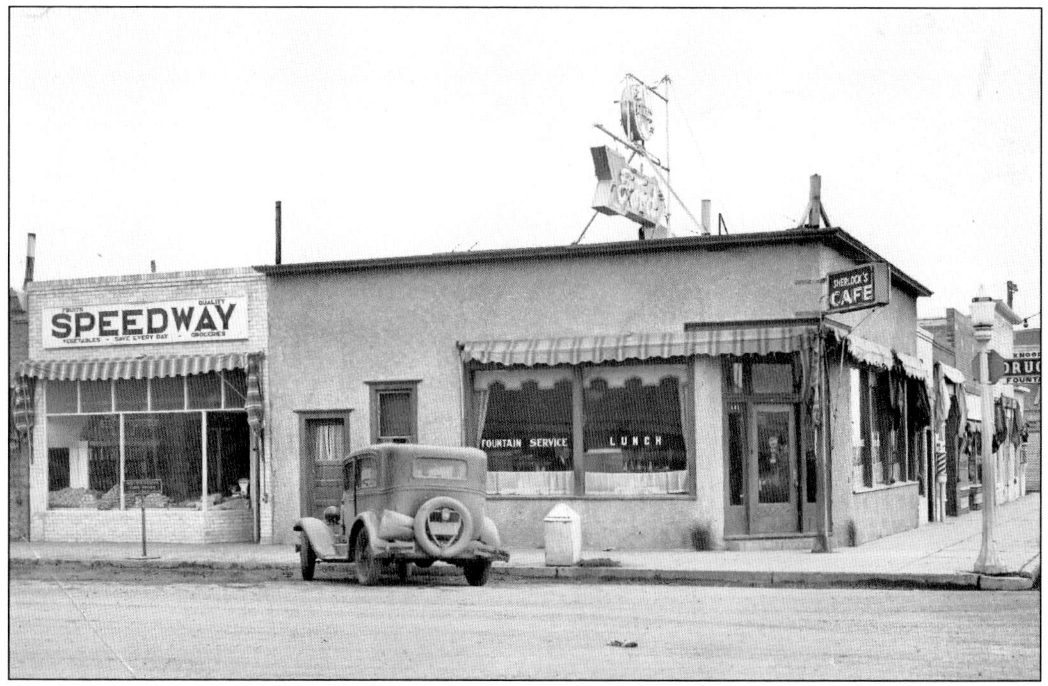

Sherlock's Café, which was opened by Homer Sherlock in 1936, offered a variety of food and drink options for nine years before it was sold to Sherman McCarten in 1945. At that time, it became known as the Stockman's Café. Speedway Groceries can also be seen next to the café.

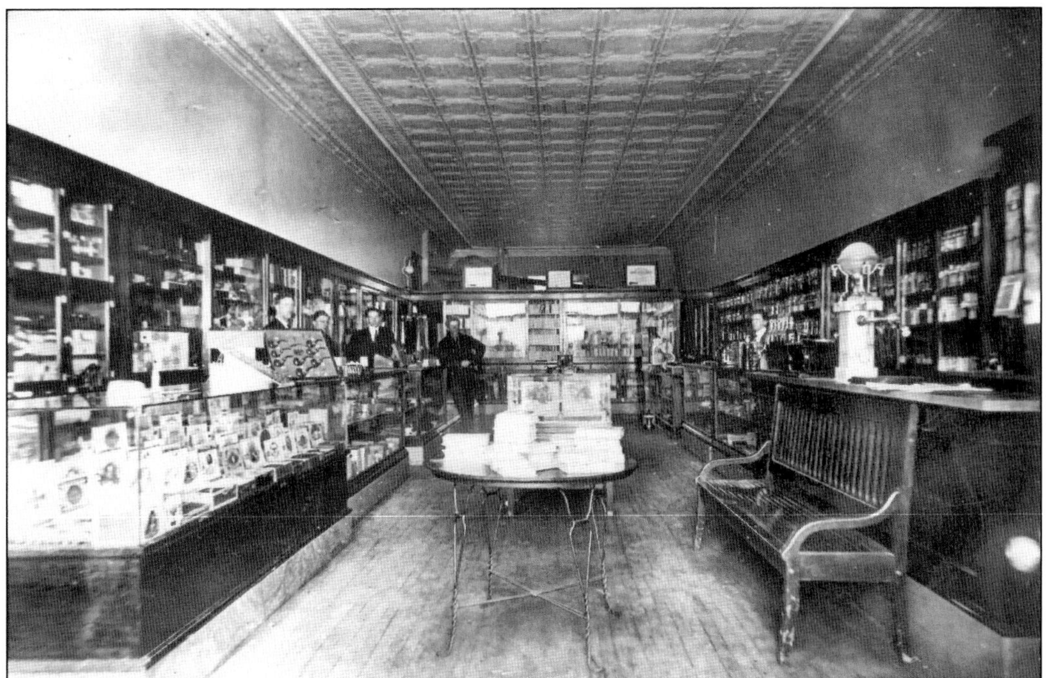

Sidney has never had a shortage of drugstores and pharmacies. Turner Drug, which was located in the First National Bank building, was founded in 1909 by brothers James and Henry Turner. The picture above shows the interior of Turner Drug in the First National Bank building. The store continued to flourish in that location and in 1949, when the Lalonde Hotel opened, a second Turner Drug opened on the lower level and was known as the hotel pharmacy. Sidney Drug and Jewelry Store, on the other hand, was founded by Walter Knoop in 1920 and opened on East Main Street. Originally, Knoop had a partner who worked as a jeweler, but when he died a year into their venture, the jewelry was dropped. The original store was replaced in 1936 by new construction in the same location.

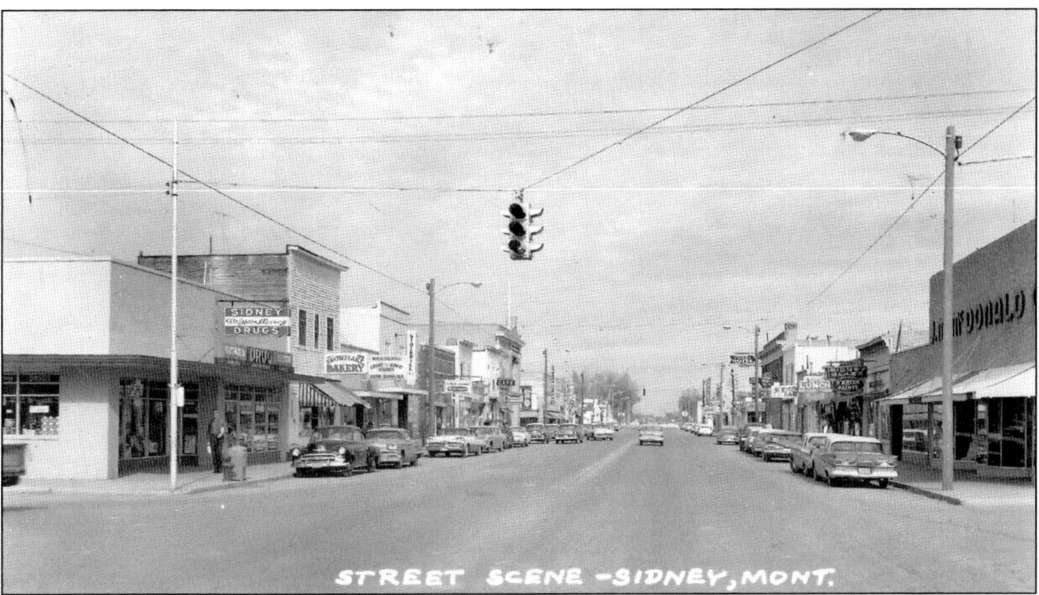

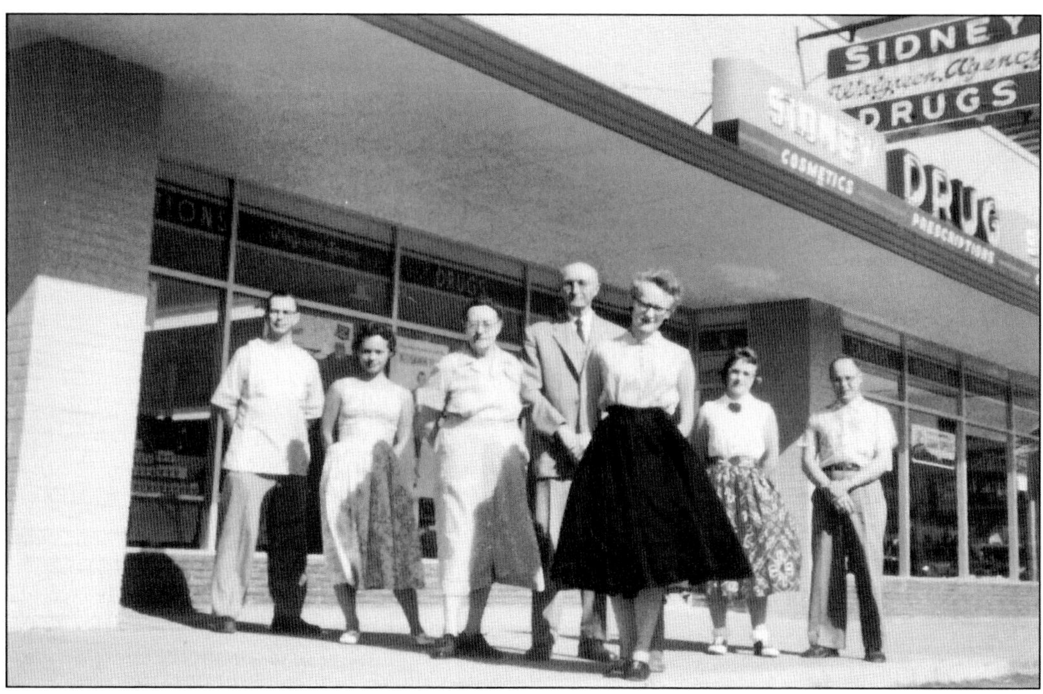

In 1957, Sidney Drug moved to a new location on Central Avenue. The photograph above shows the store on September 7, 1957. Walter Knoop's wife, Anna, continued to have a shop in the East Main Street location. Additionally, Anna had become a registered pharmacist and worked alongside her husband for many years. Knoop's son, John, who went by Jack, also went to school to become a registered pharmacist and took over the business from his father in 1975. Walter died in 1976, and Anna died in 1978. A third-generation Knoop, Jack's son, Stephen, also became a pharmacist and joined the family business in 1981. In the late 1980s, after celebrating nearly 70 years in business, Sidney Drug closed, and an accounting firm took over the building.

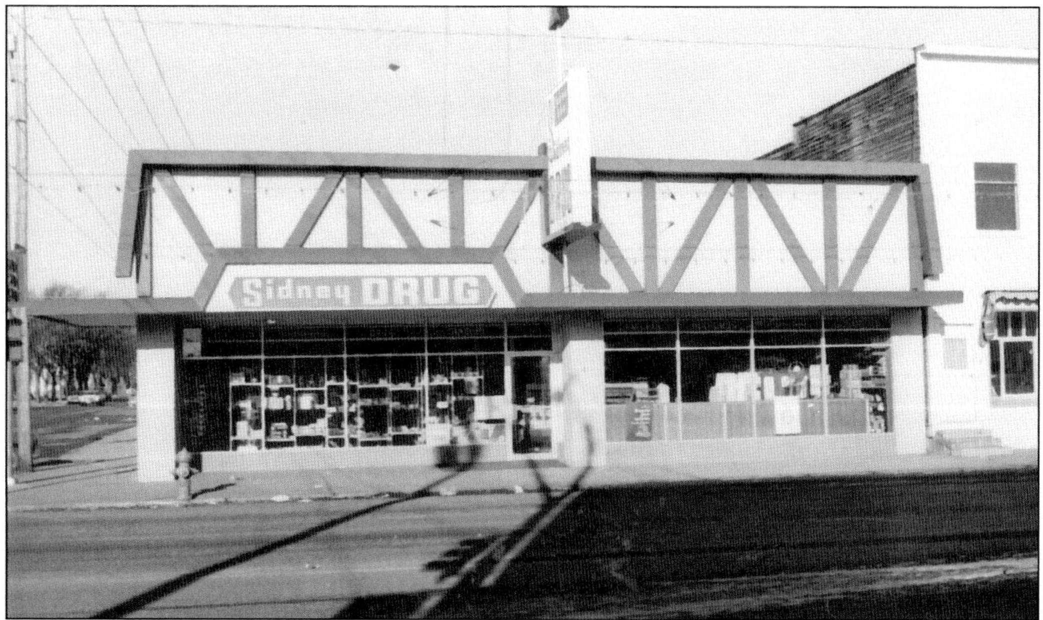

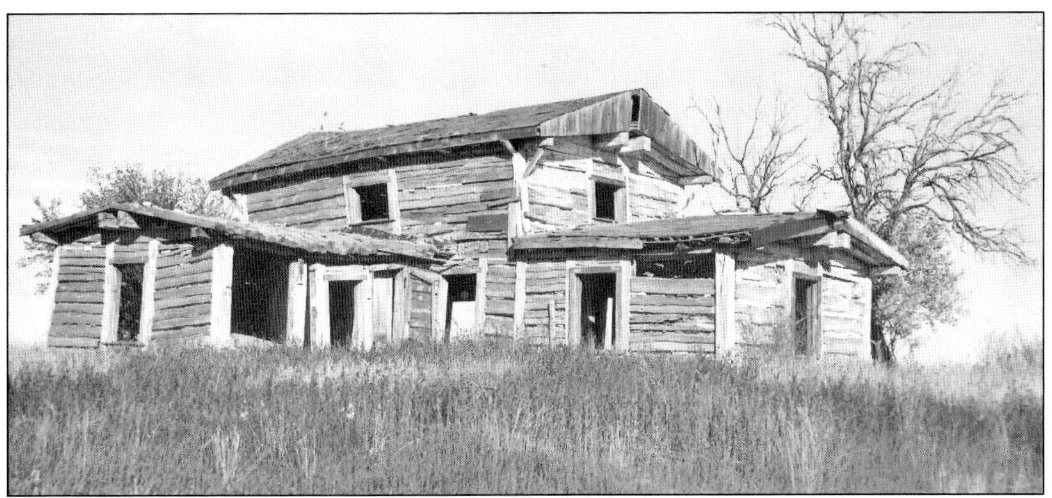

The O'Brien Stage Stop opened in 1881 just south of Sidney near Fox Creek. It was opened by John O'Brien and was one of the earliest general stores in the area. O'Brien built several structures on his property, and it became a popular stop along the ranch road. The photograph here shows the main building in disrepair after the stage stop closed.

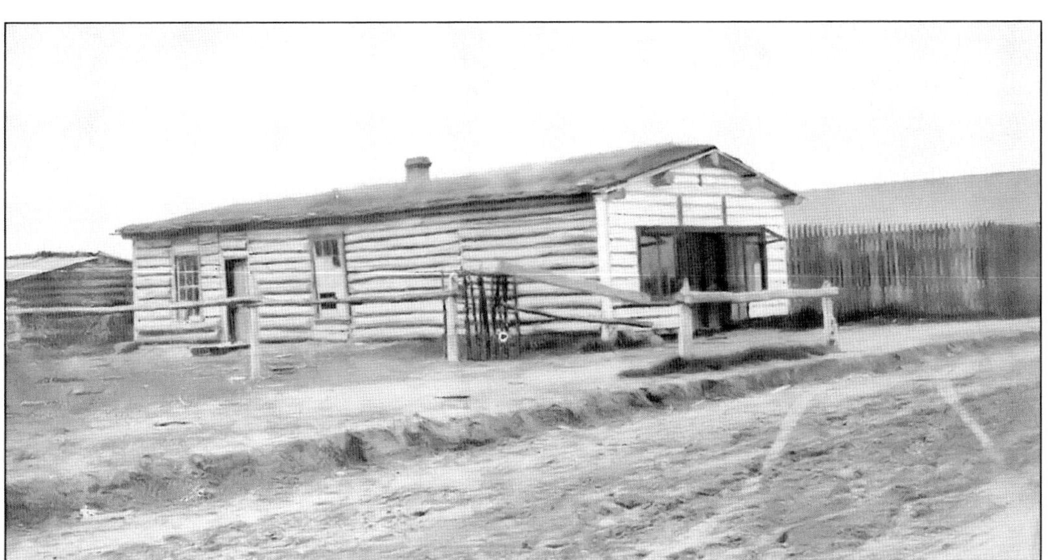

The Kenoyer Store was built on the west side of Central Avenue by Edgar Kenoyer in 1900. It was run by Kenoyer until 1904 when he sold it to Joe Ferris. Ferris ran the store for about five years before closing the store. Ferris's son, Arnie, talked to some of his friends about renting it as a bachelor clubhouse, and soon bridge sessions were held there.

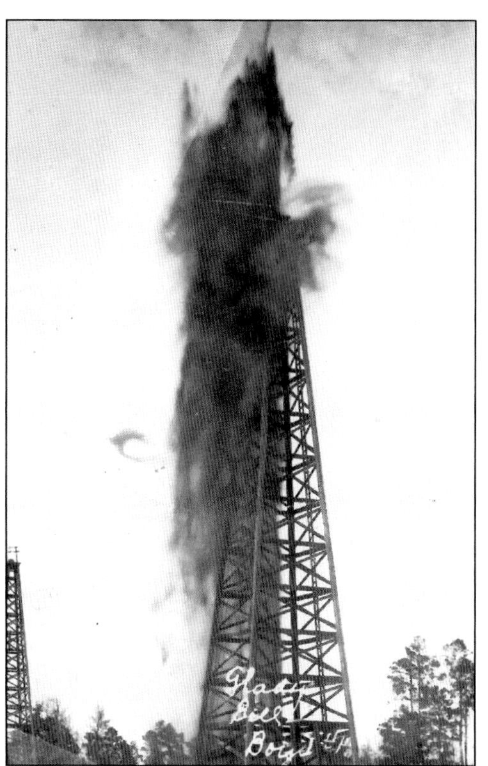

The Williston Basin, in eastern Montana and western North Dakota, is known for its rich petroleum deposits. Oil was originally found in southeastern Montana, but it was not until large fields were discovered in the 1950s that oil production began in northeastern Montana, including in and around Sidney. Production peaked in the mid-1980s and started again in the 2000s as different drilling techniques became available.

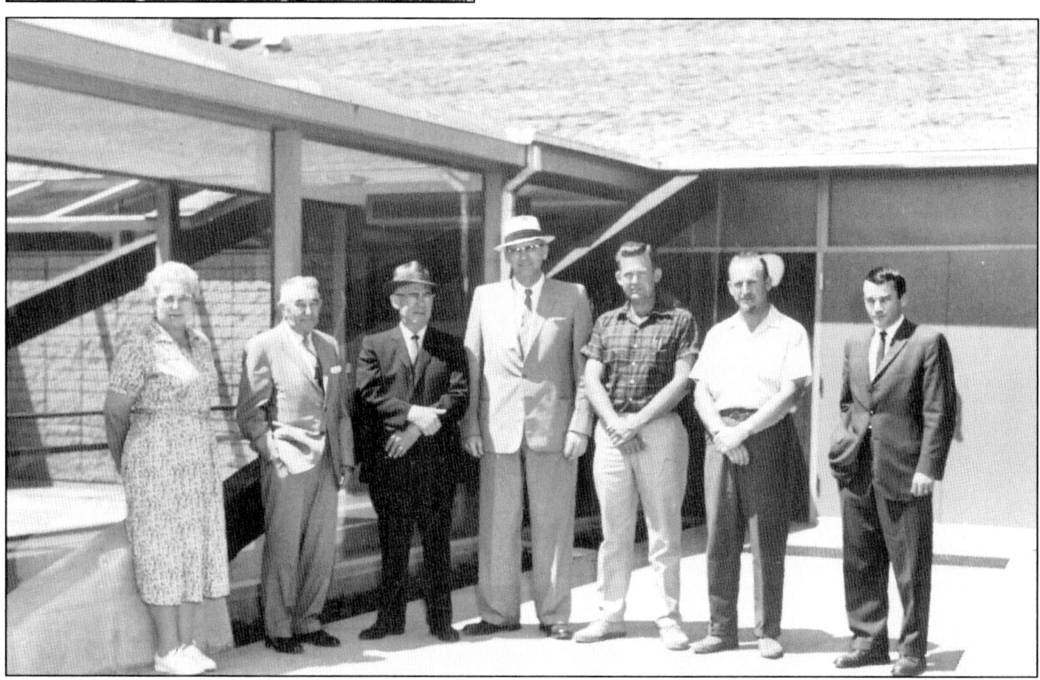

Richland Homes was a nonprofit, nondenominational Christian home for aging men and women that was created on March 19, 1957. The home, which was designed to house 64 people and needed a staff of 28, opened in May 1961. The organization is still in business today as part of Sidney Health Center's extended-care facility.

Dr. R.A. Morrill was one of the first doctors in Sidney. When the construction of the Lower Yellowstone Irrigation Project began, he was appointed by the government to be the official physician for the construction crews. Because of his knowledge of typhoid fever, his experience was welcome in the area due to widespread outbreaks at the time.

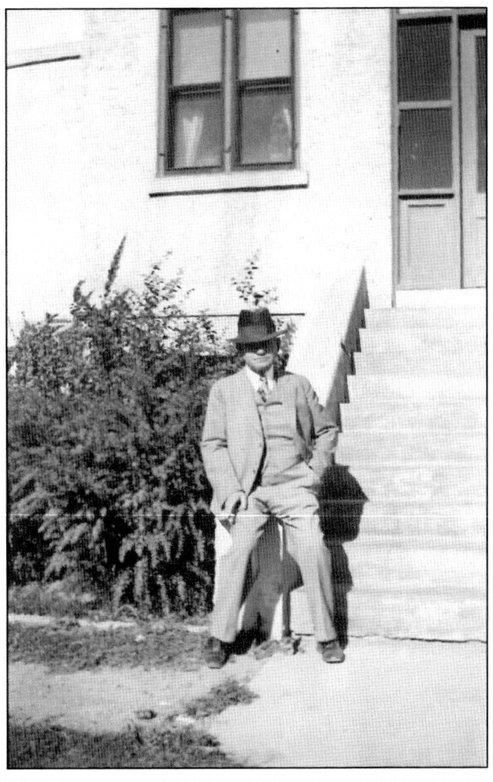

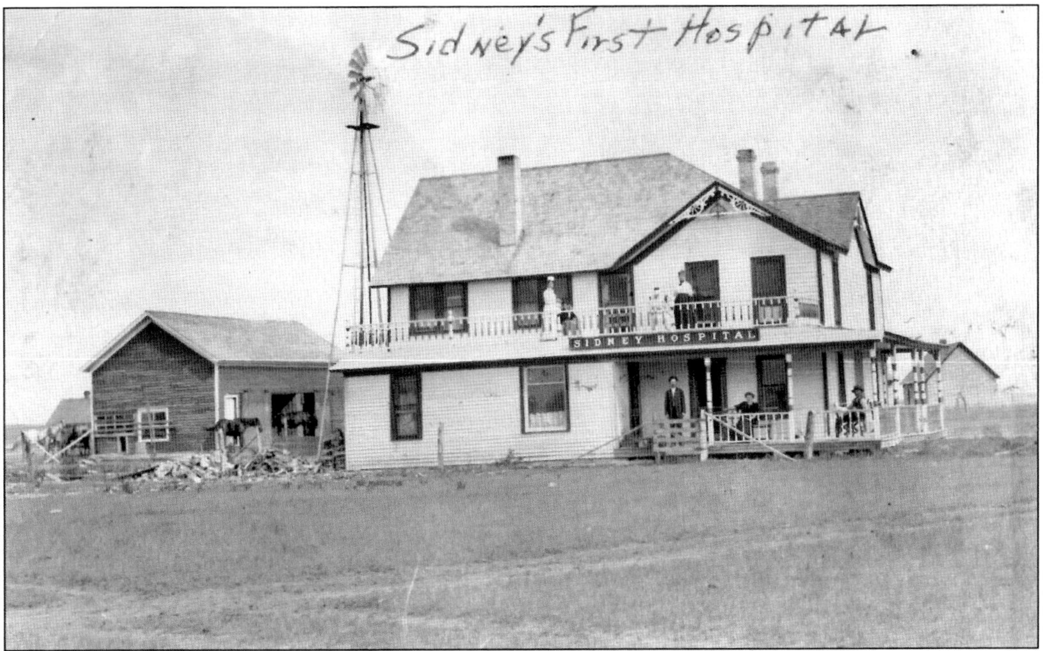

Dr. J.S. Beagle, another of the earliest doctors in Sidney, ran his practice out of rented office space. As the town grew, the small offices became inadequate, so in 1907, the first hospital in Sidney was run out of William Meadors's two-story home. The nurses who helped to run the hospital occupied a small cottage near the property.

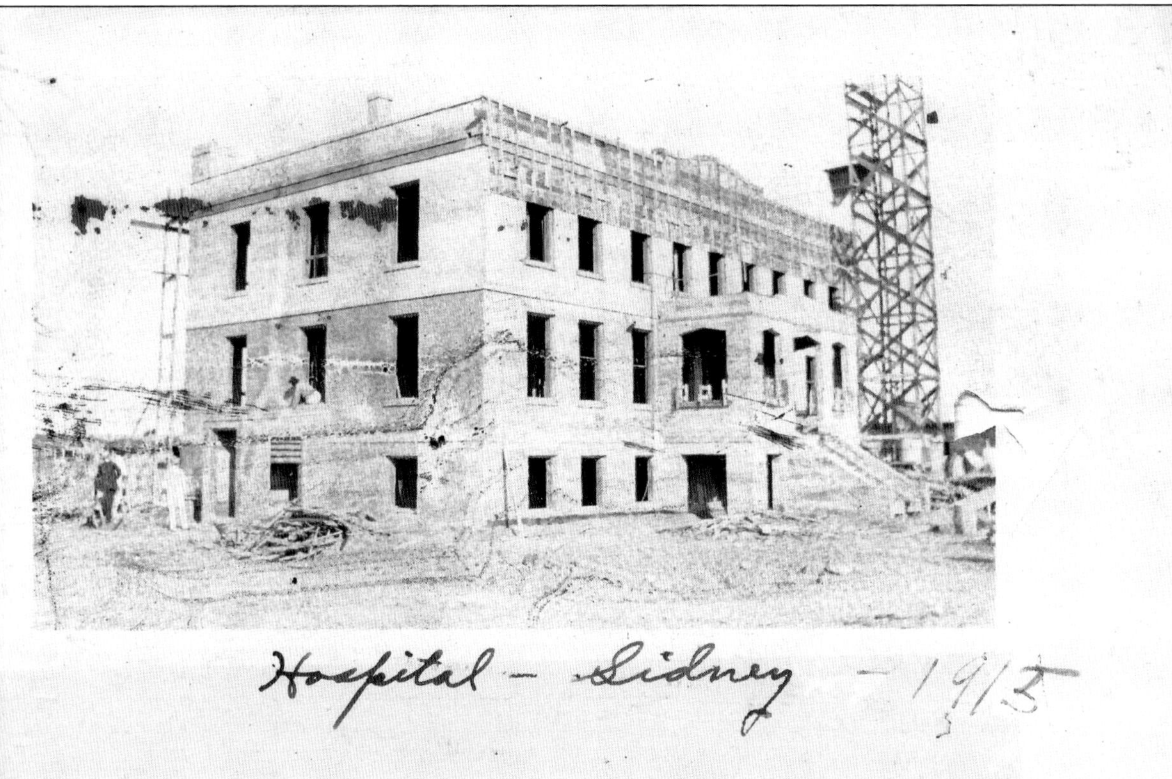

In 1913, Dr. F.A. Gowdy, Dr. Beagle's cousin and a surgeon, joined Beagle in his practice in Sidney. By that time, Dr. Beagle's offices were located above First National Bank, where he continued to practice until his retirement in 1958. The pair was continuously busy, often making trips out across the river and into the badlands in the middle of the night. Concerned about the lack of space for their growing number of patients, Dr. Beagle and Dr. Gowdy began working on plans for a new hospital. To prepare for the construction, Dr. Beagle visited numerous small hospitals and sent out for countless blueprints until he found a plan that he thought would work perfectly for Sidney. In 1915, construction on a large new hospital began with C.J. Weston, a contractor from Miles City, at the helm of the project.

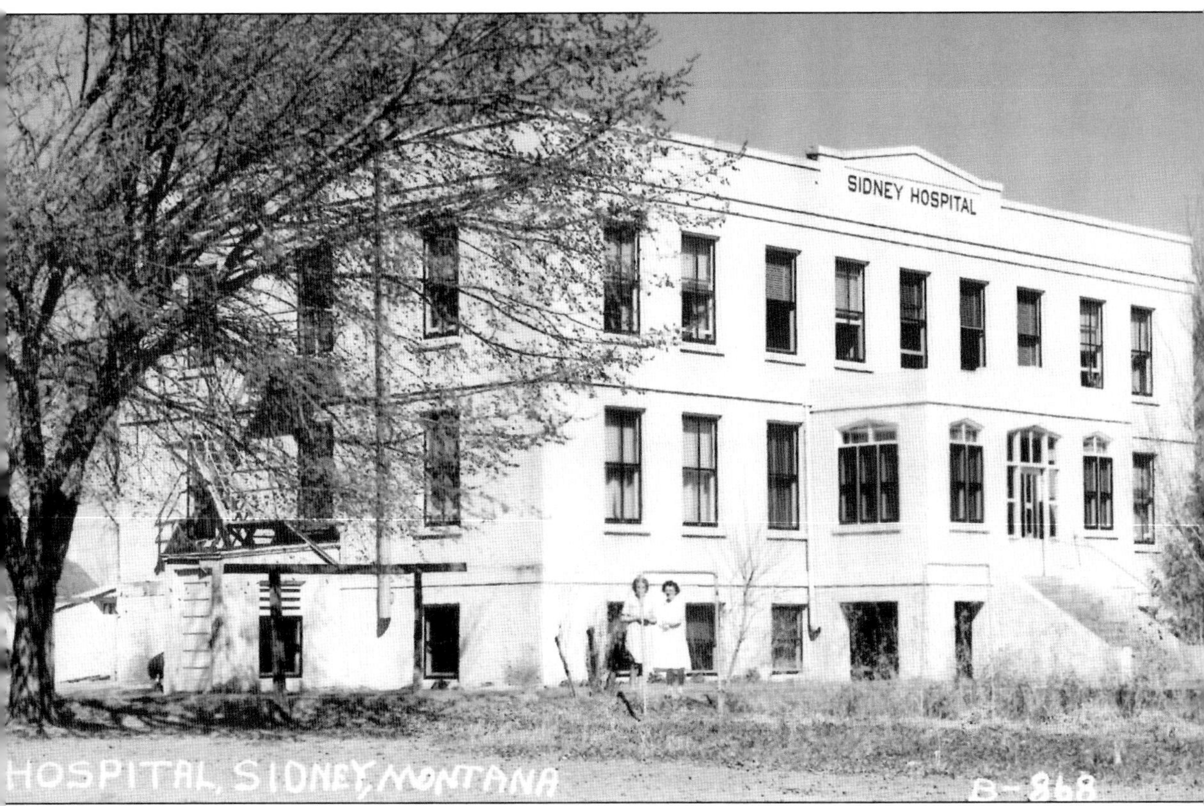

In 1915, Dr. Beagle was able to convince Dr. H.H. Parsons to come to Sidney from Glendive, where he had been a surgeon at the Northern Pacific Hospital, just in time for the new Sidney Hospital to be finished in 1916. The basement contained a laundry, kitchen, and dining room, as well as nurses' quarters. The medical wards were on the first and second floors, and an updated surgery was built on the second floor. Additionally, a dumbwaiter was installed as an added convenience. A nurse training school was created at the hospital where Dr. Beagle would teach classes when he had time and where nurse Nettie Ray would also serve as an instructor. The first two graduates of the nursing program at the Sidney Hospital were Marian Woodard and Esther Thorson. Graduation exercises were held for them in the People's Congregational Church.

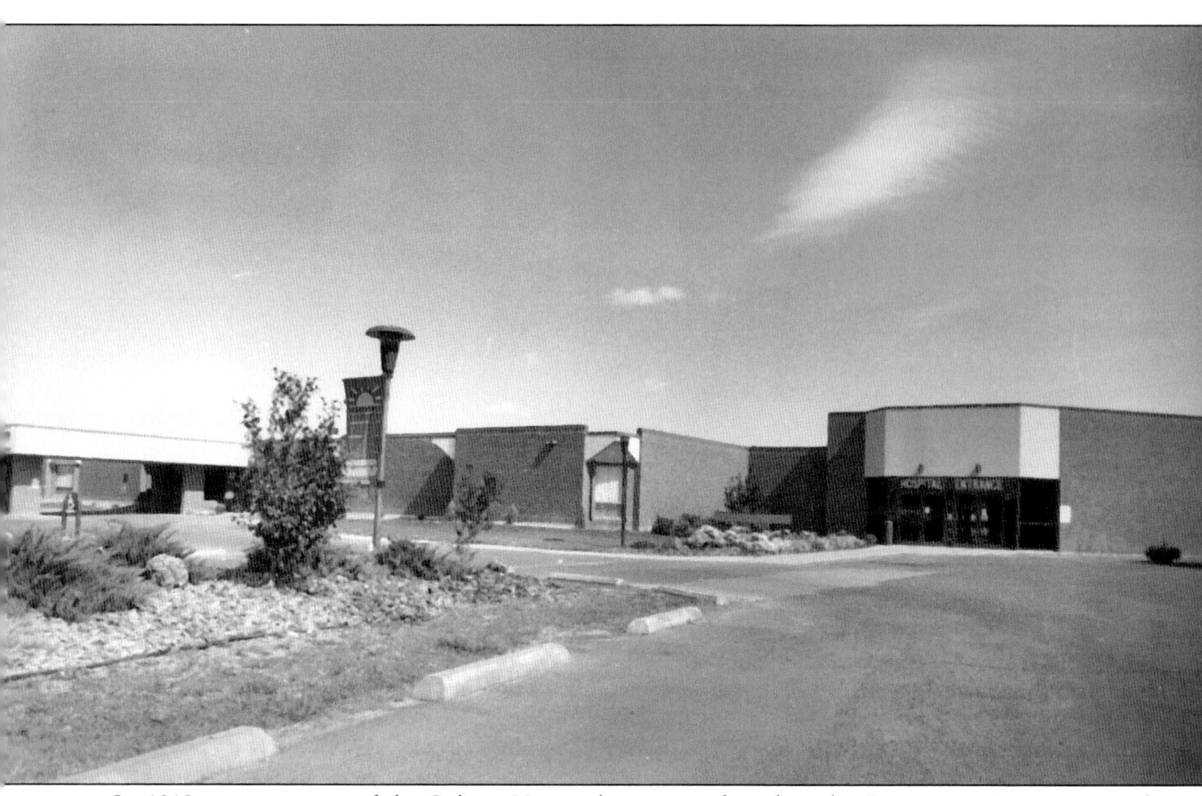

In 1919, management of the Sidney Hospital was transferred to the Deaconess Association of the Methodist Church. Monte Bane and Cora Meneley were put in charge of the hospital as superintendents at that time and were also in charge of the nurse training school located at the hospital. In 1946, the hospital reorganized as a nonprofit, nonsectarian institution, and it was renamed the Community Memorial Hospital. Additional funding was raised by the community to add to the aging building, including waiting rooms and patient rooms. As the community grew, however, so did the need for a larger institution, and so a new complex was built in the late 1960s. The hospital was finished in 1970 at a cost of $1.5 million. Additions were also made in the 1980s (seen here), in the 1990s, and well into the 21st century.

Four

Transportation in Sidney

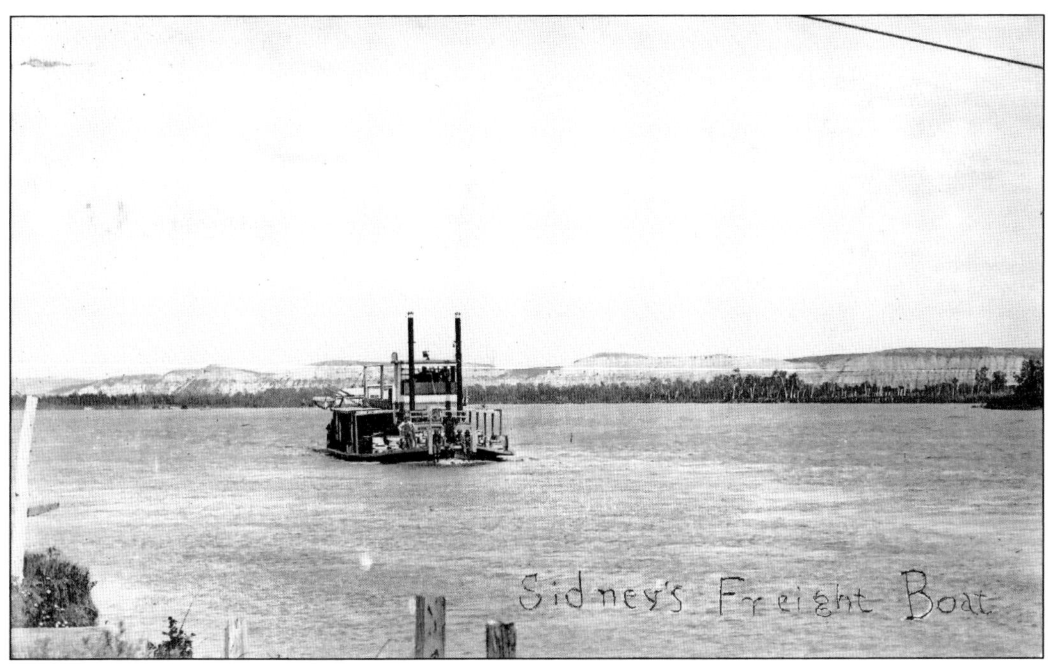

This boat, seen in 1909, was used to bring supplies to Sidney. Since the nearest railroad was nowhere near the town at the time, food, sundries, and tools, as well as other items, were loaded onto the freight ferry and floated to Sidney. Building supplies were also carried down the river on the boat.

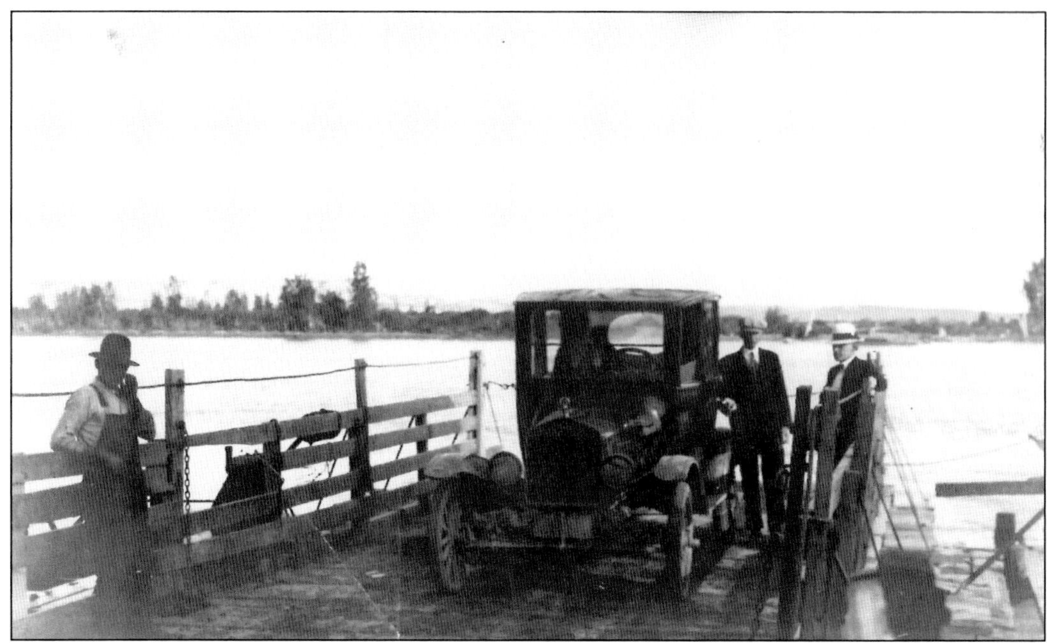

It was especially important that a regular ferry be posted in Sidney, especially for the physicians who needed to travel long distances and across the river to visit their patients. This photograph shows Dr. Beagle, right, standing next to Jim Turner and his automobile on the ferry. Trips taken out into the hills would have likely taken too long for doctors without access to a car and a ferry.

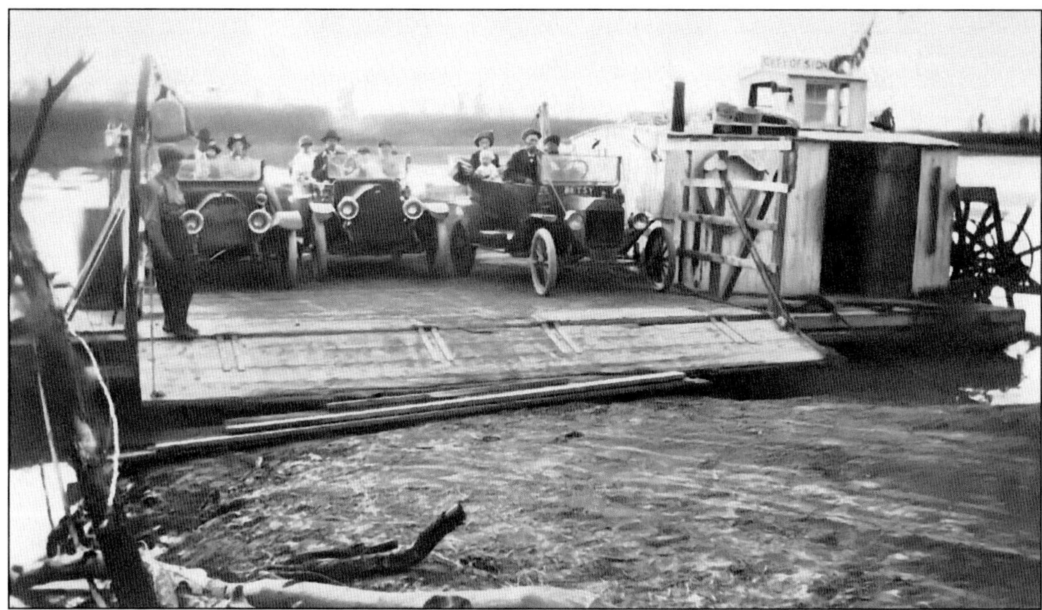

Crossing the Yellowstone River was difficult before bridges were built to span it. If the river was at low flow, riders and their livestock could ford the river, and if it was frozen solid, they could cross over on the ice. However, a boat was necessary during high flow or when automobiles needed to get across. This photograph shows a ferry bringing autos and passengers across the river in 1915.

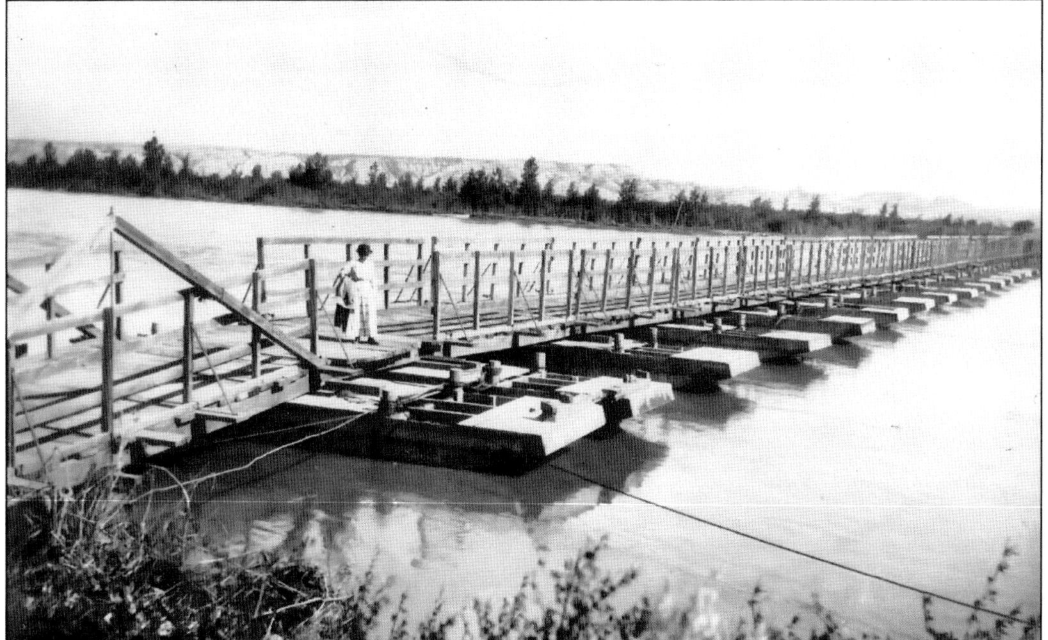

In 1916, John Meadors and Billy Combes installed a pontoon bridge across the river, which added great convenience to those who frequently made trips across the Yellowstone. Once the river froze and then thawed, however, the ice flowing downriver hit the bridge and caused the cable holding the bridge in place to break. The bridge was then abandoned.

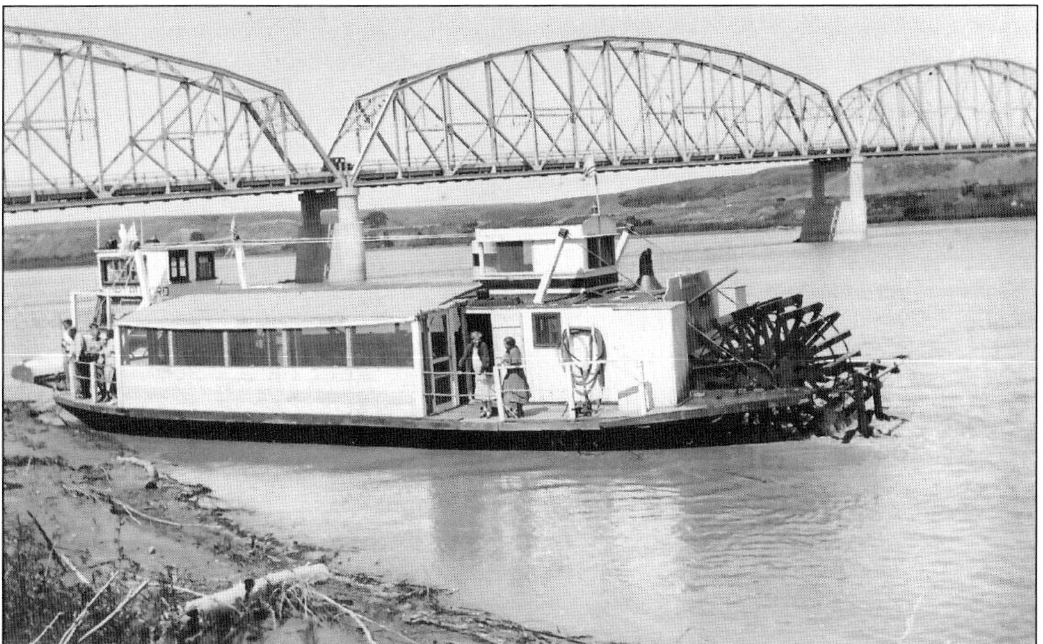

Once bridges were built across the Yellowstone River and travel to the other side was improved, there was not a need for the ferryboats that had long been shuttling autos and passengers across the river. Fort Buford decided to turn a ferryboat into an excursion boat. It could be rented by the day or for weeks at a time and could be used for vacations, parties, and dances.

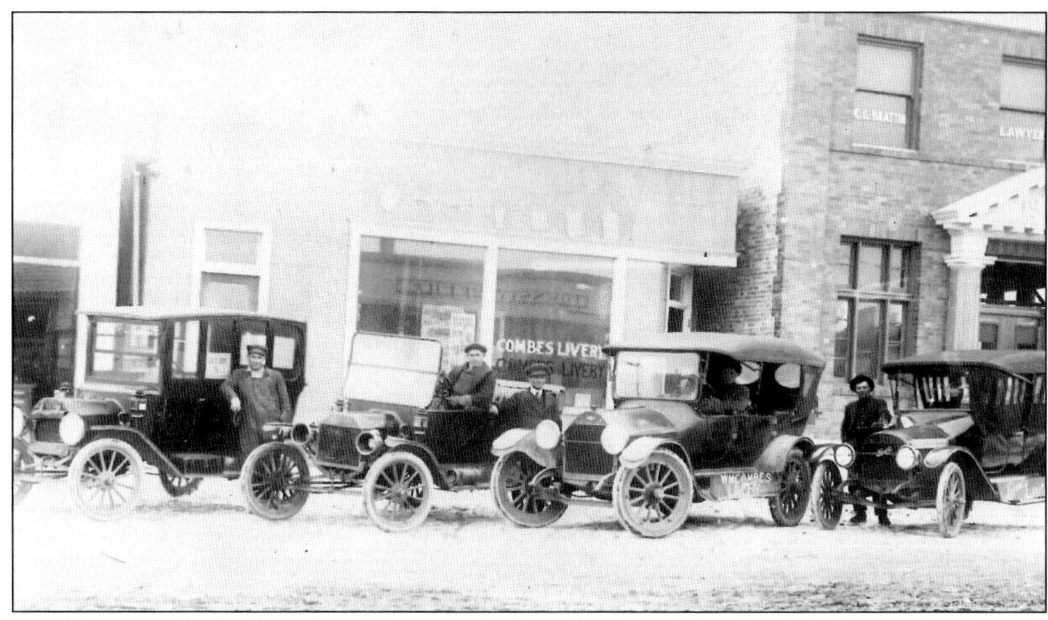

Combes Livery, located next to Sidney National Bank, offered one of the earliest taxi services in Sidney during the early days of automobiles. Billy Combes opened the first local auto dealership in 1907. Between 1913 and 1914, Gilbert Durand owned what he called an auto livery, and Gem City Motor Company was established during that same time. In January 1921, Gem City was officially incorporated, and it is still in existence today.

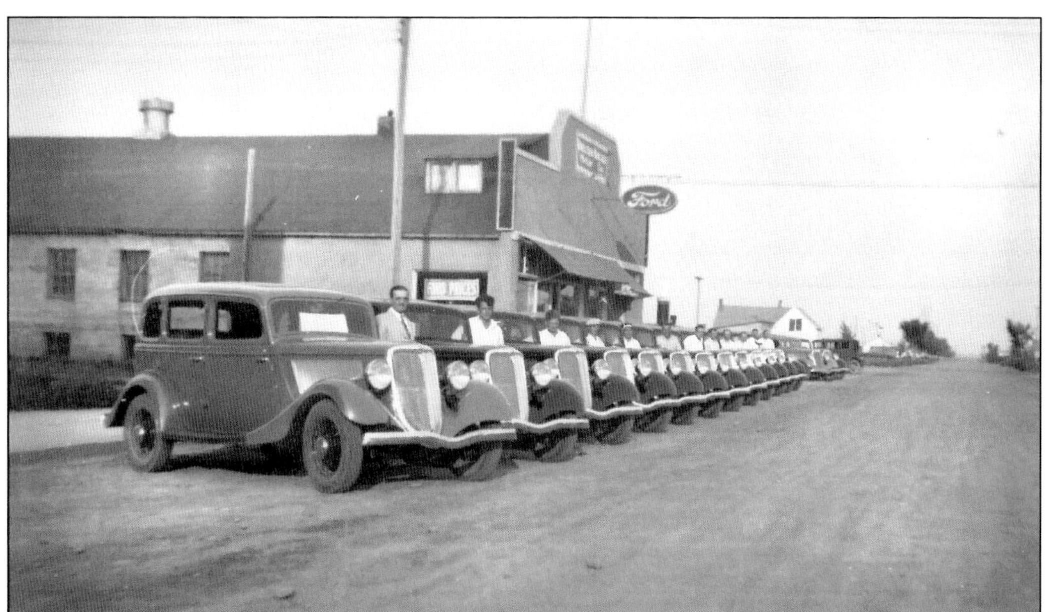

As automobiles became more and more popular and affordable, dealerships began to open in Sidney. In 1916, the town's first Ford dealership was opened by William Ball. He owned it for less than a year before selling to Ira Bendon. Ball never sold a car during his ownership. Bendon Auto and Supply Company ran from 1916 to 1947 and is shown here in 1932 with a line of brand-new Fords.

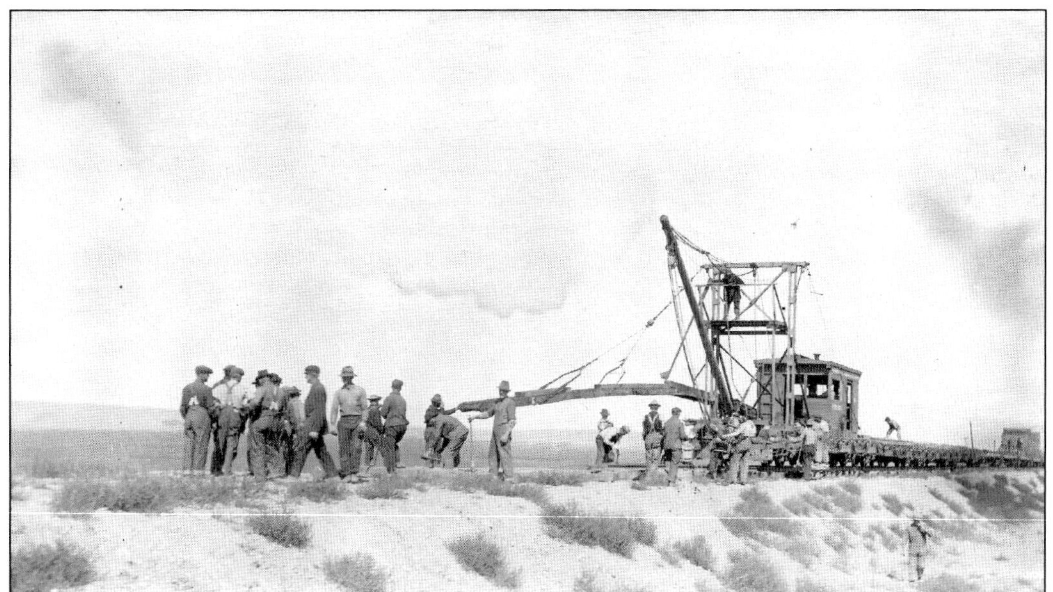

Famous railroad executive James J. Hill's Northern Pacific Railway had been built across Montana in 1887, but it was not until 1911 that surveyors visited the area for a branch line to Sidney. In early 1912, the first tracks were laid for the line, which was finished by June of that year.

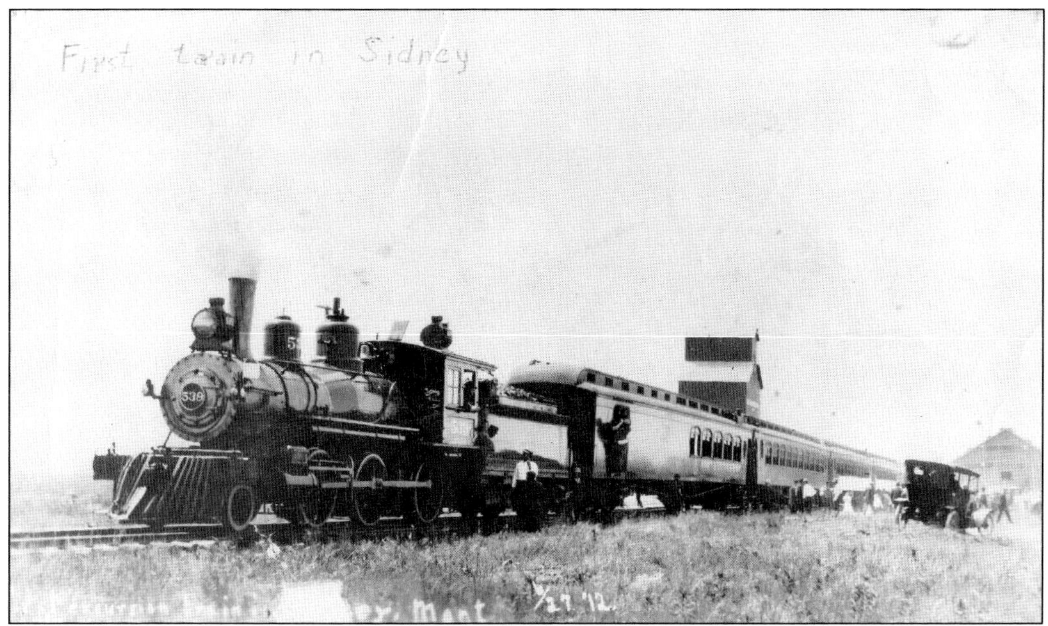

On June 27, 1912, the first train pulled into Sidney. The excursion train allowed anyone who lived along the line between Glendive and Sidney to have a ride there and back for free. Reportedly, there were 3,000 people at the station to watch the train arrive, and the depot was not even finished for the first ride.

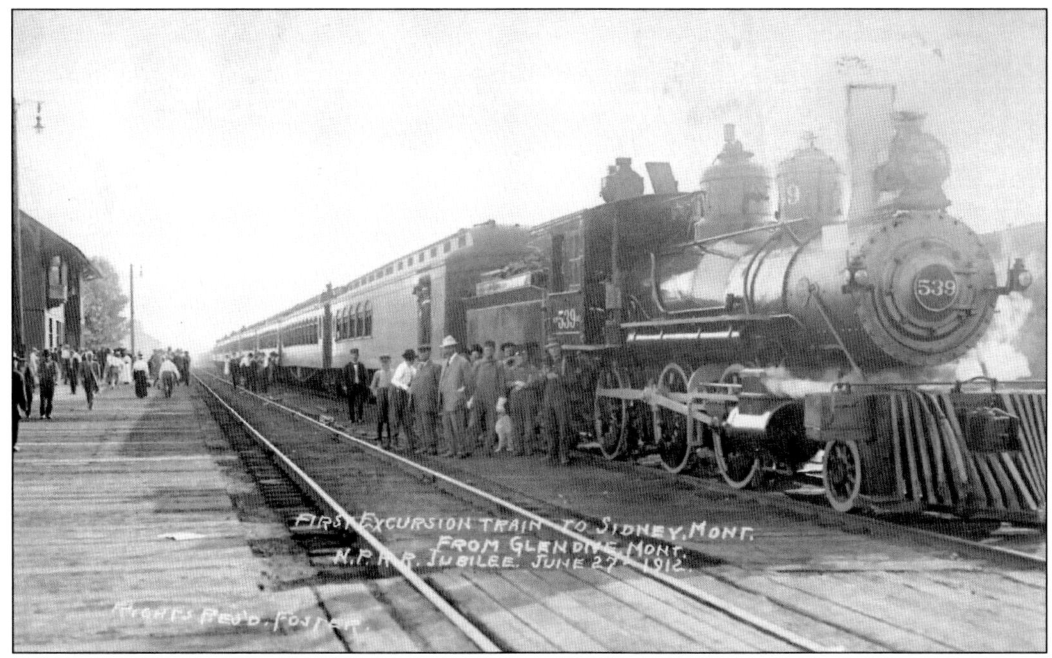

The Glendive Special carried 565 passengers to Sidney to join the celebration, known as the Railroad Jubilee, for the completion of the Northern Pacific line between the two towns. Additional passengers were picked up along the way from the Stipek, Intake, Burns, and Savage stations, including the Savage Band and the Savage Commercial Club.

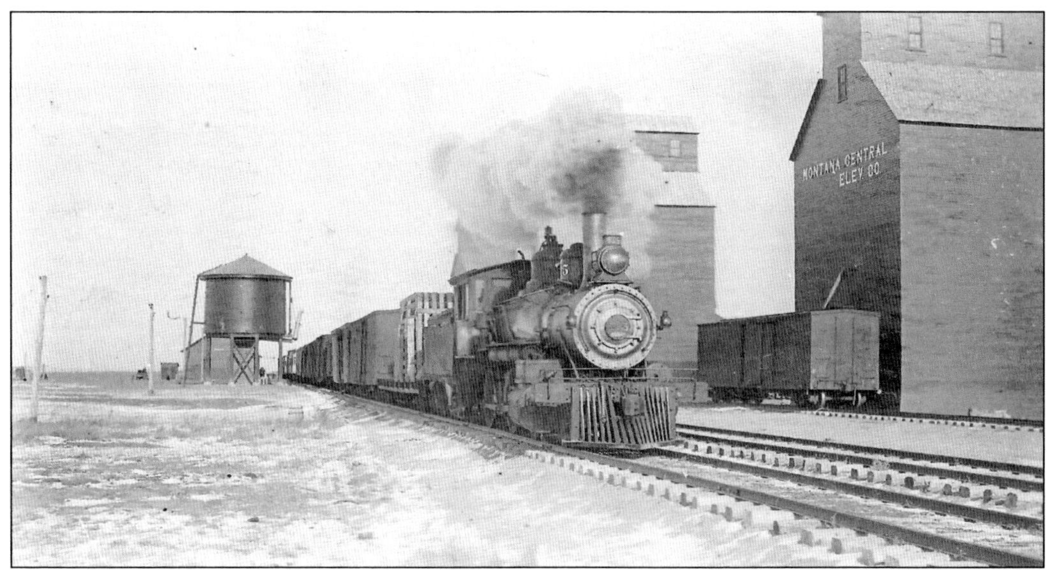

The citizens of Sidney plus all of the train passengers held a huge celebration in the streets of Sidney. Concerts played throughout the day, and a vaudeville performance took place in the afternoon. A dance also took place in the evening before the train whisked its passengers back south, arriving in Glendive by 10:30 p.m.

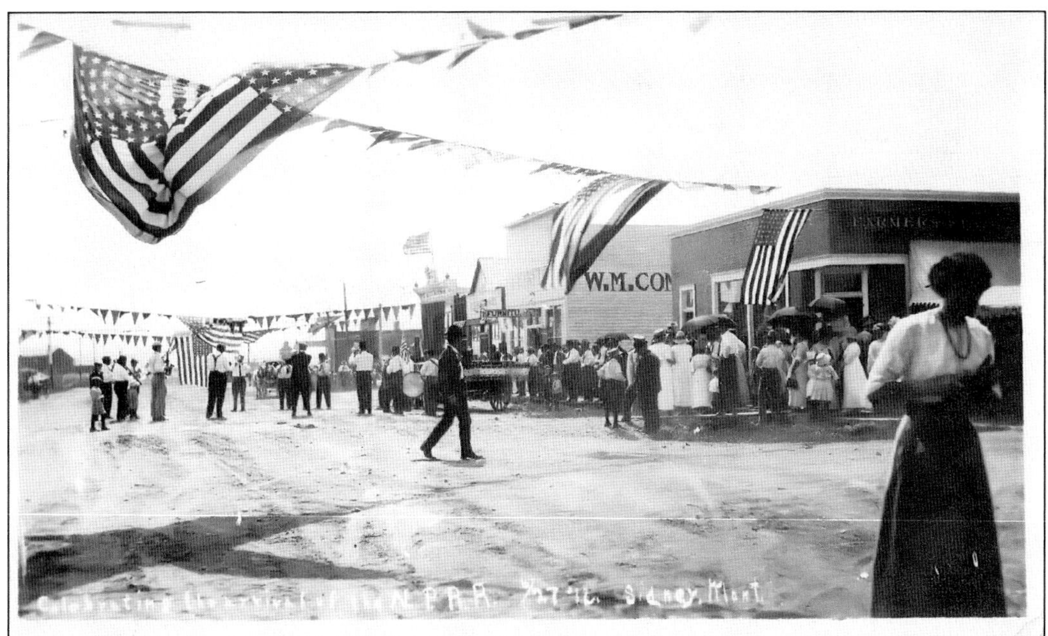

All of the festivities were free on June 27, 1912, as the Railroad Jubilee took place. A band played joyous music in the nicely decorated streets on the day that the excursion train pulled into Sidney. The townsfolk dressed in their finest to partake in the day's happy celebration.

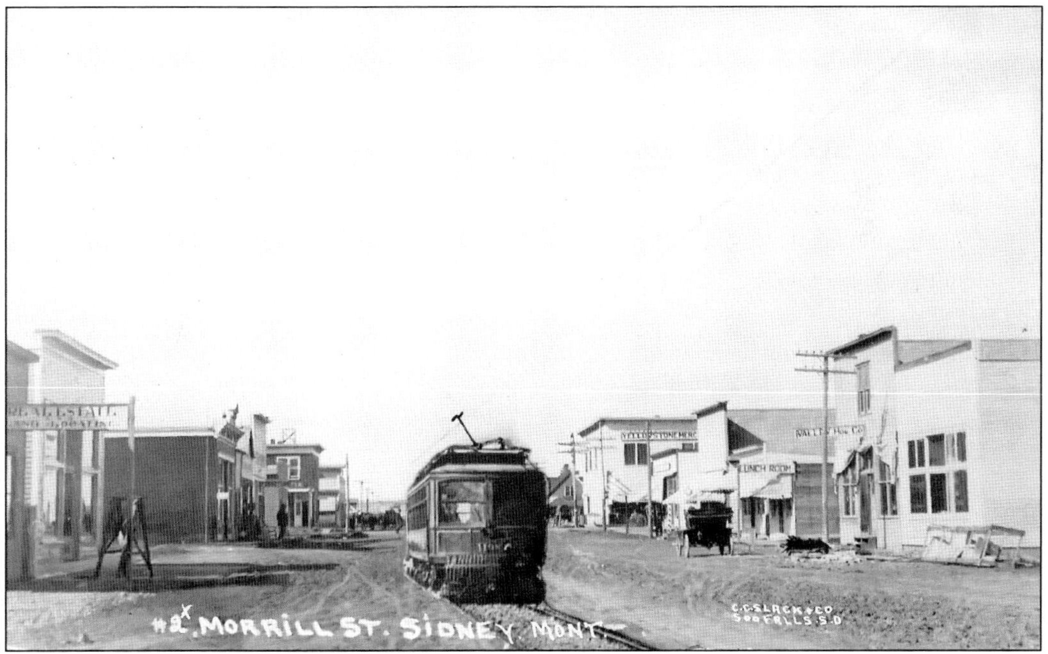

With trains rolling into town regularly and industry quickly growing on the east side of Sidney, citizens might have thought it would be nice for the city to install a trolley on Morrill Street, now Main Street, as it is shown in the photograph. Unfortunately, this photograph was doctored to show a trolley that was never built. Records do not make mention of a trolley ever being planned in Sidney.

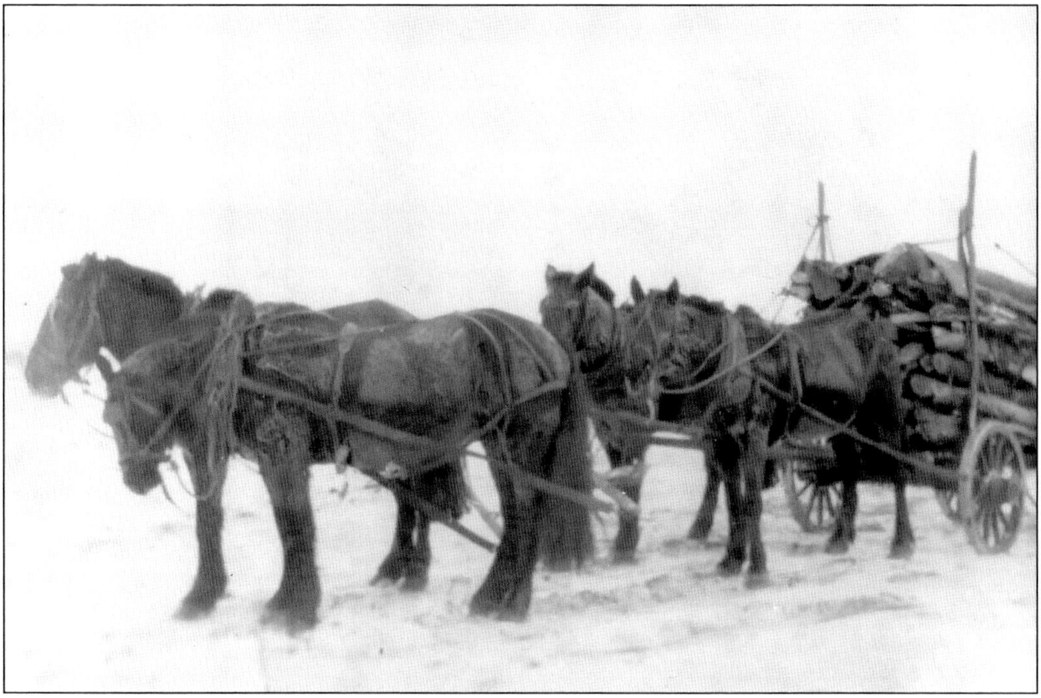

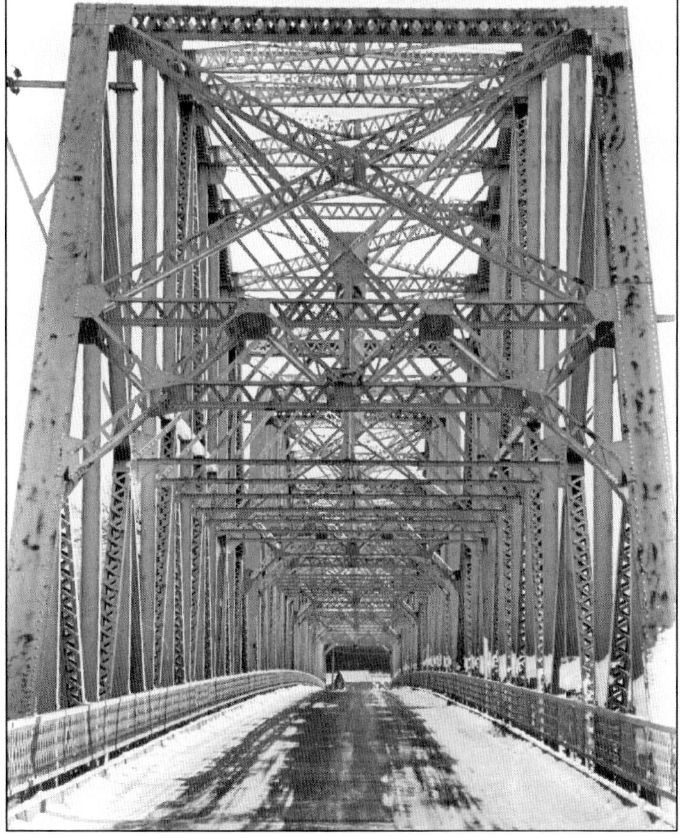

Even as boats, trains, and automobiles began to descend upon Sidney, horse-drawn wagons still provided a feasible and practical transport for travel and business. This photograph, taken in the fall of 1917, shows horses hauling wood up from the banks of the Yellowstone River. A large supply of wood was not readily available in Sidney, and it was harvested from other areas for use in town.

By June 30, 1932, a vehicular bridge across the Yellowstone was completed. Work had begun the previous year in April, starting with some excavation for the main piers. Work continued through the year, but in February 1932, two young men fell to their deaths. The scaffolding on which they stood slipped and, most likely due to ice, the men were not able to hold on.

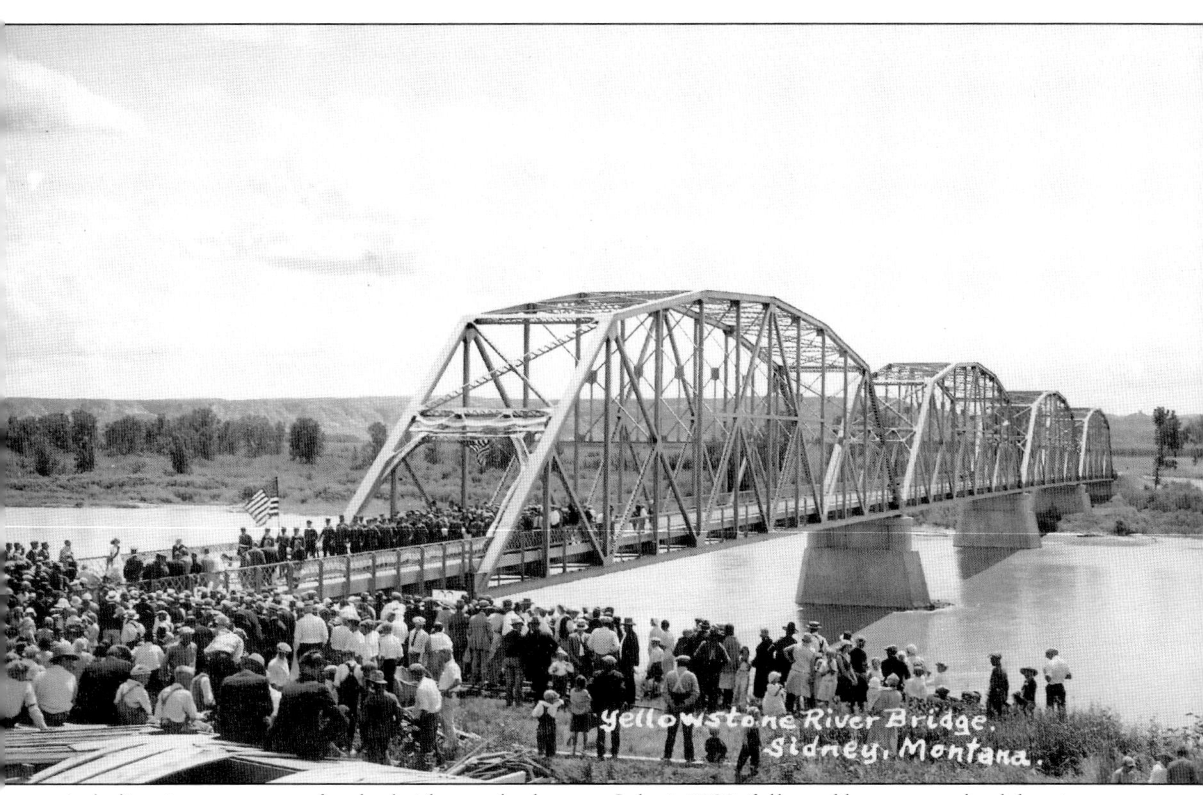

A dedication ceremony for the bridge took place on July 4, 1932, followed by a general celebration and barbecue. North Dakota and Montana officials attended the event, including Gov. George Shafer of North Dakota and Lt. Gov. Frank Hazelbaker of Montana. The bridge, more commonly referred to as the Sidney Bridge, was also known as the Yellowstone Bridge and the Montana-Dakota Utility Bridge. It was constructed using one 80-foot steel girder, four 275-foot steel truss spans, and one 40-foot concrete T-beam span, giving the bridge an overall length of 1,231.28 feet, according to the *Sidney Herald*. It cost a total of $288,985.20 to build, which was a reasonable price considering that the footings needed to be installed 40 feet deep into the water. The Sidney Bridge served its purpose for 62 years. After being deemed unsafe for travel, the bridge was torn down in 1994.

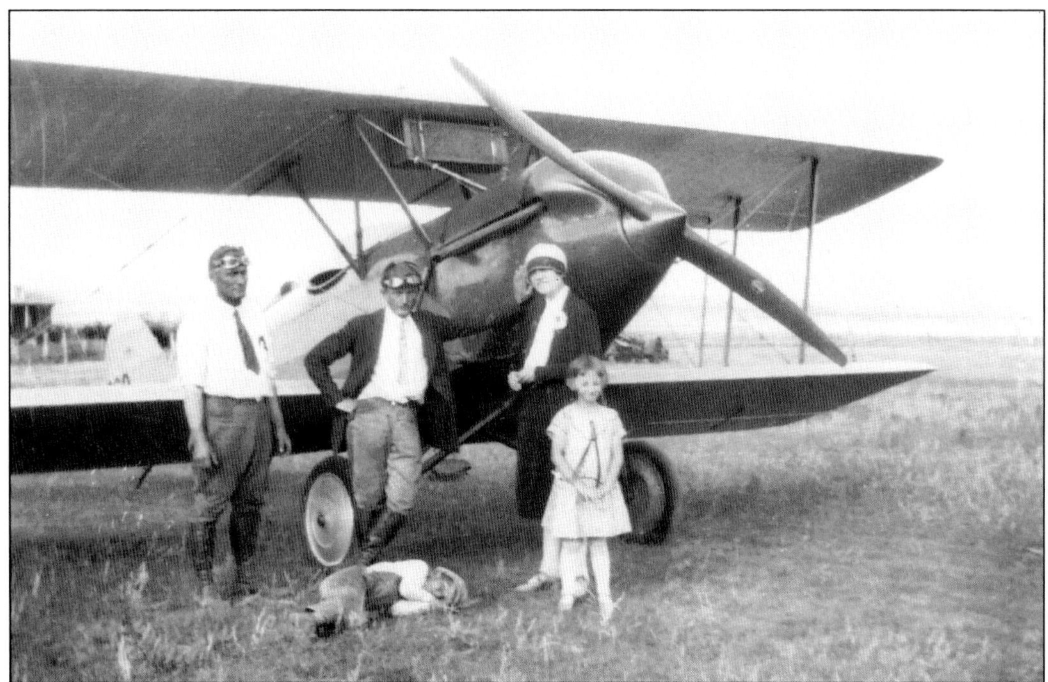

Early Sidney residents loved to watch airplanes, especially during the first Richland County Fair. When given the chance, there were also a few thrill-seekers who jumped at the chance to take a trip in a plane. This photograph shows plane owner Earl Vance, back center, with his bi-wing plane. Joining him are Bill Combes and Bess Ralston in the back row and Henry Miller Jr. and Helen Foss in front.

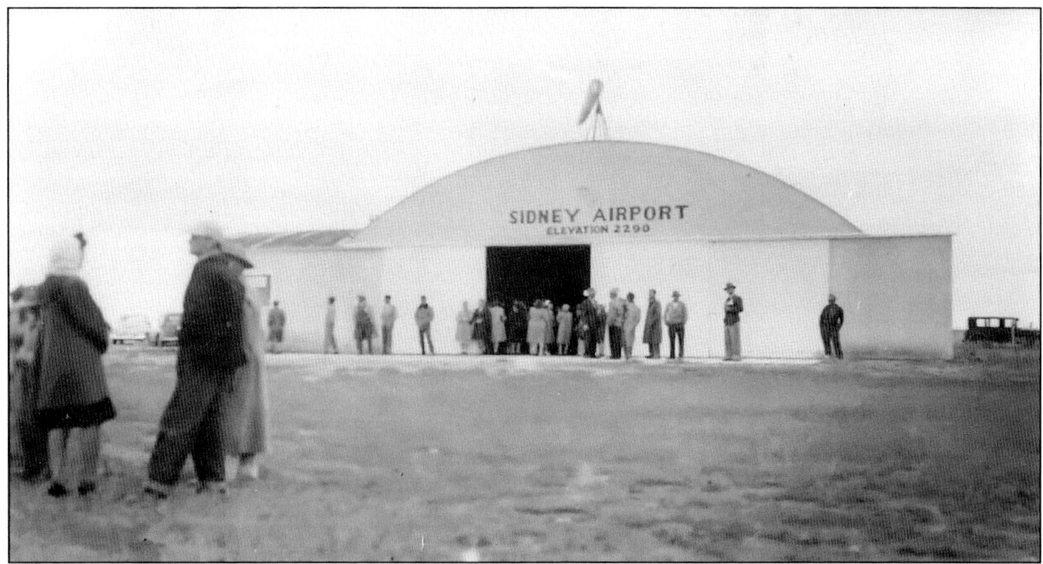

Just to the west of Sidney sat the original airport. This photograph shows the airplane hangar of the original airport during the 1947 Montana Air Tour. In the 1950s, the airport was moved into Sidney, just west of the Richland County Fairgrounds, where it remains today, run by the Sidney Richland Airport Authority.

Five

CATASTROPHE IN SIDNEY

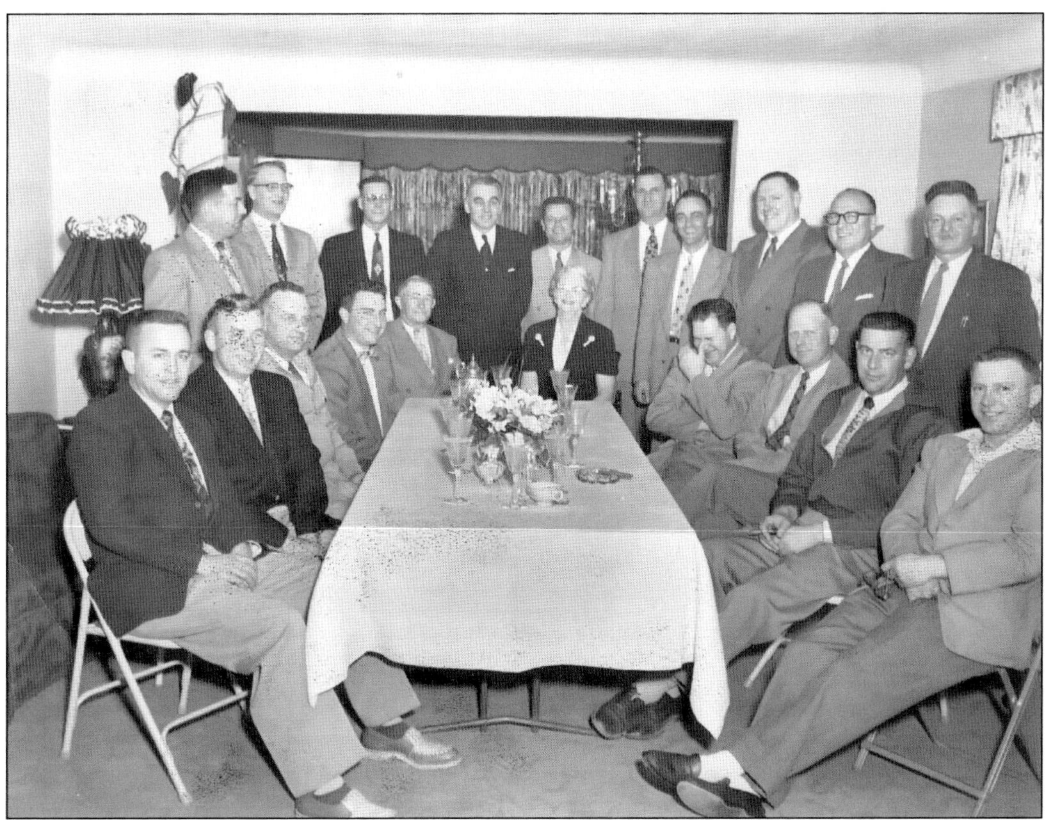

Just before Christmas 1950, a dream of Nels and Anna Bach's came true: a new house was built on their farmstead. On April 7, 1955, however, a heater started a fire in their nearby barn. Thanks to the quick-acting Sidney Volunteer Fire Department, their house and barn were saved. At a dinner in their home, Nels and Anna, sitting at the head of the table, thanked the firemen.

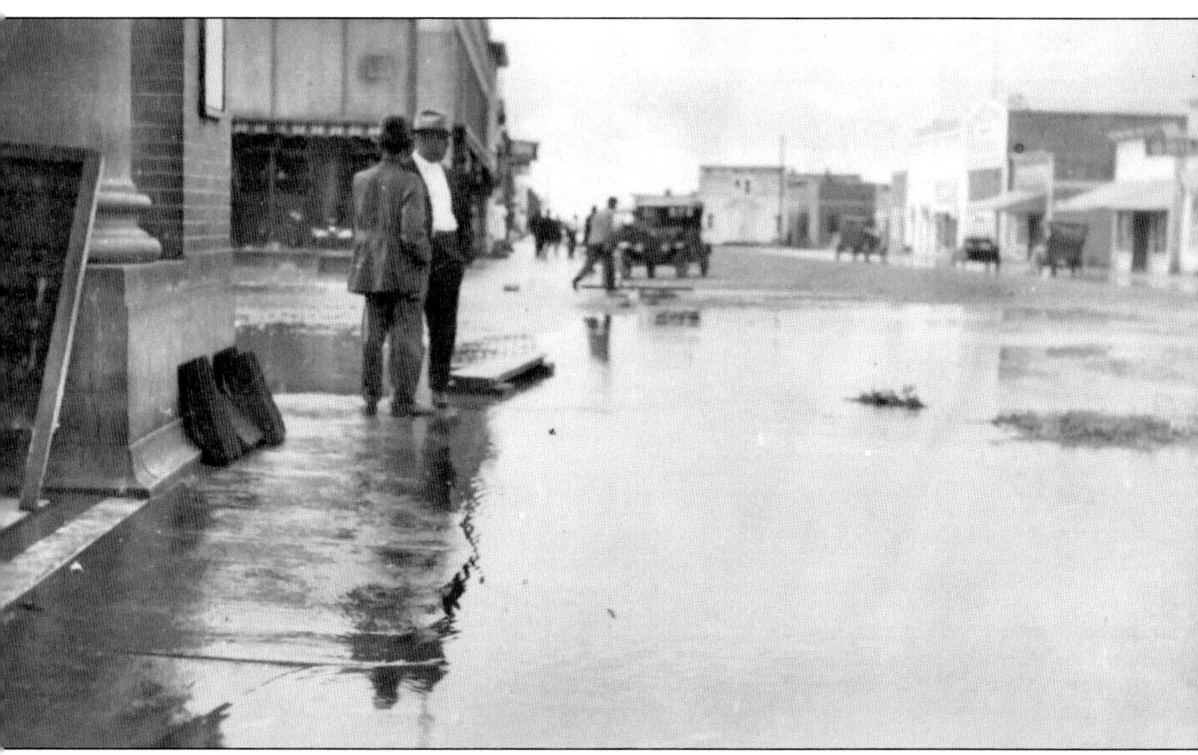

The summer of 1918 was especially hard on the farmers of Sidney, who were struggling to grow crops through a long drought. Assistance from the government was requested to help those hardest hit by the disaster. The *Sidney Herald* reported that farmers in the affected areas would receive $3 per acre but no more than $300 total. The money would only cover the cost of fall planting, but discussions were still taking place to help tide the farmers through the winter. To make matters worse, torrential rains blew through Sidney on August 15 and continued nonstop over a three-hour period. Nearly seven inches of rain accumulated over that time, flooding roads in town, as well as residential basements and businesses. Power was also lost for most of the day. Damage estimates were in the thousands of dollars, especially for the loss of grain because of the storm.

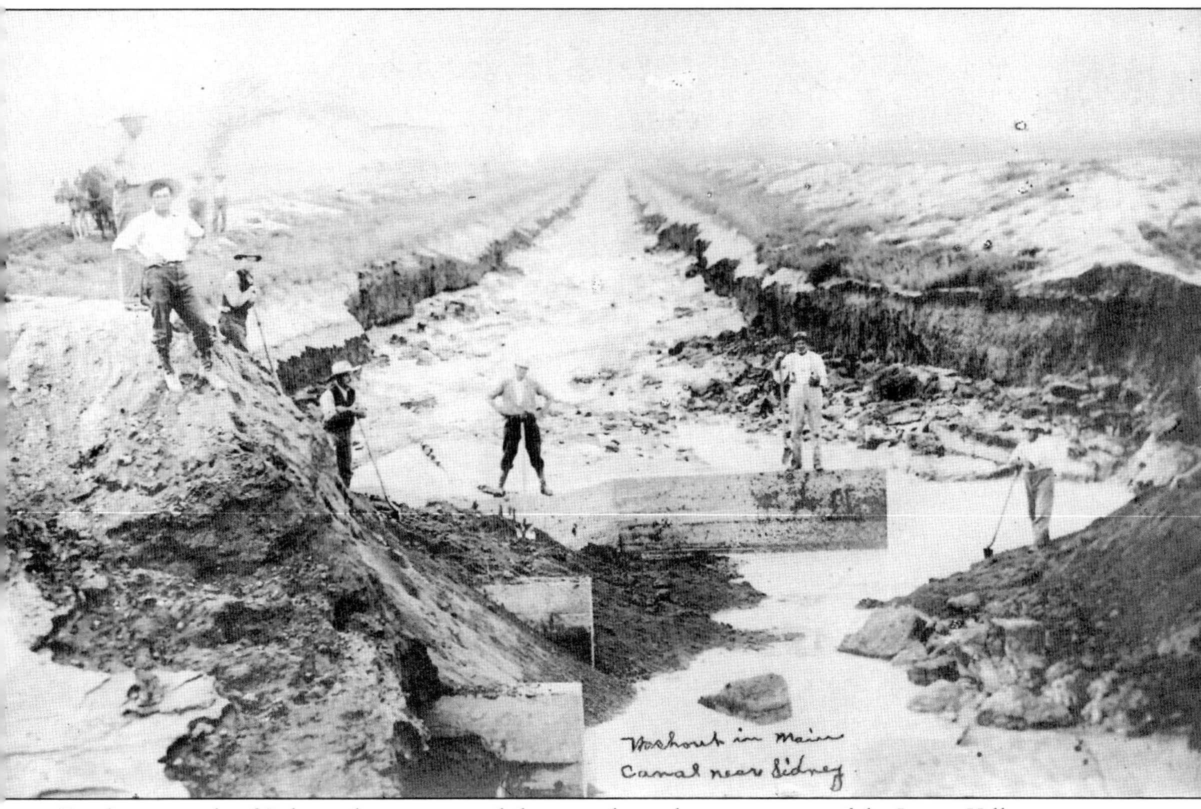

On the west side of Sidney, the main canal that ran through town as part of the Lower Yellowstone Irrigation Project was damaged in the flood. The heavy rains caused the canal to be washed out, which in turn led to more severe flooding in parts of town. Farmers in the area were the biggest losers of all. Those who had hoped to salvage some of their only surviving crops were completely devastated. Many farms surrounding Sidney were covered with standing water. According to the *Sidney Herald*, there were instances where entire fields of grain were washed away and were considered to be a total loss. Out of the thousands of dollars in damage due to the rain, most of the cost was due to the loss of grain late in the growing season.

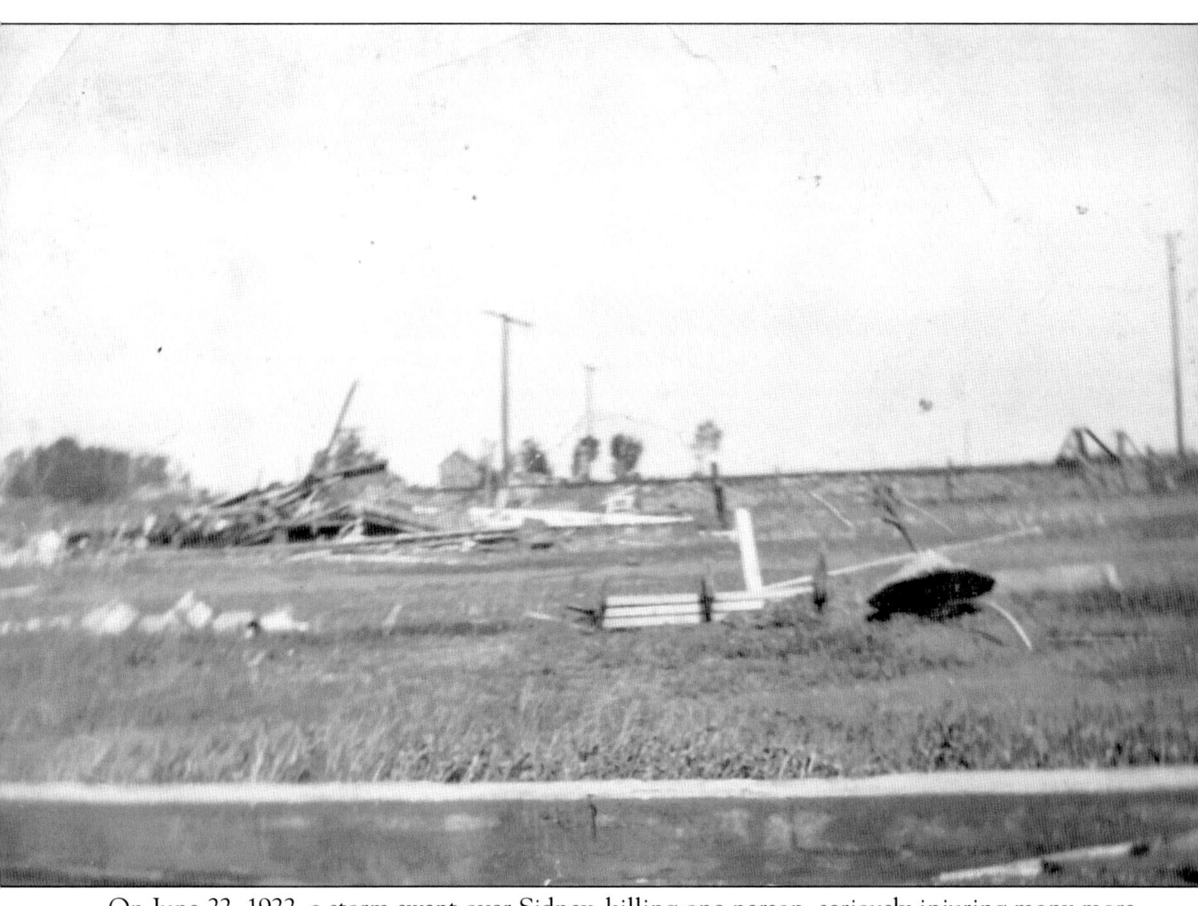

On June 22, 1922, a storm swept over Sidney, killing one person, seriously injuring many more, and caused damage to the tune of thousands of dollars in the area. A tornado first roared through town heading northwest, tearing the roof off a building and knocking down chimneys on several residences, as well as the post office. A dance pavilion in Sidney was completely destroyed, and the wreckage was blown across town. Windows in several businesses were shattered, including the Farmers Café and the Yellowstone Mercantile, and the grandstands at the fairgrounds were partially damaged. To make matters worse, severe winds and heavy rain continued for about an hour after the tornado touched down. Once the townspeople were able to look farther outside of the city, they also discovered that Ridgelawn School, just north of Sidney, had been completely destroyed. Even though there was significant property damage, residents were happy that the damage to their crops was minimal.

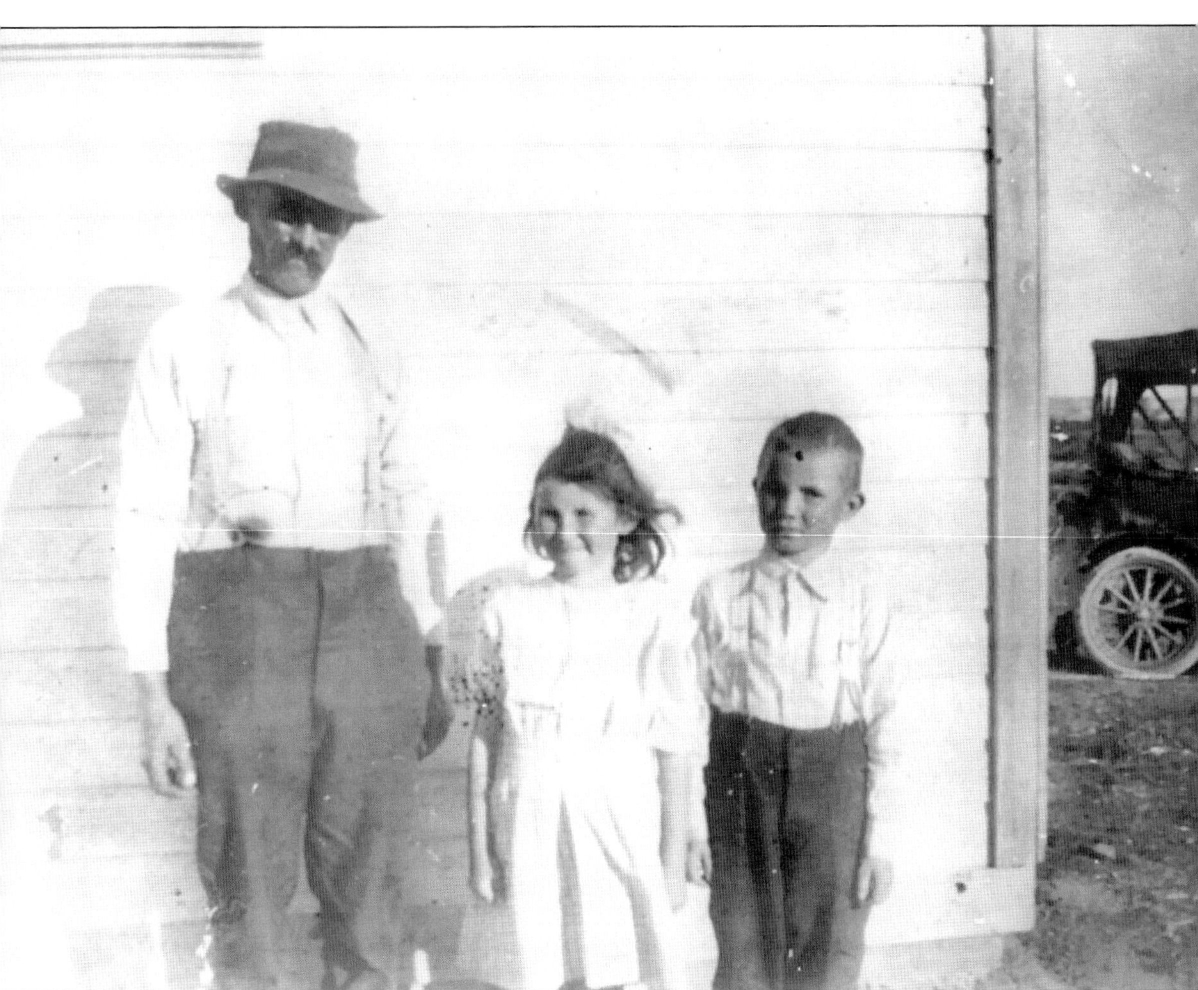

The Olson Farm was located north of Sidney and was in the direct path of the storm. The farmhouse, barn, and other outbuildings were completely destroyed by the tornado. The Olsons lived in a log house with a newer addition, and on the evening of June 22, they had already gone to bed. Ole Olson had gone to sleep with their youngest son in the original part of the house, and Josephine Olson with their two daughters was in the addition. Hours after the storm, Ole and his son were found in the wreckage, unhurt but pinned under heavy debris. The Olsons' two daughters were found about a quarter-mile from where their home once stood and were trapped underneath a mattress. They both had severe injuries and were taken to the hospital to be treated. It took a few more hours to find Josephine, who had been killed instantly when a heavy piece of timber struck her in the head after being torn from their log home.

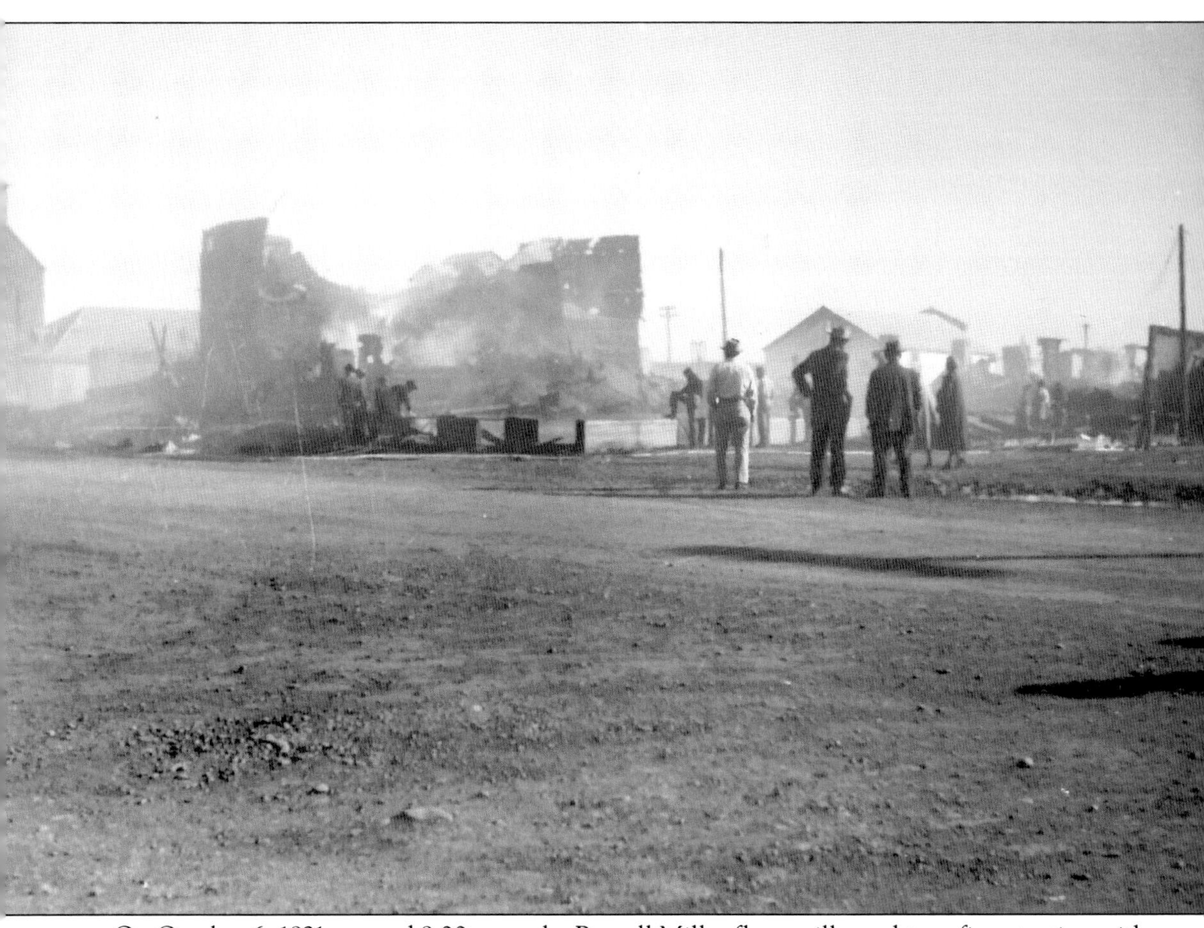

On October 6, 1921, around 9:00 p.m., the Russell-Miller flour mill caught on fire, starting with the top of the middle elevator. The cause of the fire was assumed to be wheat dust that had accumulated in the cupola of the building. The Sidney Volunteer Fire Department was able to make it to the scene in just three minutes, although there was little it could do to help combat the flames. The mill was located outside of the city's improvement district, where no water mains or hydrants had been installed. The loss included 34,000 bushels of wheat and tons of flour, as well as the destruction of the mill. As the flames began to threaten nearby buildings, a volunteer bucket brigade began work to prevent the fire from spreading. The estimated total loss came to $140,000, and the mill was rebuilt.

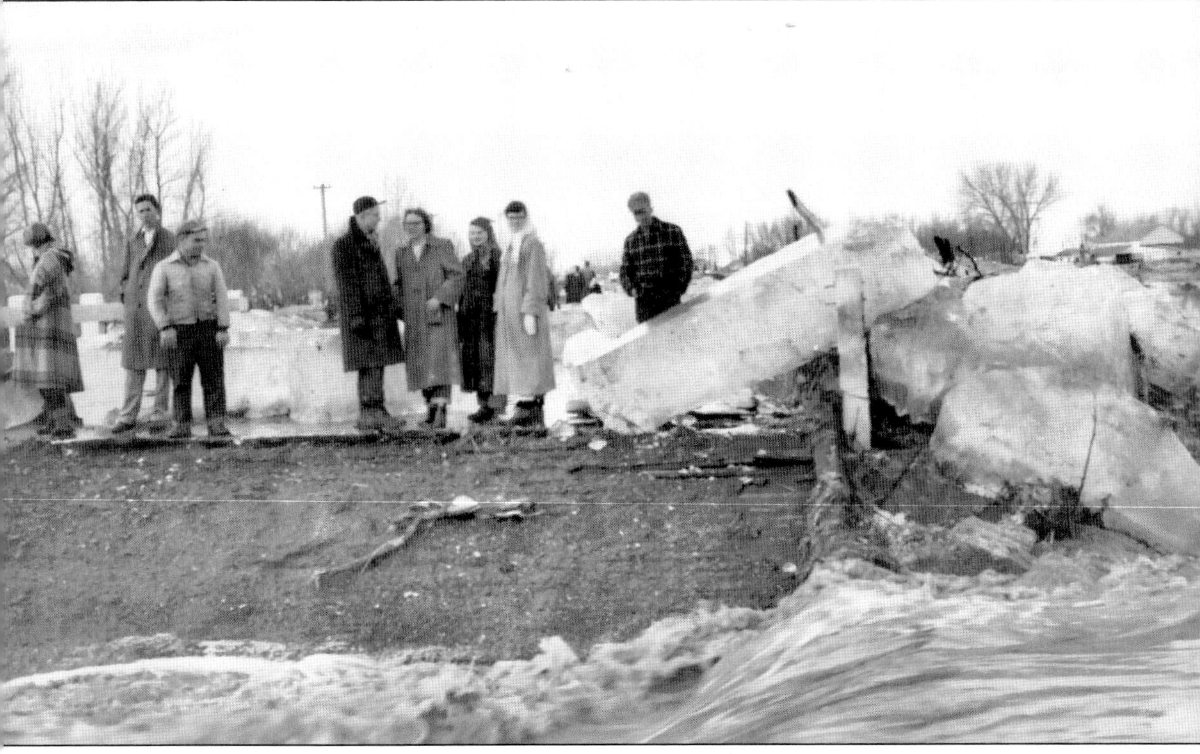

In 1936, August Vaux, one of the early pioneers of Sidney, built the lower dam across Lone Tree Creek. In 1944, a higher dam was built to reinforce the first dam, which had begun to deteriorate. A few years later, the upper dam was enlarged and a spillway was added to divert overflow from the creek into the north fork. On the evening of Easter Sunday, March 25, 1951, a warning went out to residents closest to the dam that it might break. Those nearest the dam began to move into town, some staying with relatives or friends out of the danger zone. The dam broke early on Monday morning, March 26. Days after, people were still cleaning up the area. Damage was estimated to be in the hundreds of thousands of dollars within four days of the flood. Homes were destroyed, businesses damaged, vehicles rendered useless, and livestock lost.

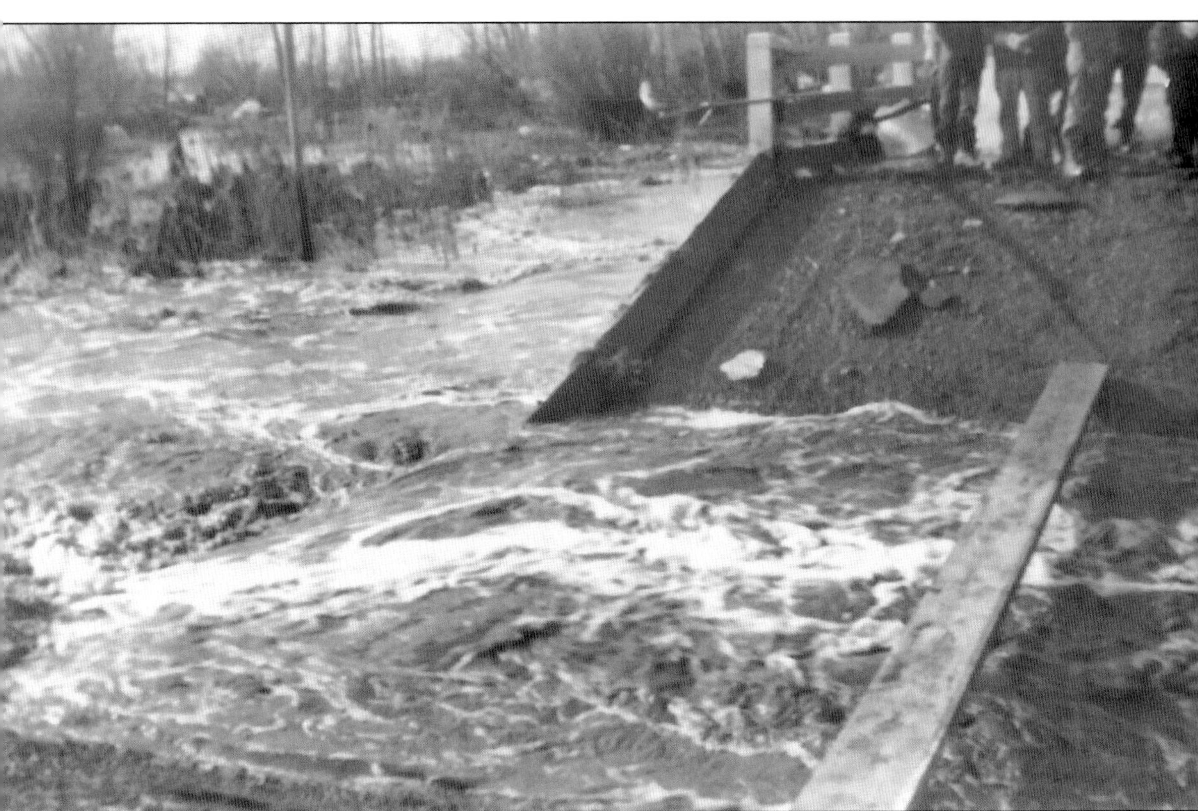

Clifford Jenson, a ranch owner near where Vaux Dam was located, was interviewed by the *Sidney Herald* as the town went to work to clean up after the flood. He said that he noticed that water was elevated and rushing through the spillway around 9:00 p.m. on Sunday night. He immediately took action, trying to contact the other ranchers in the area, as well as letting the local police department know about the possibility that the dam might break. One of the nearby ranchers, S.A. Anderson, made his way over to the spillway to see how high the water had reached, and while he was there, water that had begun to run over the spillway washed out the approaches to the bridge just above it. It was not long after that when the middle span of the bridge collapsed into the spillway, causing water to back up.

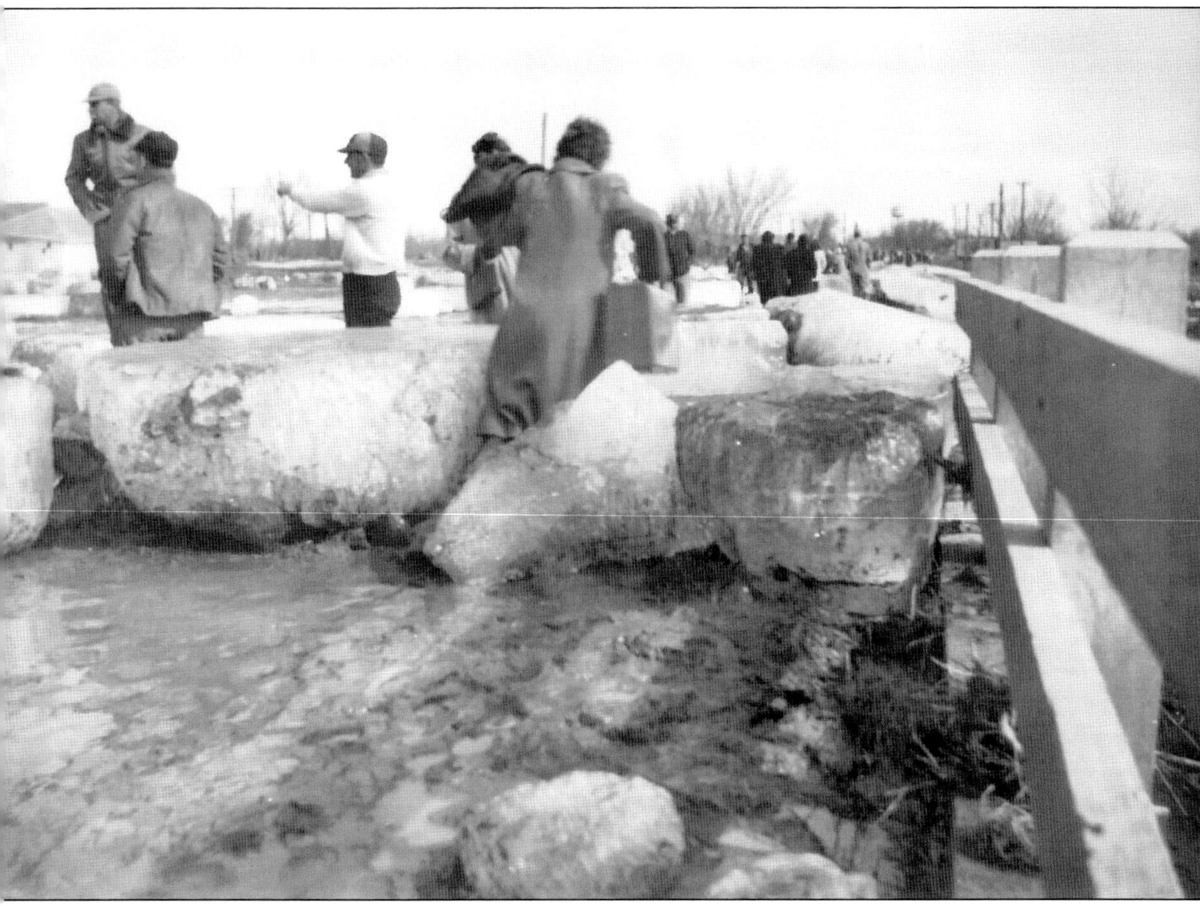

The flood hit Sidney around 2:30 a.m. and crested shortly after. Water and ice from the collapsed dam flowed through the streets for an hour. Work began on the cleanup process as soon as the water started to recede. The Sidney Volunteer Fire Department was put to work right away running gas pumps to pull water out of local homes and businesses. The Sidney Police Department traveled by boat around town, rescuing those who were not able to make it out of their homes in time. One family had made it into their truck, but the water had made it impossible to start. As the water rose, the family was forced onto the top of the cab of the truck and finally into a tree. They were only dressed in light clothes with no shoes on their feet, and it was two hours before they were rescued from the tree.

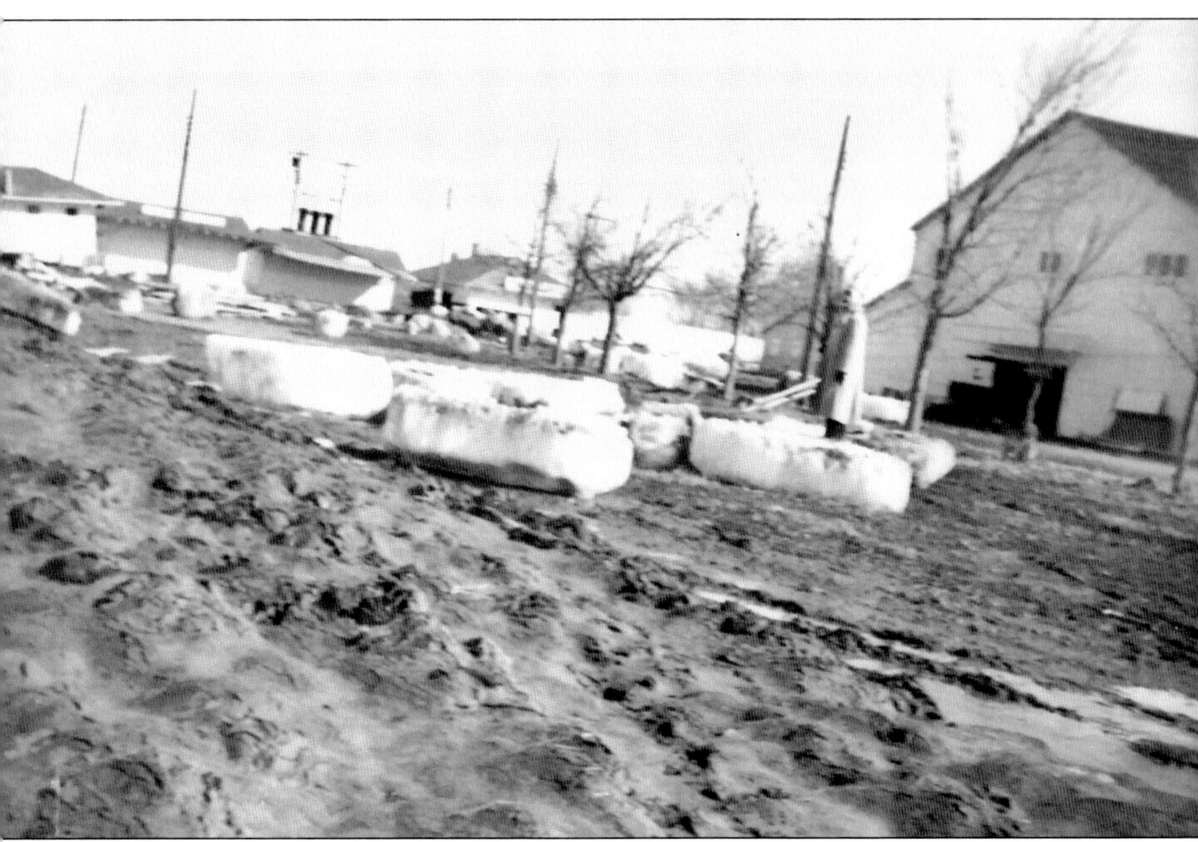

As the floodwaters began to recede, the townspeople of Sidney were left with huge chunks of ice to clean up, as well as rolling fields of mud. Those residents who lived nearest to where the water and ice burst through the dam reported damage to their homes or, at the very least, to their basements. According to newspaper accounts, common sights around town after the floodwaters went down included furniture sitting out on lawns, some covered with mud and some that had been cleaned and was drying in the sun. Additionally, clotheslines were filled with mud-covered, soaked clothing, curtains, and rugs. To make matters worse, Mondays were usually wash days. Many families had a whole week's worth of clothing in the basement ready to wash when their homes were flooded, making the cleanup process even more strenuous.

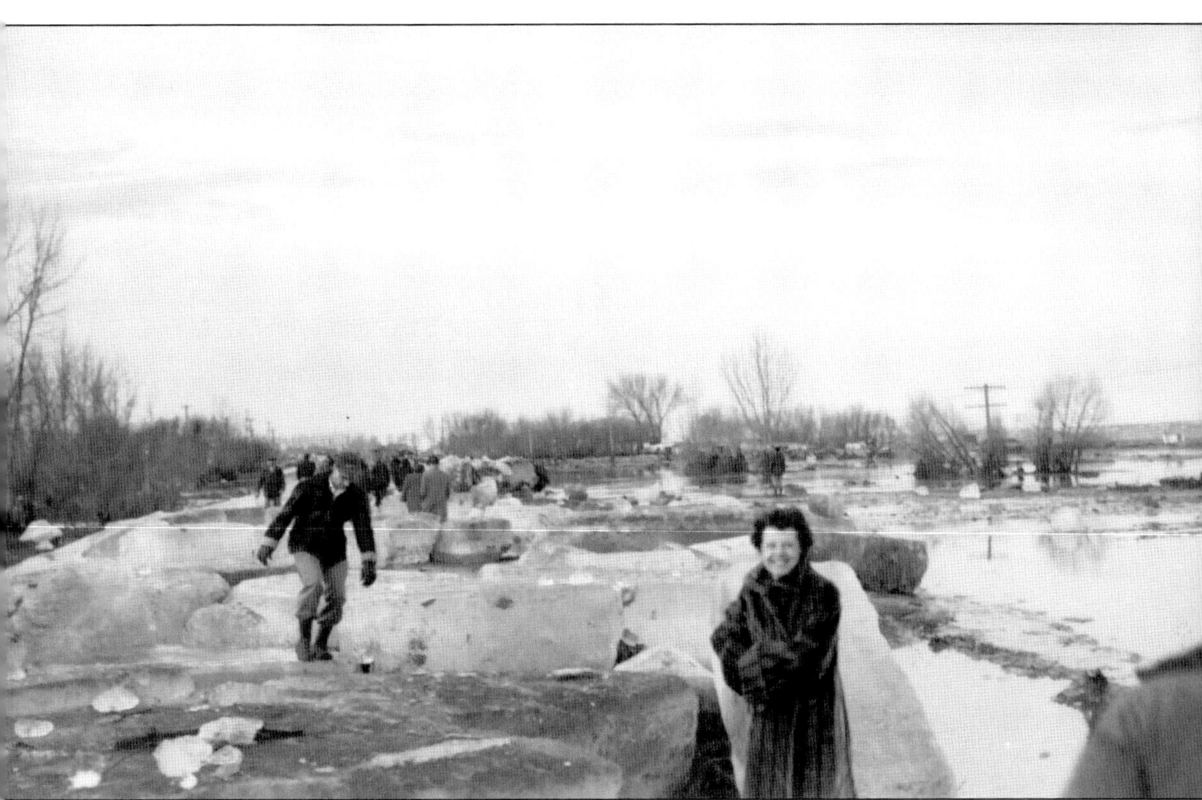

Crowds gathered the morning of March 26 to view the breadth of the damage in and around Sidney. As cleanup went on, many businesses were able to profit from the disaster earlier in the day. Those people not willing or able to deal with washing clothes that were dirtied in the flood dropped them off at local dry cleaners. There, they told the cleaners "do the best you can with it." Chamber of commerce chairman Ed Admondson, via a newspaper interview, made sure to let townspeople know that all the merchandise they needed could be found in the local stores and that shopping should be continued. Additionally, townspeople were also encouraged to gather an unlimited number of fish from around town. The dam had been highly stocked with various types of fish, and residents reported seeing them in nearly every part of town. According to the *Sidney Herald*, nine-year-old Craig Price strung up 10 fish to bring home, all gathered near the fairgrounds. Bobby Jensen and Gordon Dige also gathered large amounts of fish from around town.

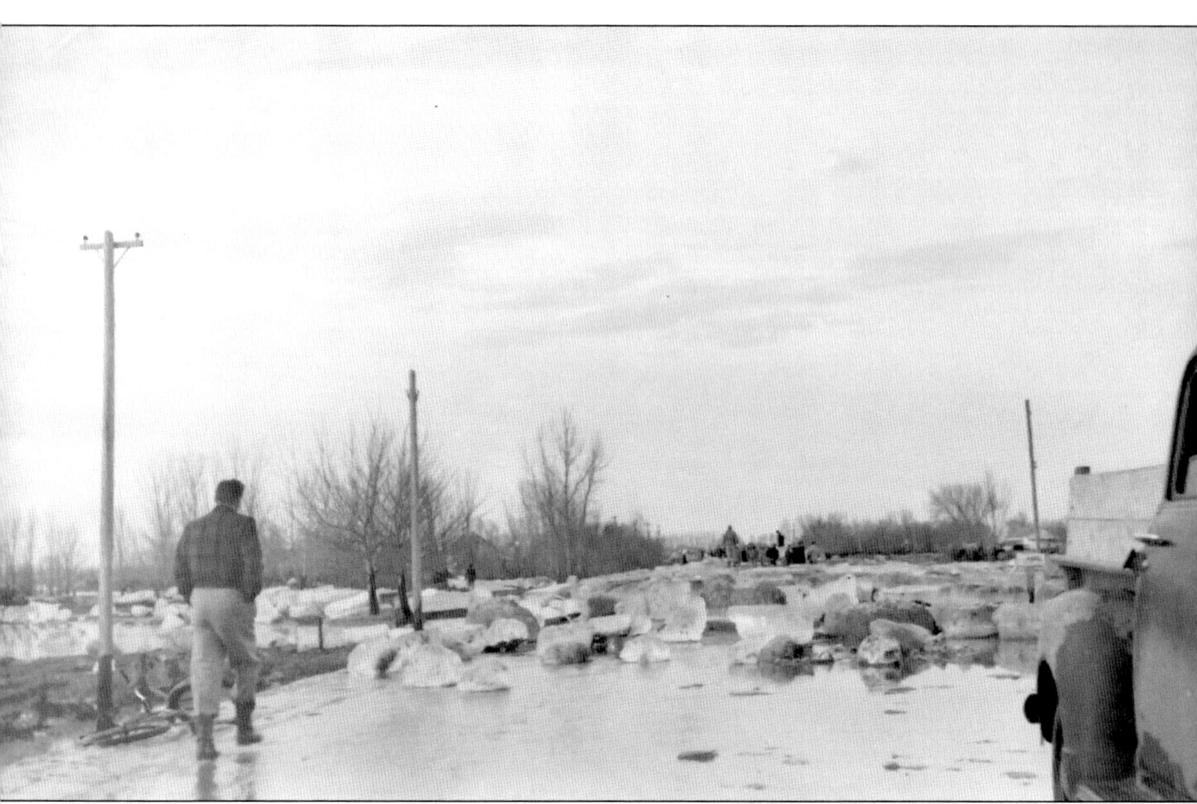

In addition to damage from ice and water around town, another problem that the flood caused was the overflowing of gasoline storage tanks in Sidney. According to the *Sidney Herald*, more than 7,000 gallons of gasoline was forced out of the tanks at the Farmer Union Oil Company station. Lloyd Radke, manager of the station, said that the area was in danger of catching on fire because there was a quarter-inch of gasoline resting on top of the standing water in the area. Radke estimated that his losses, including the gasoline and the merchandise in his shop, would be between $7,000 and $10,000. Another business, the Centre Theatre, was also damaged by floodwater, causing the theater to be closed for the first time in 20 years. Crews there worked to pump water out of the theater and clear debris. Walter Knoop, owner of Sidney Drug, also reported damage to his store. Loss of damaged merchandise at the business was estimated at $3,000.

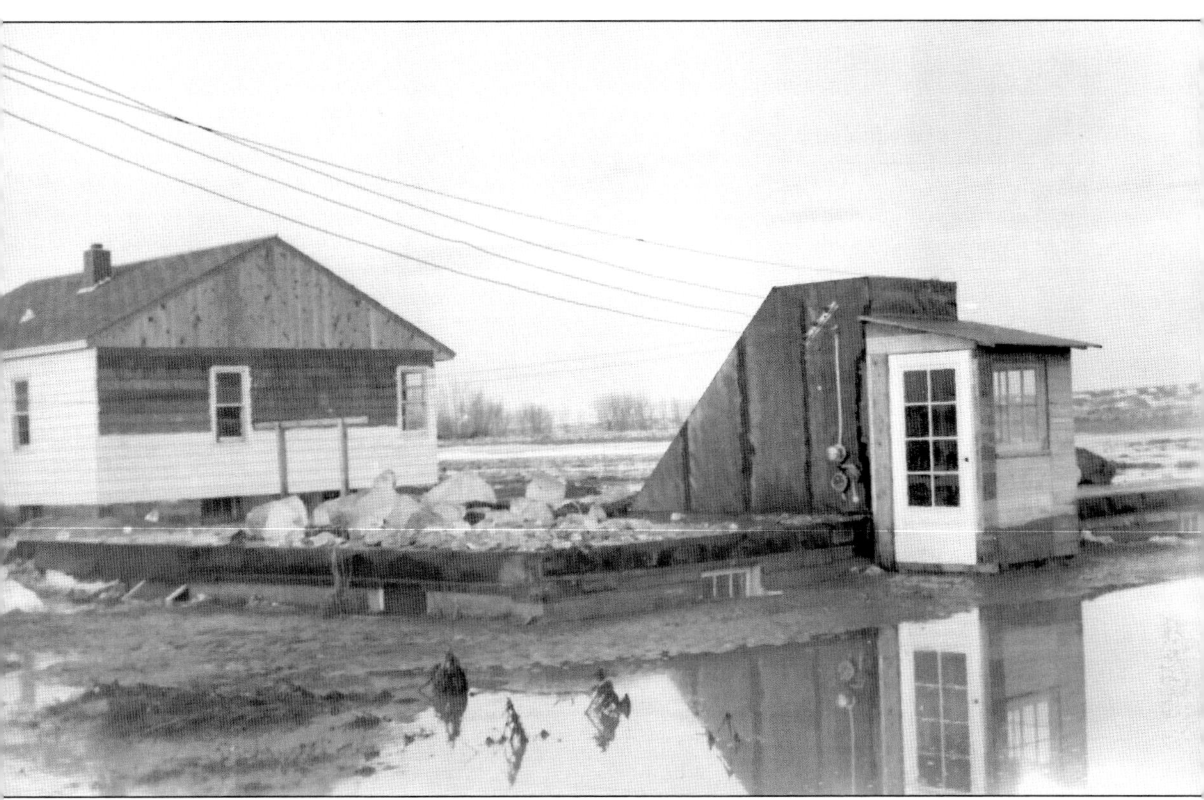

Families around Sidney had houses under construction as the floodwaters rolled into town. The Coke Eckley family had been living in the basement of their home while the upper levels were being constructed. The family was awakened in the middle of the night as the basement of their new home filled with water. Dressed only in their nightclothes, the Eckleys barely escaped as the water rose higher and higher. The Arthur Hall family was also awakened in a basement, in this case the basement apartment that they occupied. Ervin Johnson woke them up just as water began to pour into their home. The Halls were also dressed only in their pajamas and made their way to their car, only to find that it was floating away on the rising water. They were eventually trapped near an unfinished home until 5:00 a.m. Suffering from cold and exposure, Arthur ultimately carried his family home, one at a time, through high water.

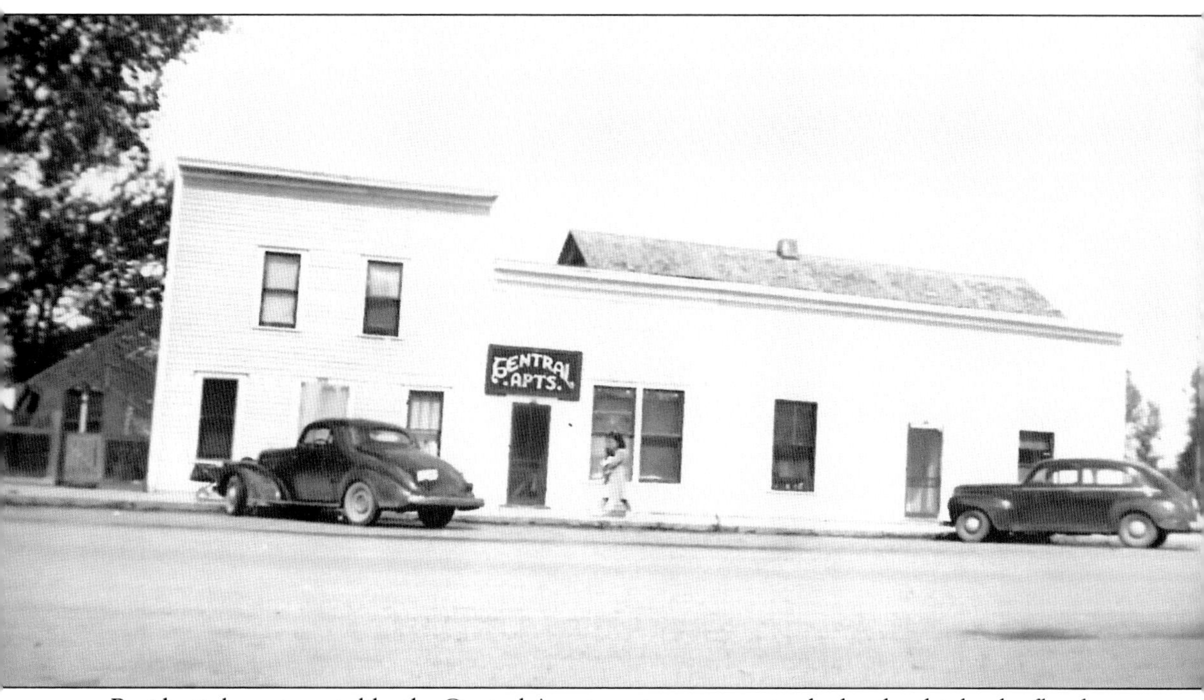

Residential apartments like the Central Apartments were among the hardest hit by the floodwater and ice, especially those apartments in the basement of the building. Residents who were forced out of their homes by the flood were urged to contact the Red Cross immediately. The relief organization set up offices on the third floor of the Richland County Courthouse in order to help those most affected by the disaster. There, they were able to offer cash assistance to help with the rehabilitation of flood victims. They also had a committee on hand who could survey individual situations and assess how they could move forward. All persons who were in need of food, clothing, and medicine were told to visit the temporary Red Cross offices at the courthouse directly, where officials would be waiting to help those in need as soon as they could.

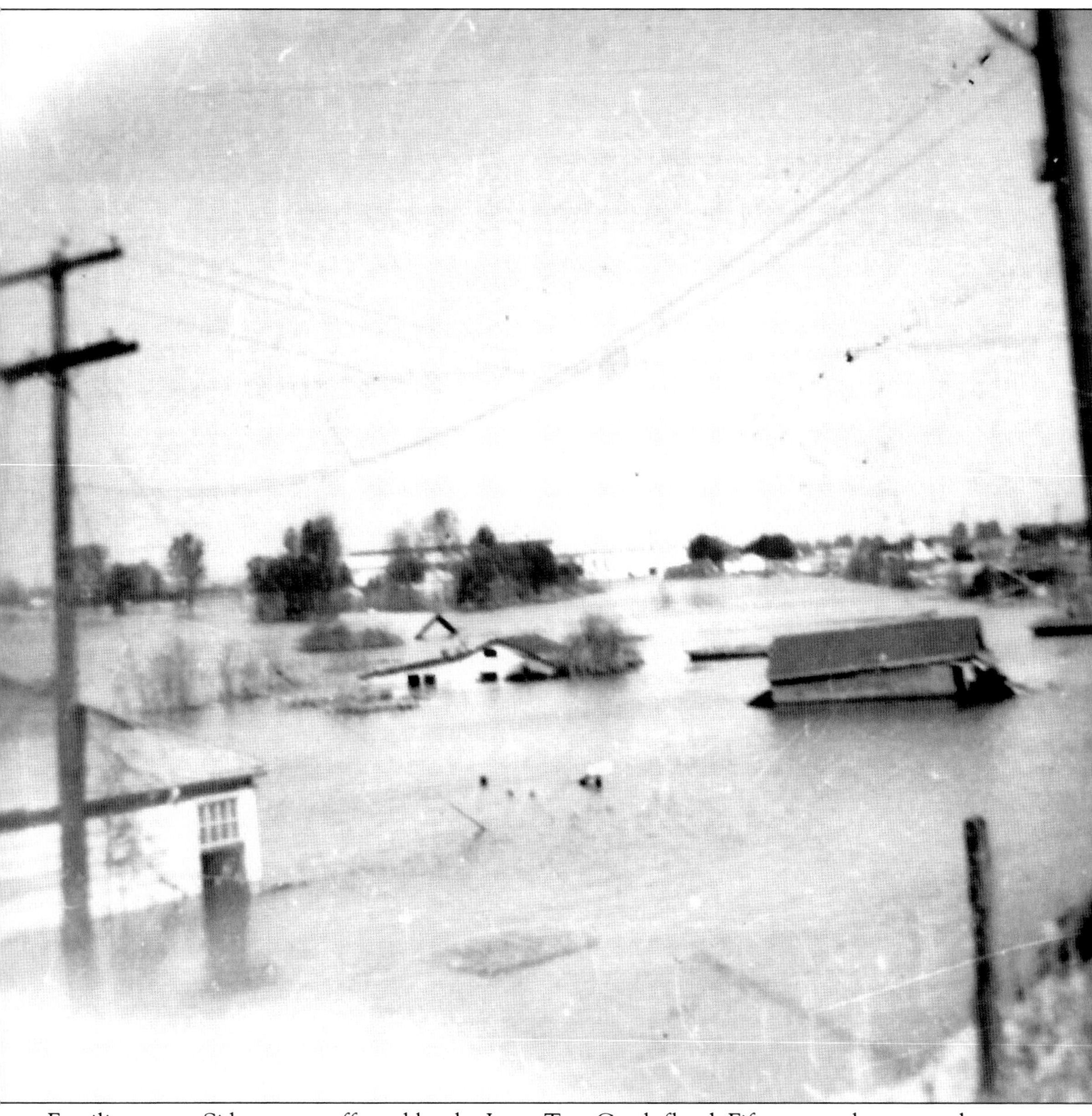

Families across Sidney were affected by the Lone Tree Creek flood. Fifteen people managed to make it to a truck to get out of the danger zone, but the truck stalled on Holly Street, stranding all of the passengers. The six families, including adults and children, were stuck, cold and shivering, until a kindly resident, Pat Chase of Fairview, showed up in his boat and took them to the home of Al Johnson. Those rescued were so thankful to their savior that they took an ad out in the *Sidney Herald*. It thanked Chase for rescuing them and taking them to the Johnson home, where they "were served coffee." Interestingly enough, there were also families completely unaffected by the flood, even with the crashing ice, roaring floodwaters, and fire alarms echoing through the city. The *Sidney Herald* reported that there were even those who slept right through the events of the night.

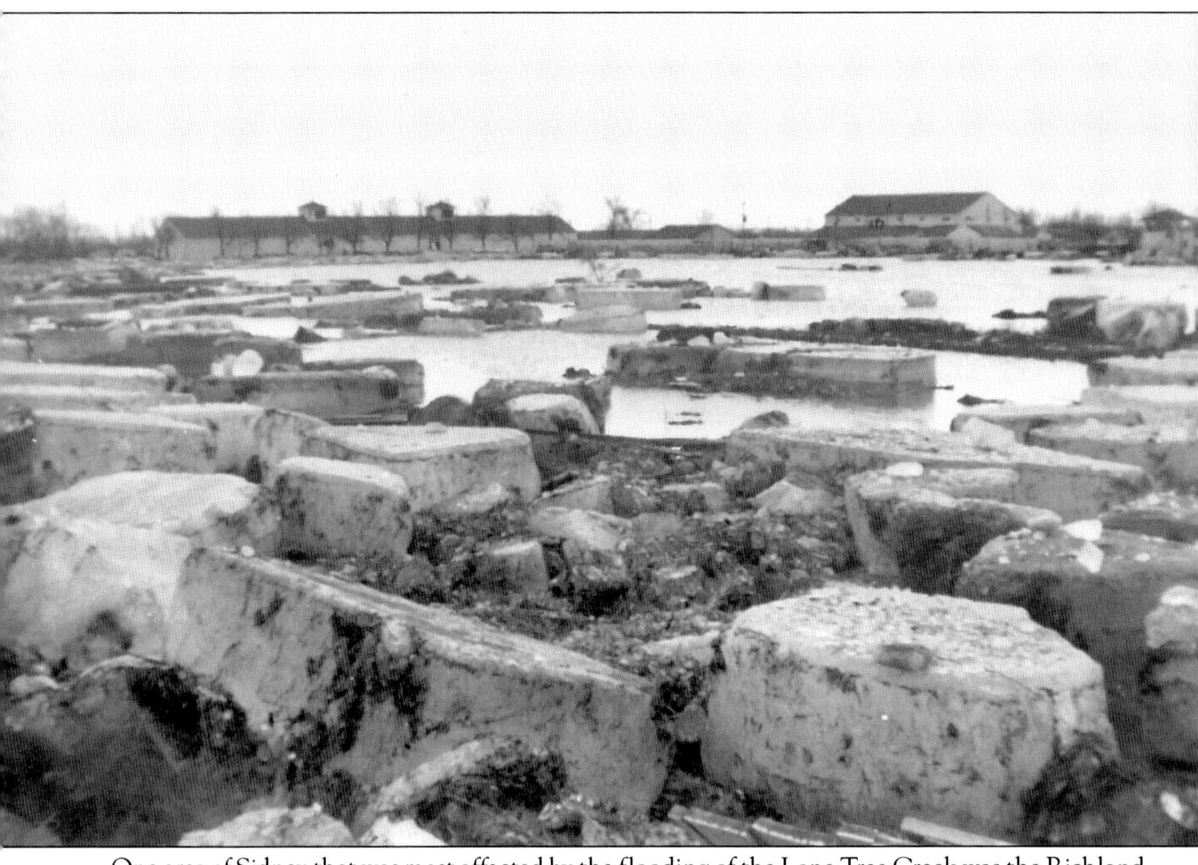

One area of Sidney that was most affected by the flooding of the Lone Tree Creek was the Richland County Fairgrounds. The swift-moving ice swept across the fairgrounds, breaking down the door of the exposition building. Ice filled the building in several layers, surrounding two new trucks and a station wagon that had been stored there. Ice and water also caused considerable damage to other buildings, as well as to the racetrack. Crews worked diligently to clear the surrounding roads and to move the ice, but just four days later, the Richland County Fair Board met. The board decided to cut back on some of the activities planned for the fair because of the unexpected expense of cleaning up the damage to the fairgrounds and buildings. Features of the fair that were continued that year included 4-H activities, the carnival, and the rodeo.

Six

Religion and Recreation in Sidney

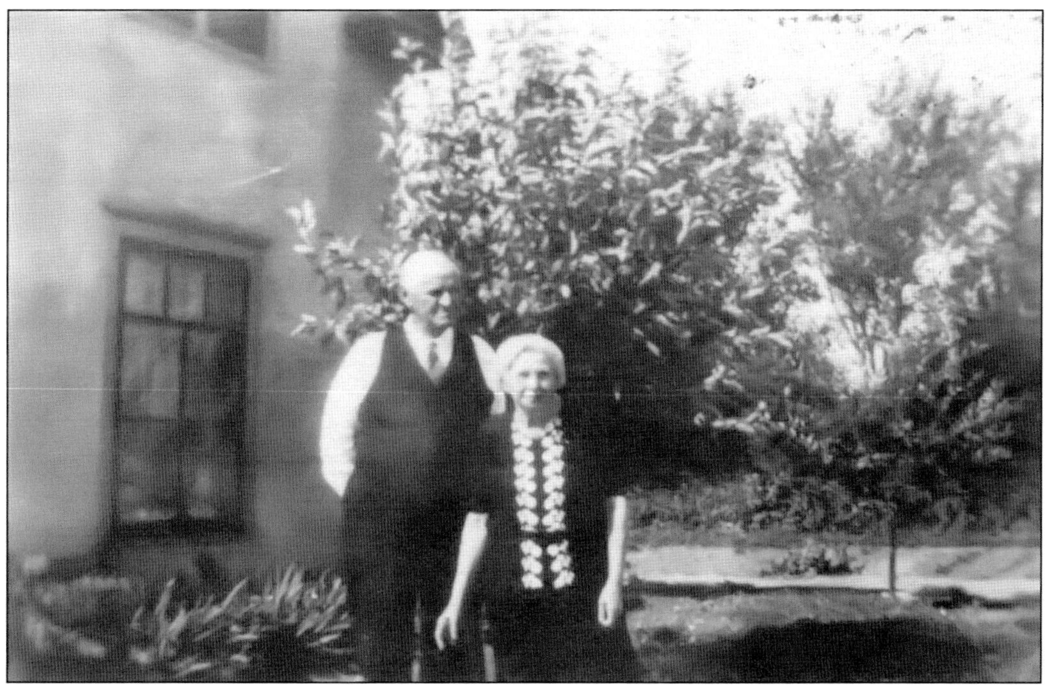

The first Methodist church services in Sidney took place in the log schoolhouse in 1892. Walter Kemmis was the first preacher. As the congregation grew, Kemmis requested that the Methodist Conference appoint a full-time pastor to continue the work. Rev. Melvin Rumohr was appointed to the position in 1899. Here are Kemmis and his wife, Jensine, in 1945.

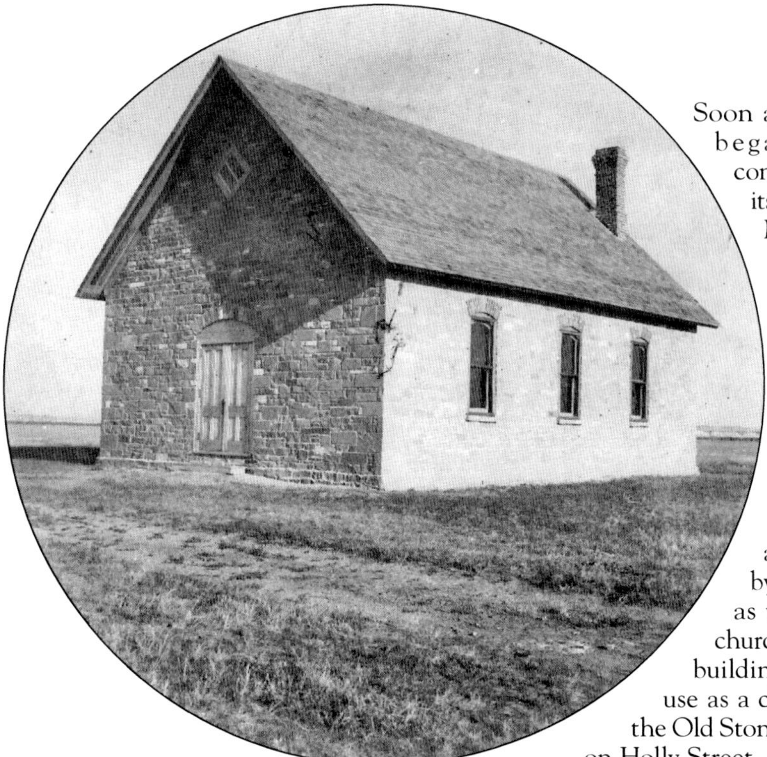

Soon after Reverend Rumohr began his work, the congregation began building its own church. In 1900, the Methodist church, known as the Stone Church, was built. Dave Stewart, from the nearby Crane community, served as the contractor. The stone for the church was blasted and peeled from the rock beds west of Sidney and hauled by a team of horses pulling a sled that was handled by stewards of the church as well as many men from churches across the valley. The building, which is no longer in use as a church, is now known as the Old Stone Church and still stands on Holly Street.

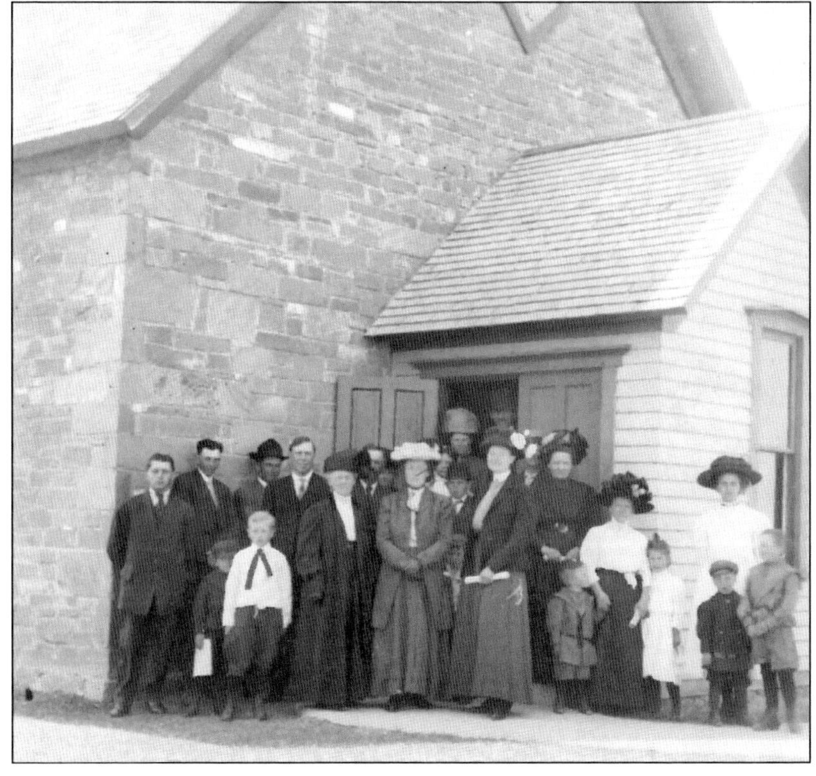

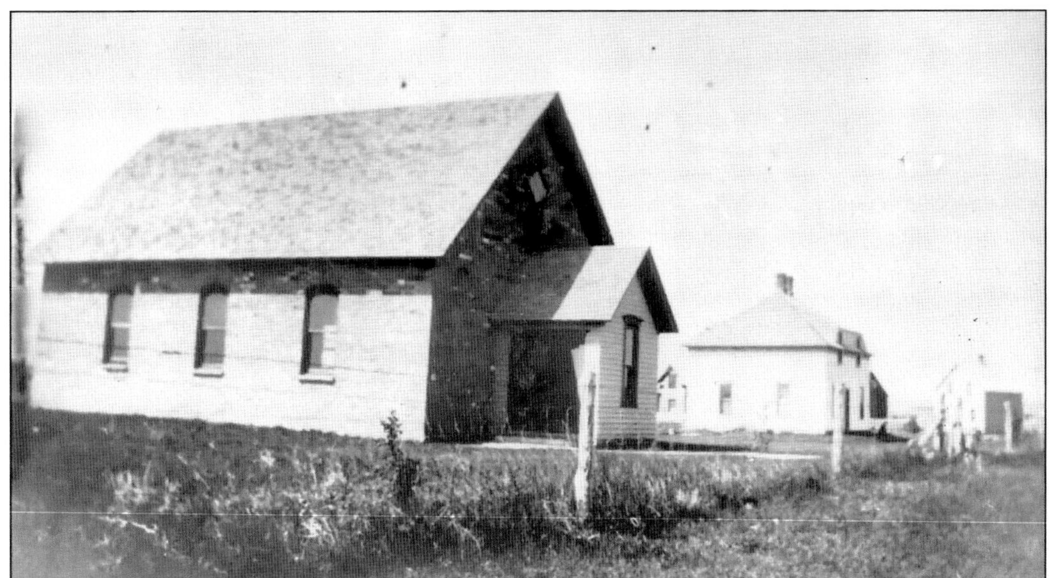

In 1900, when the Old Stone Church was completed, it was officially dedicated by the congregants. At the time that the church was built, there were only 30 members, so the Methodist congregants allowed other denominations to hold services there. By 1917, however, the congregation had grown enough that a new church was warranted. Land was acquired and the Lonsdale Methodist Church was finished in 1924. The church continued to grow, and in 1953, a parsonage was built. In addition to having living space for the reverend, there was also classroom space built in the parsonage basement. In 1964, Lonsdale created plans to build an addition onto the church towards the parsonage. The addition included 14 rooms: a library, parlor, office, chapel, and kitchen, as well as more classroom space.

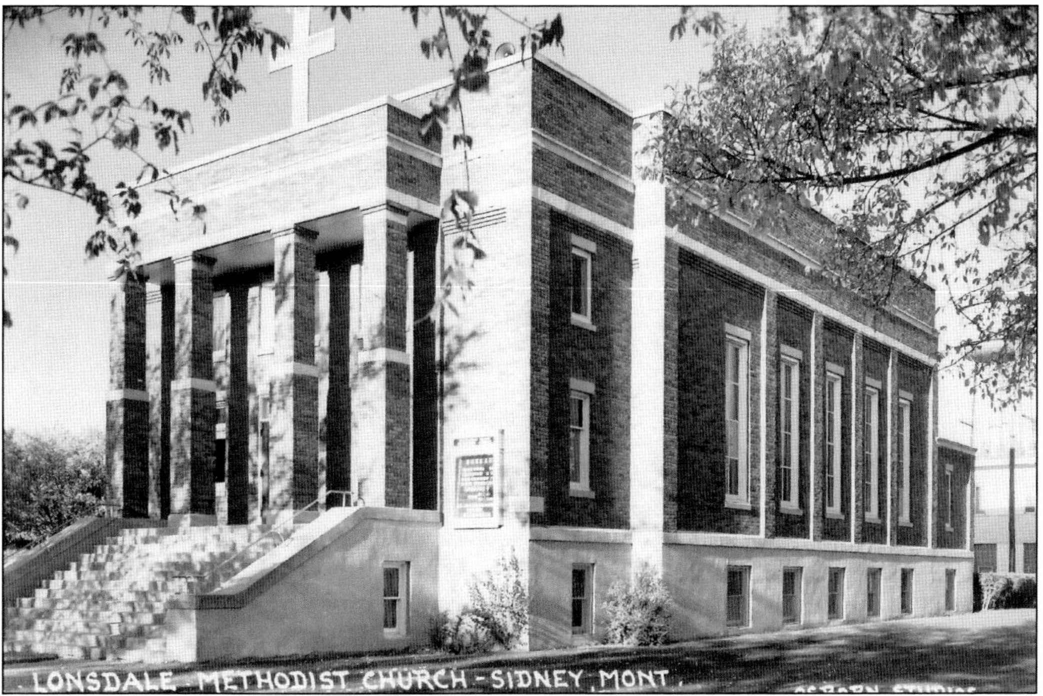

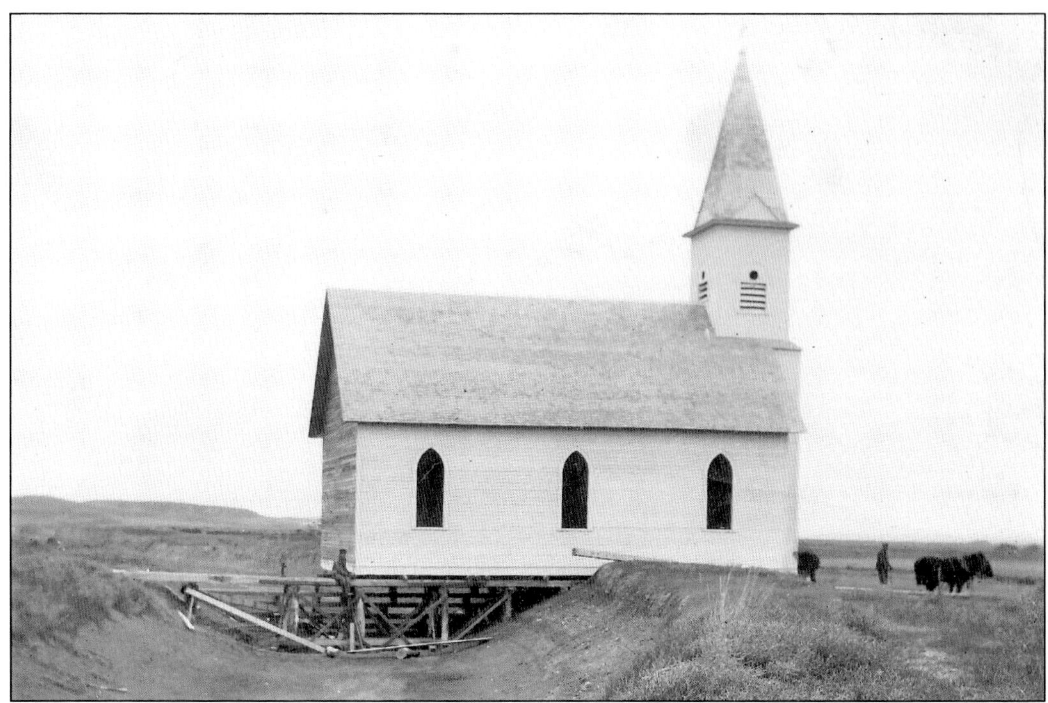

In 1906, a group of 75 Danish settlers established a Danish Lutheran church. A resident pastor was contracted in 1907, and in the follow years, the congregation grew so quickly that a church was built to house them all in 1910. In 1913, that church was moved into Sidney, and it is now known as Pella Lutheran Church.

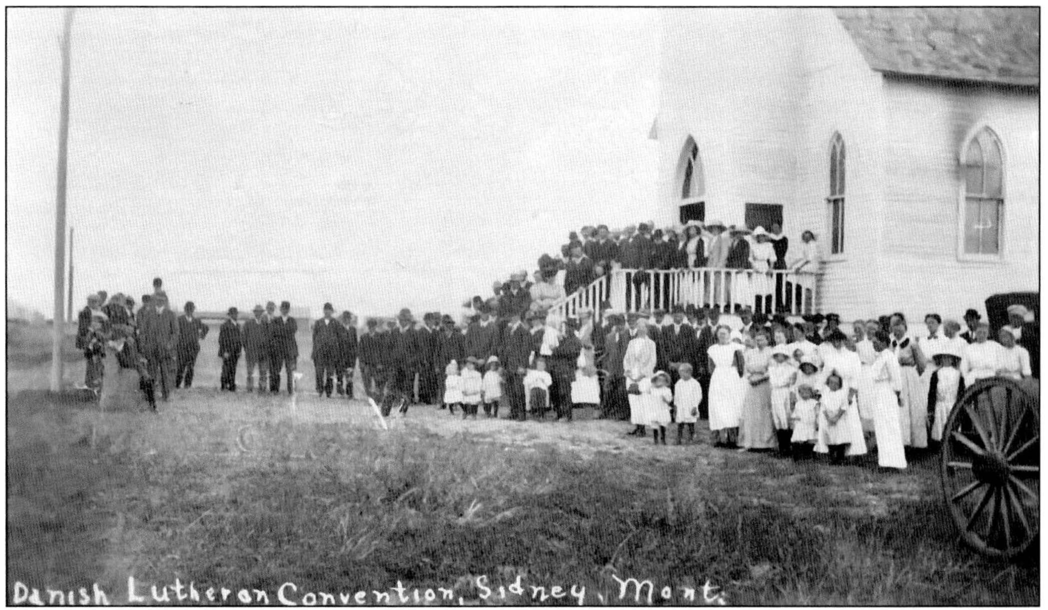

As Pella Lutheran Church grew, the congregants were able to host a Danish Lutheran convention in their new church. By 1925, the Danish settlement had grown to over 700 people, many choosing to move to the Sidney area, not for riches, according to the *Sidney Herald*, but for a sense of community.

Pella Lutheran Church continued to grow rapidly in its early years, especially during the time that Rev. P.C. Jensen (shown here) served as pastor from 1929 to 1938. At one point, it became impossible to fit all of the church members in for services at the same time. It took many years of fundraising before a new church, parking lot, and parsonage were finished in 1949.

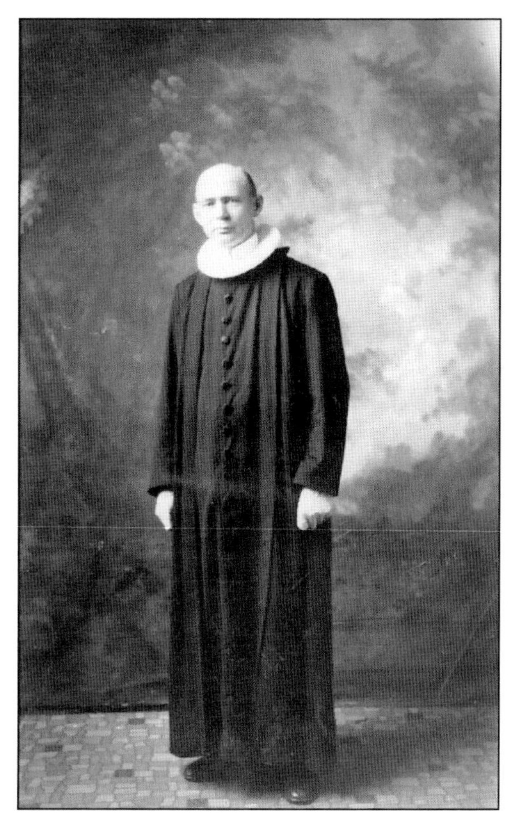

According to church records, the People's Congregational Church in Sidney was created due to a casual conversation with the superintendent of Congregational churches. The first service was held in an abandoned saloon in 1908; by 1910, the congregation had raised $2,400 to build a church. A parsonage was added in 1913. The church and parsonage were sold together in the 1960s, when a new People's Congregational Church was dedicated.

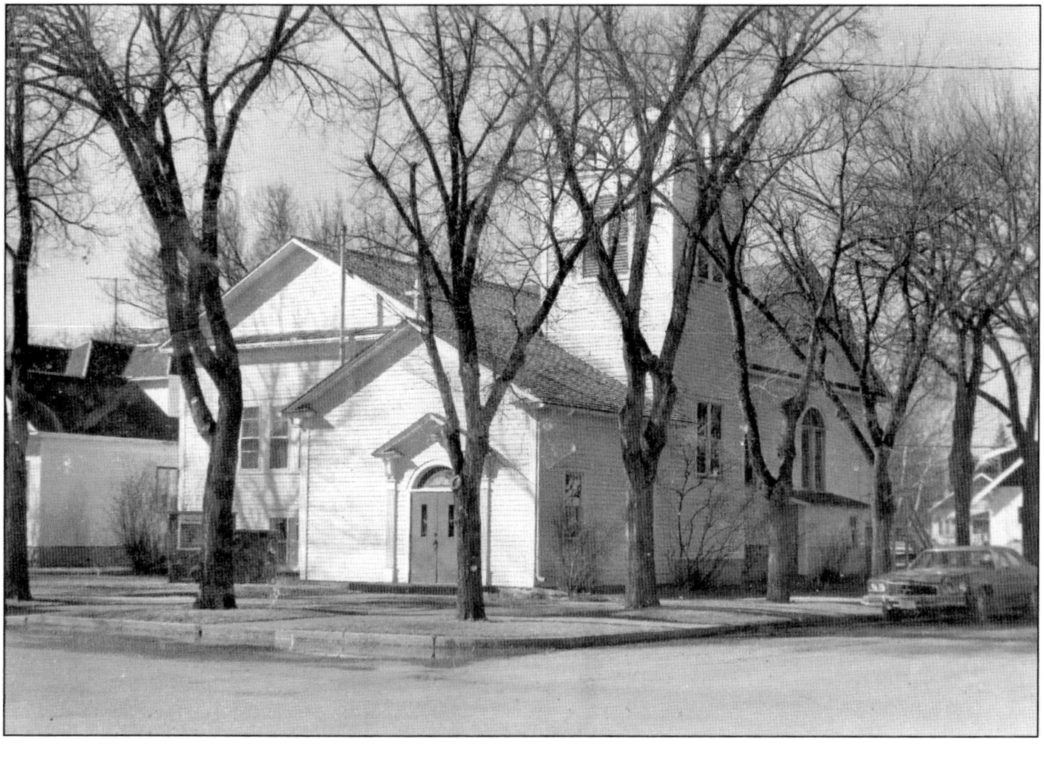

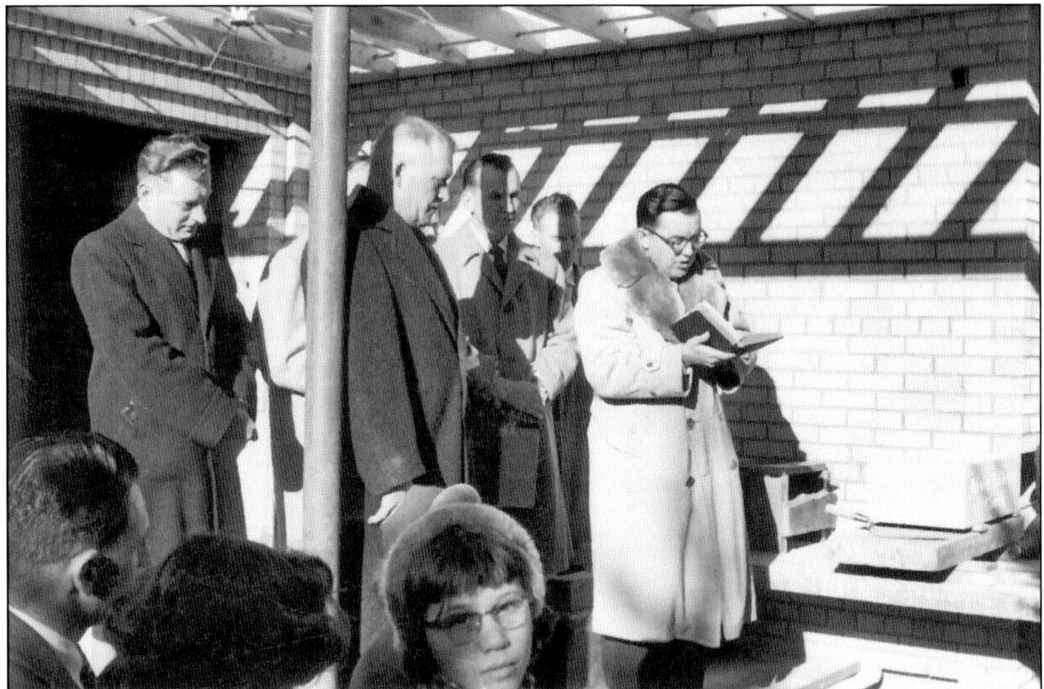

Trinity Lutheran Church was officially organized in 1928. An abandoned schoolhouse and an empty lot were purchased, and on May 28, 1928, Trinity's first house of worship was dedicated. A new church was dedicated in 1935, and as the congregation grew, a third church was needed. On July 24, 1955, Pastor John Chambers and the members of Trinity Lutheran dedicated their new church.

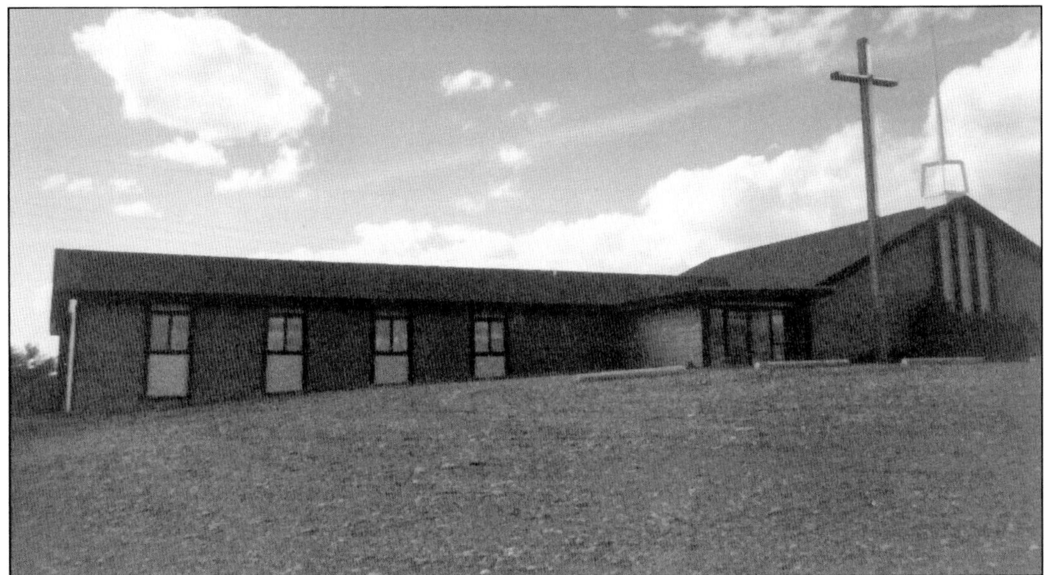

The Church of the Lutheran Brethren of America announced that it would be building a new church in Sidney in 1967. It would be called the Sidney Lutheran Brethren Church. The governing board for the newly formed church applied for membership that same year, and it was approved unanimously.

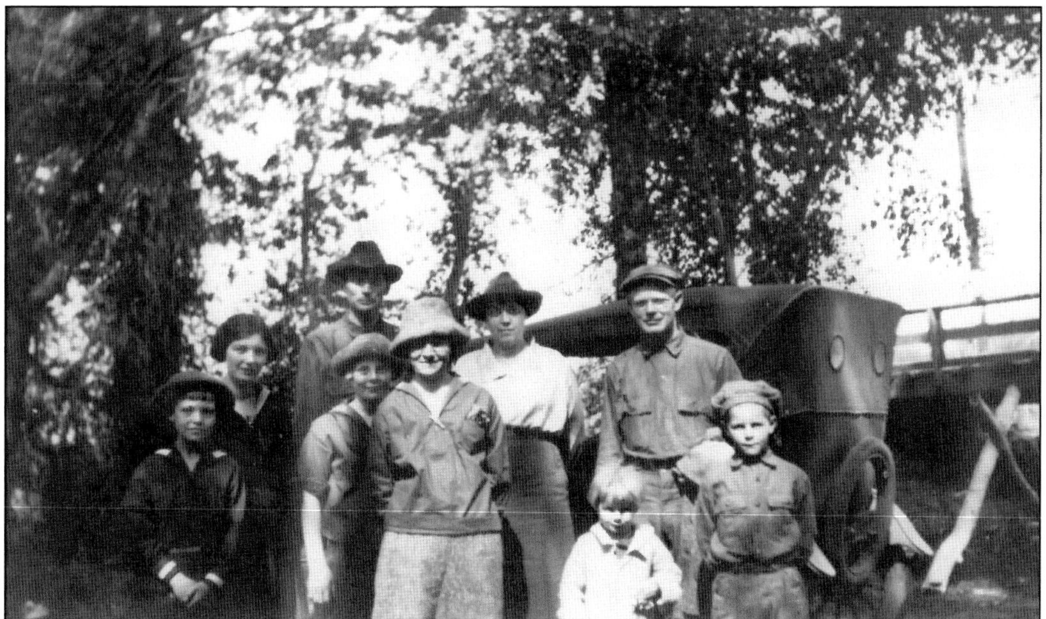

One way that the residents of Sidney could enjoy the outdoors was by having a picnic. Friends and families could get together, bask in each other's company, and relax. Here, the J.H. Nevins and Earl Varco families pose for a photograph together to commemorate their outing, along with Edna Brown.

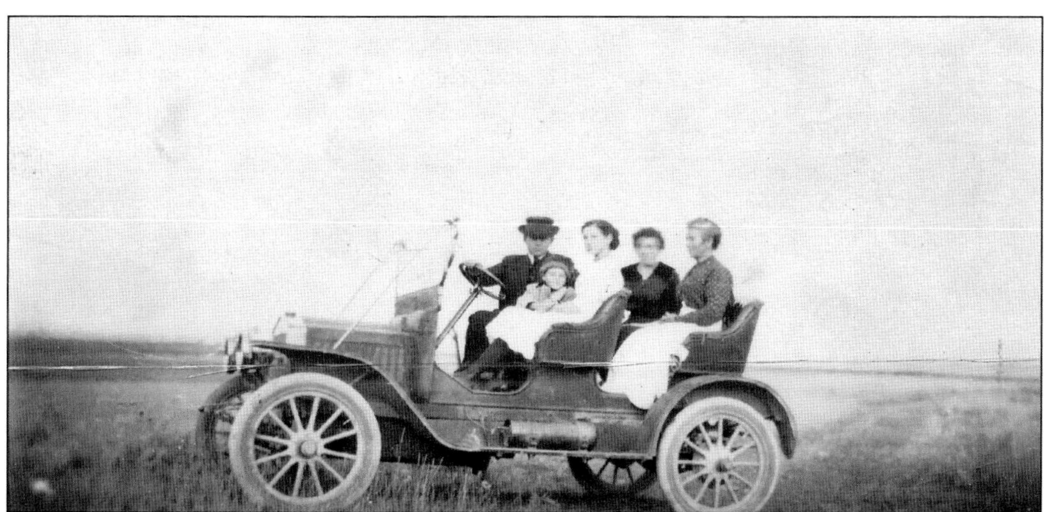

A good time was had by all when taking a car for a joyride, especially when cars were scarce in Sidney. Adults and children alike vied for a chance to ride in the car of Dr. R.A. Morrill, who is shown in the driver's seat in this picture. From left to right in the car are Bob Morrill, Julia Kelly Niehenke, Dorothy Briggs Morrill, and Bridget "Grandma" Kelly.

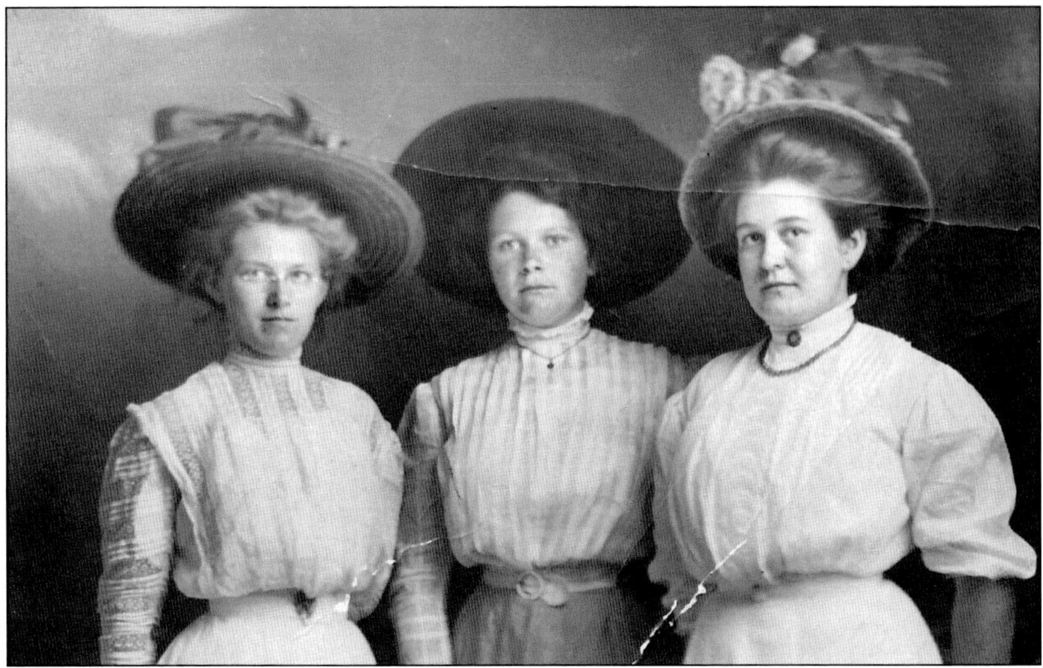

The Fourth of July was always a momentous time in early Sidney. The women shown here in 1909 are dressed to the nines to celebrate the holiday. From left to right are Georgia Adams, Rache Woodard, and Nettie Ray. The parade in Sidney that year was described by the *Sidney Herald* as "one of the swellest, niftiest, most scrumptious, elegant and splendiferous parade ever seen."

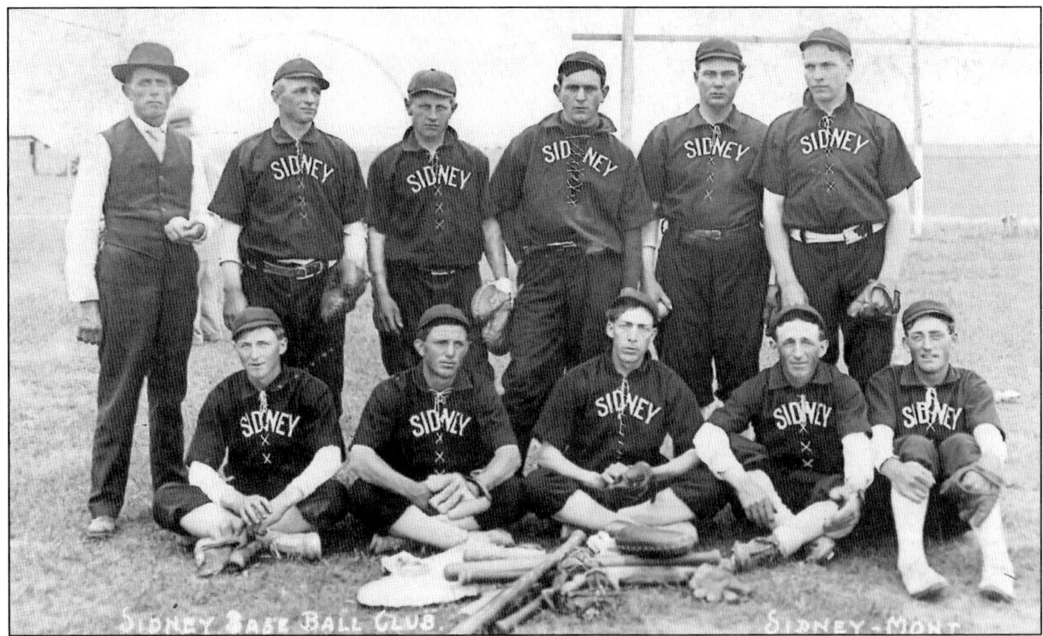

Baseball is known as the national pastime, and in early Sidney, it was no different. The hometown team, the Sidney Reds, is shown in the photograph. In the back row, second from left, is Fred Hurst. Fred Hurst became the chief of police in 1915 and served in that position until 1941. Also in the back row, at right, is Hank Turner, co-owner of Turner Drug.

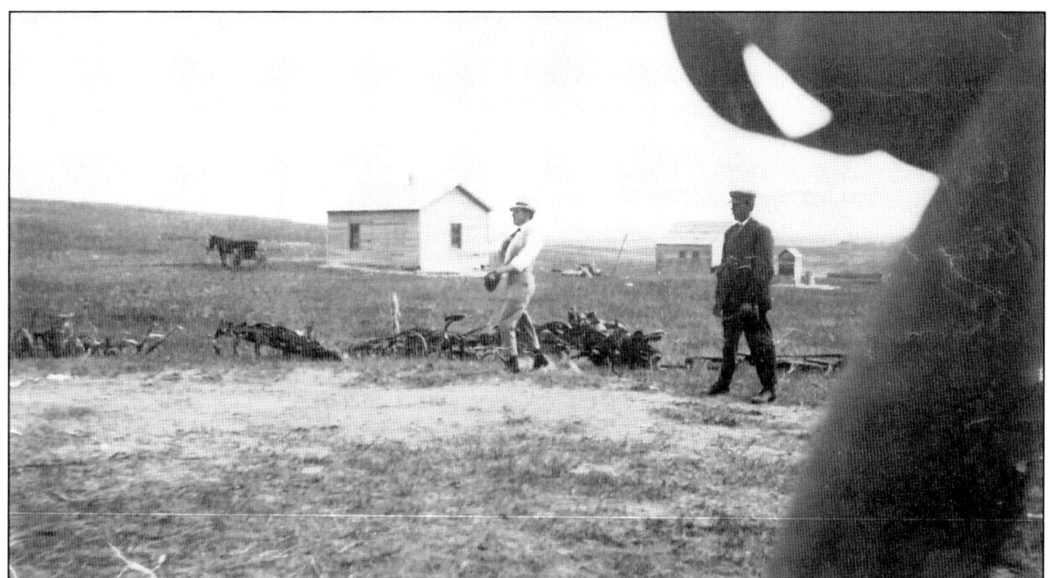

In the early days of baseball in Sidney, the teams did not have uniforms. In this photograph, taken in 1911, men dressed in their Sunday best play on a small patch of land with farm equipment littering the ground behind them. Sidney played the Fox Lake baseball team on the day this photograph was taken.

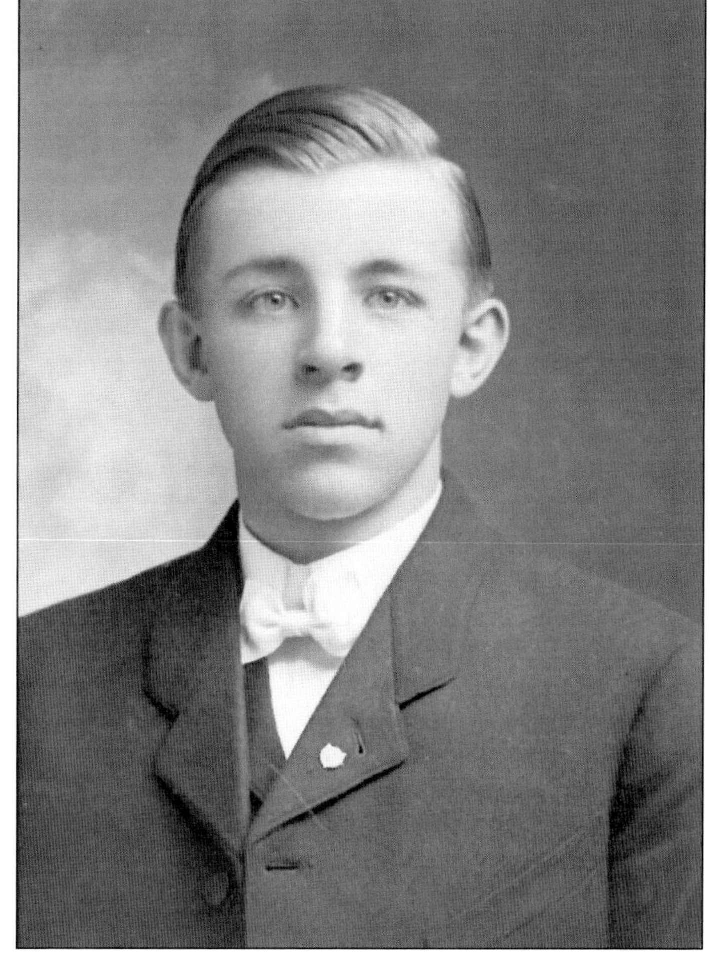

Carl Brattin practiced law in Sidney for over 50 years. In addition to serving as a lawyer, Brattin was on the Montana State Board of Education and the first president of the Kiwanis Club in Sidney. Brattin joined the Masons on August 13, 1913, and served as Sidney's Master Mason in 1921. He also served as the Grand Master of Masons in Montana.

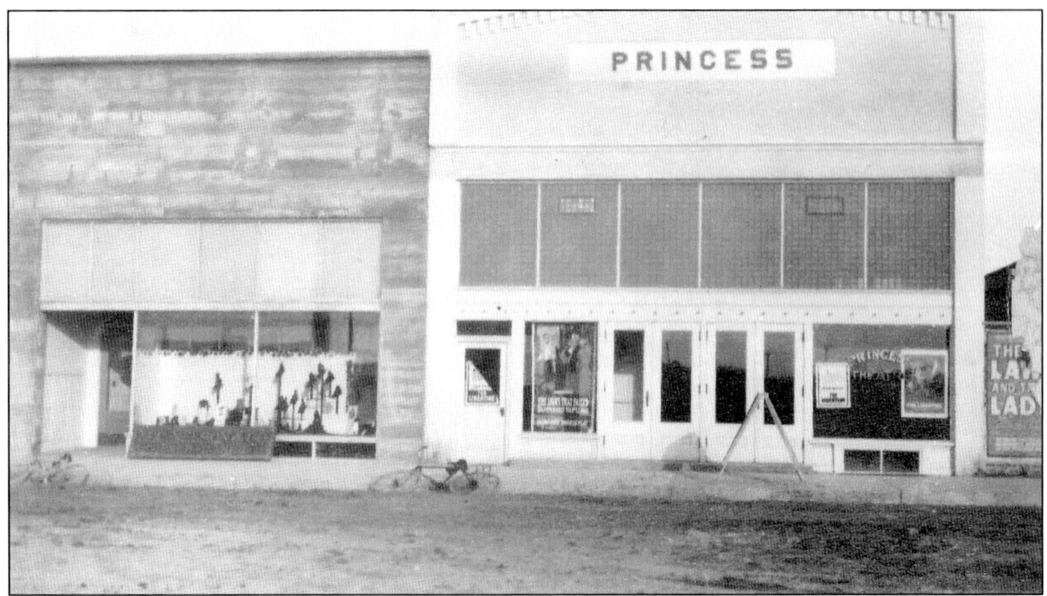

Although the Princess Theatre showed second-run movies, they changed frequently to allow guests to attend the theater at least once a week. The theater was open seven days per week, 52 weeks per year. Movies like *Snow White and the Seven Dwarfs* were popular in Sidney, as were any movies featuring Al Jolson.

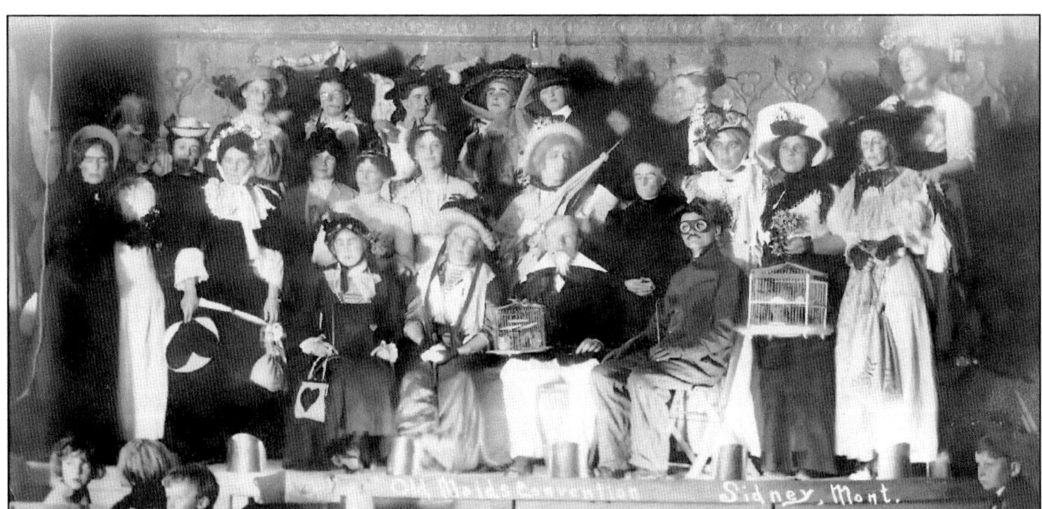

Sidney's new school was completed in December 1914, two years after the previous school had burned down. The new school had an auditorium in which plays and other forms of entertainment could be viewed. One of the first shows to be put on by the high school students was the *Old Maids Convention*.

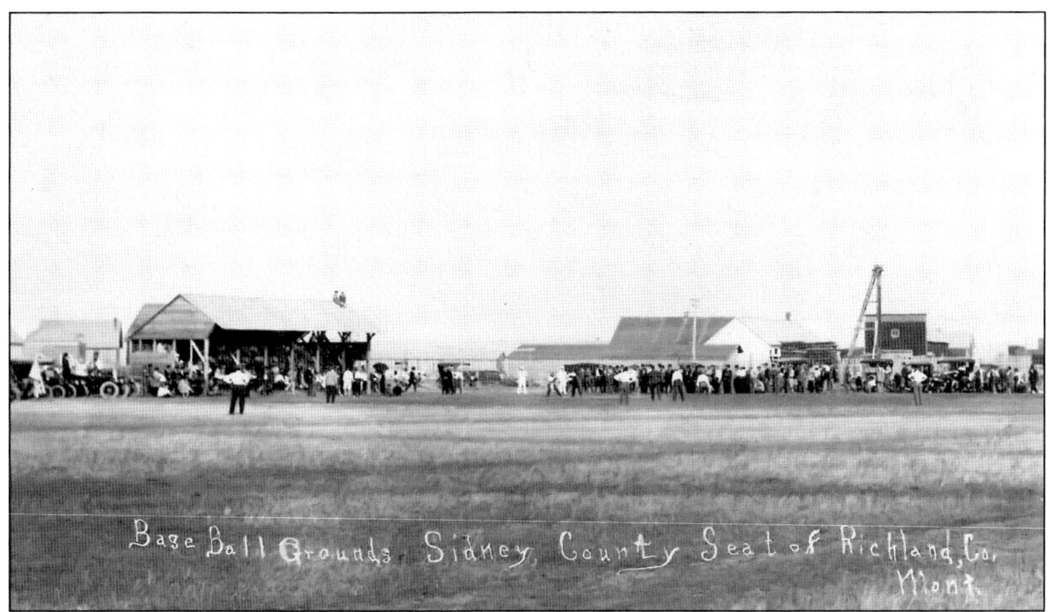

This picture shows the Richland County baseball grounds in Sidney. Locals would gather to watch their home team play, dressed in their Sunday best. This area was also where the county fair was held until it was moved further west where there was more space for the rodeo and fairgrounds.

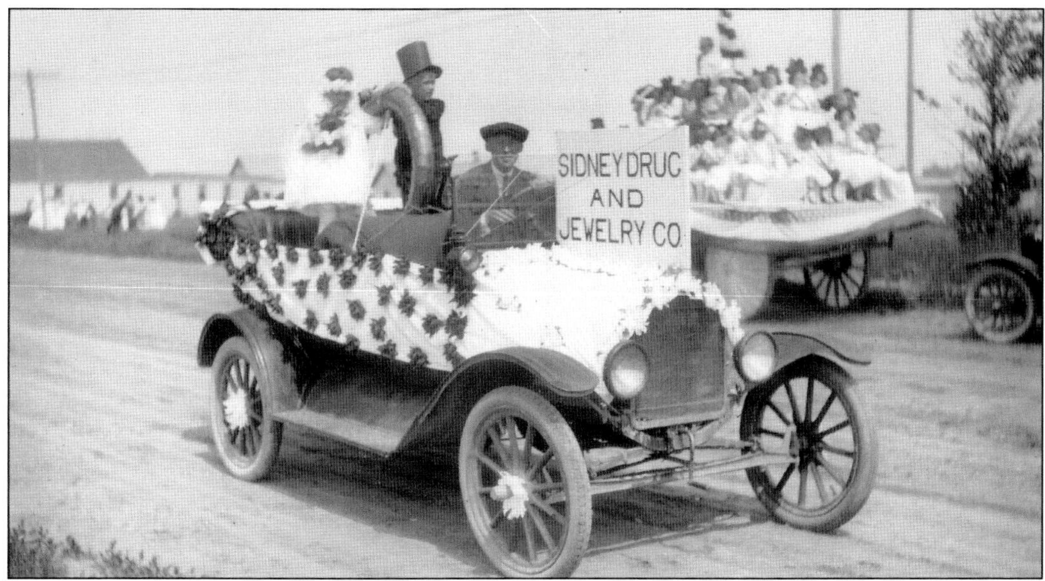

In 1916, the residents of Sidney celebrated the Fourth of July over two days, July 4 and 5. On the Fourth, a big parade was held. Veterans were invited to march in it. Local businesses participated as well. Here is a float for Sidney Drug and Jewelry Company with a large ring and two children dressed up as bride and groom.

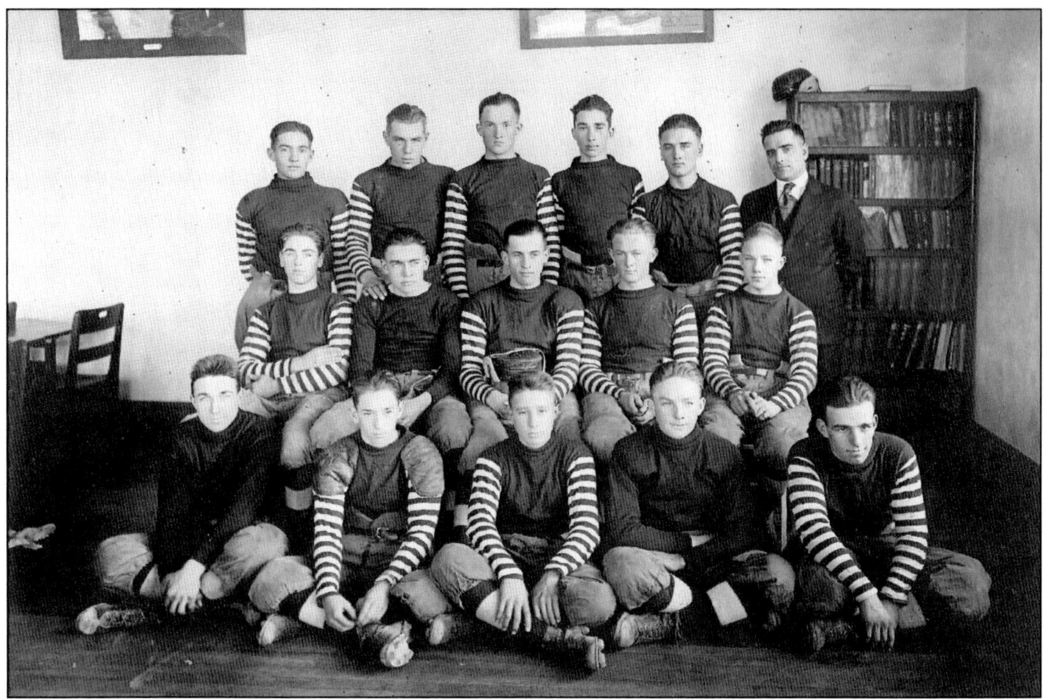

Sidney's first high school football team was formed in 1914. This photograph shows the 1919 football team from Sidney High School. That fall, the team only played four games and ended the season with two wins and two defeats. The wins were recorded against Wolf Point and Culbertson. The losses were versus Poplar and a second game with Culbertson.

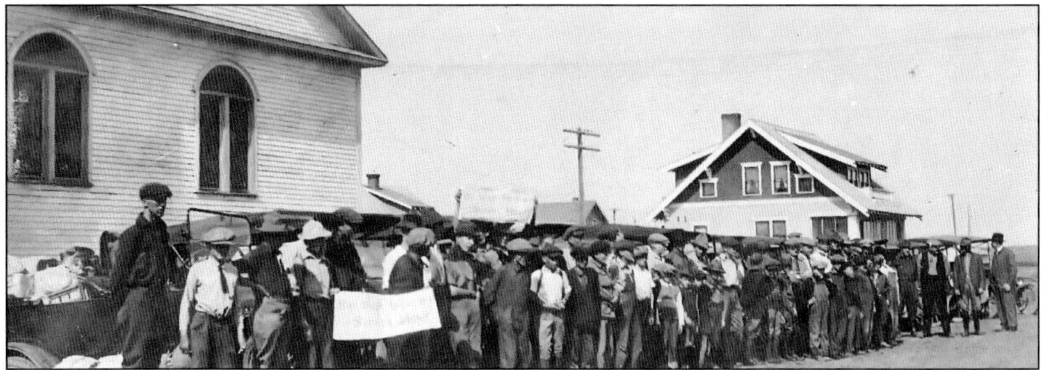

This photograph shows the local Boy Scouts lined up as they get ready to visit Brush Lake in northeastern Montana on June 12, 1922. According to the *Sidney Herald*, no Scout was prevented from attending this trip due to lack of funds. Scoutmaster James Elvin lent money to those Scouts who needed it. In return, the Scouts could work off their debts over the summer.

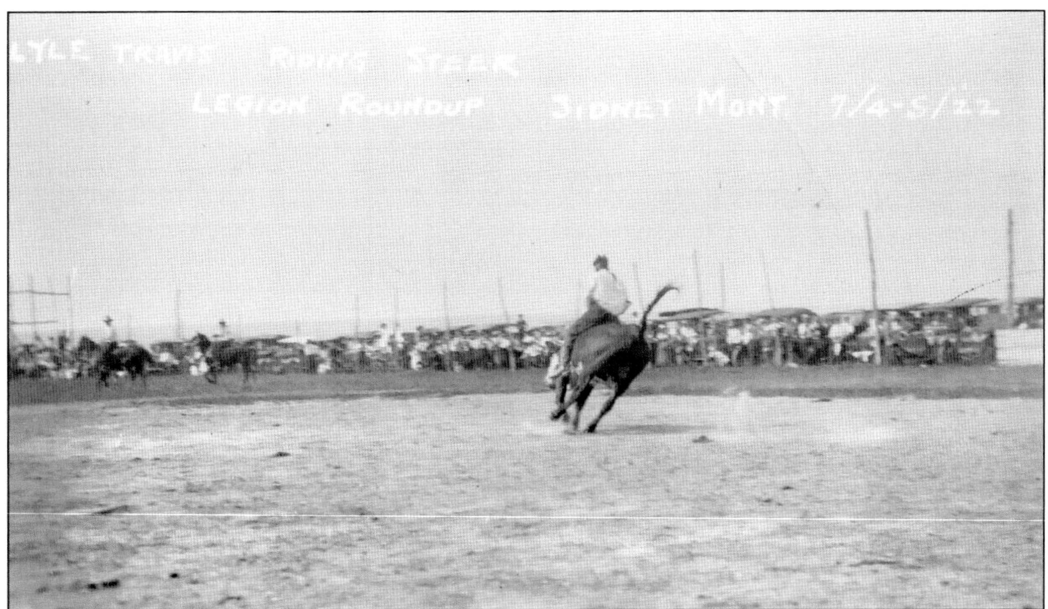

Touted as the "Biggest Event in the City's History" by the *Sidney Herald*, the 1922 Legion Roundup was highly anticipated over the Fourth of July that year. Nearly 10,000 people from across the region attended the event, which included a parade and an exhibition of riding and roping. Here, Lyle Travis rides a steer as the crowds look on.

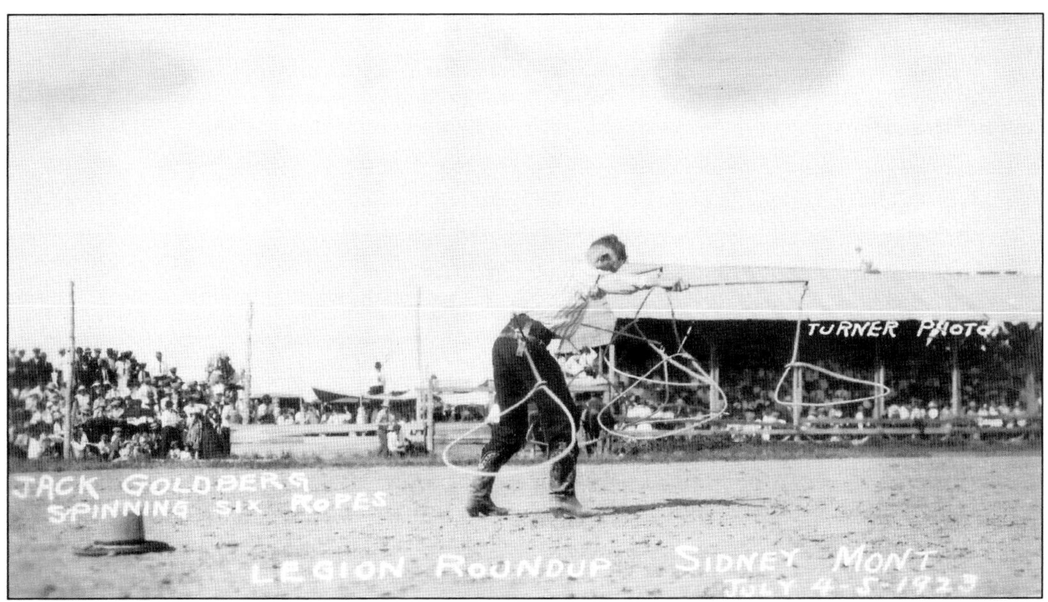

The following year, Sidney was once again host to the Legion Roundup over the Fourth of July holiday. The events on the Fourth were attended by 6,500 people, with an overall attendance of 10,000 over two days. Jack Goldberg, pictured here, was named the "Star of the Roundup" by the *Sidney Herald*. He impressed the crowds with his rope work, gunslinging, and riding skills.

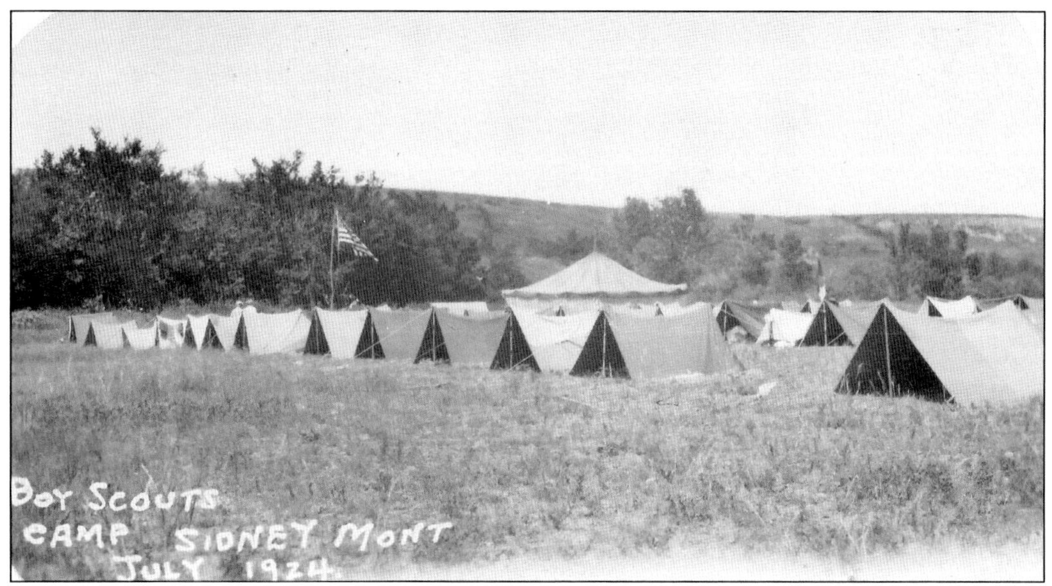

In 1924, the Sidney Boy Scouts held their summer camp in Loverings Grove, just three miles northwest of Sidney. Every boy who wanted to attend camp had to be a registered Boy Scout and had to have passed all of his tests. Each Scout also had a long list of items to bring with him, which included a pup tent, as seen in the top photograph. A list of things that were not allowed was published in the *Sidney Herald* and included bulky luggage, guns, dogs, infectious diseases, trashy novels, smutty stories, disobedient stories, and old John Grouch. The camp lasted for 10 days, and parents could write to their sons during that time or attend Visitor's Day, but they were not allowed to send any delicacies unless there was enough for the whole camp. Every day of camp was completely planned out, including making sure that the Scouts got some time to swim.

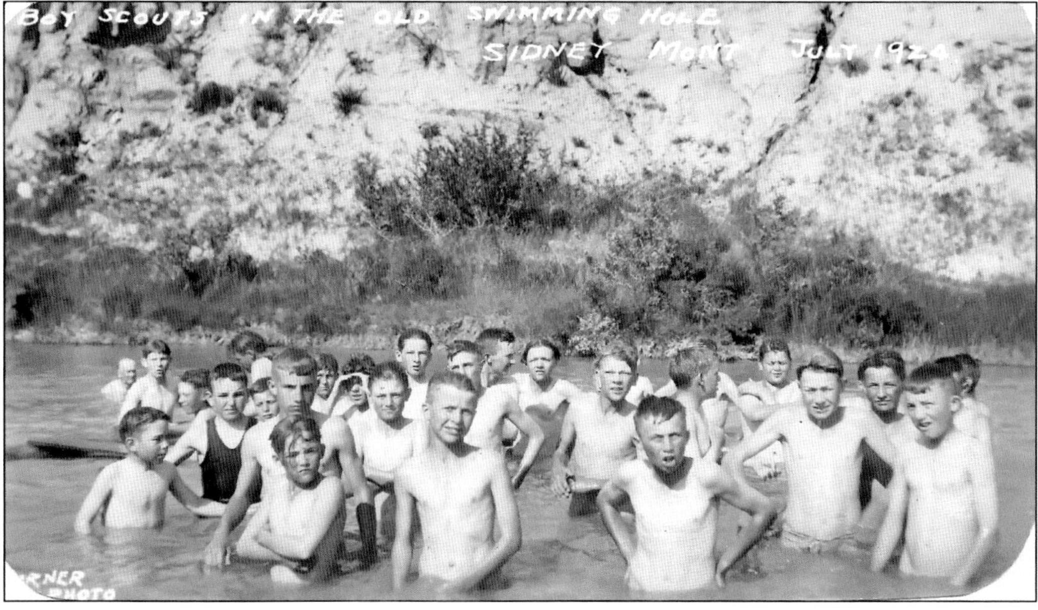

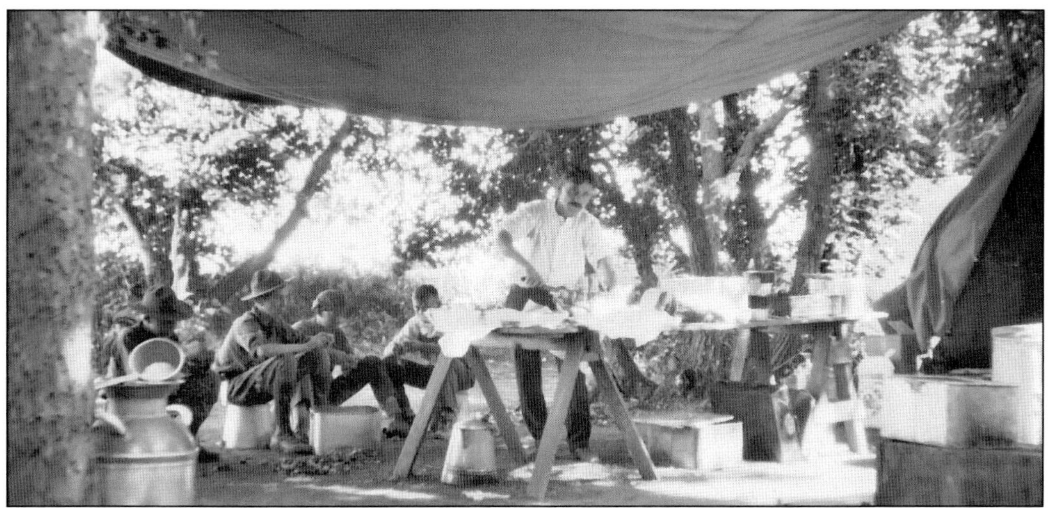

In addition to a long list of items the Boy Scouts were required to bring with them to camp, they also had to carry with them a plate, cup, bowl, knife, fork, spoon, and two dish towels. If the meals each day did not satisfy a boy, there was a camp store available. There, Boy Scouts could purchase candy and fruit, but no more than 10¢ worth per day.

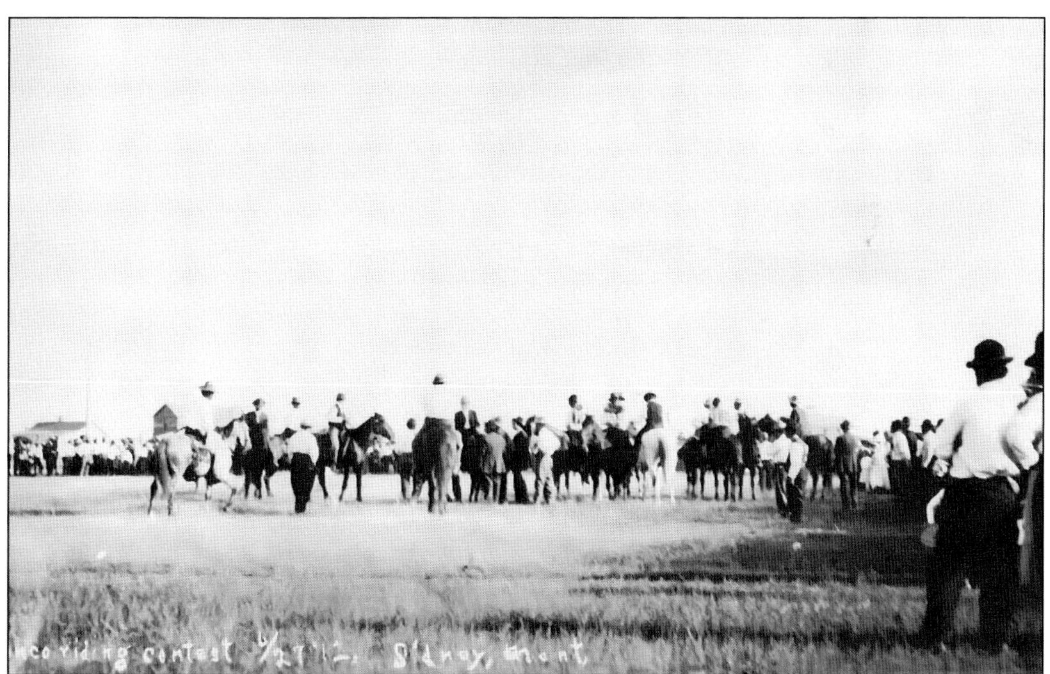

During the Railroad Jubilee, held on June 27, 1912, a bronco-riding contest was held. Four men entered the event. First place was awarded to Bill Canoy, second to Charles Remus, and Steve Douglas took third. It was said that the fourth rider, who is unidentified, allowed himself to be thrown from the horse in order to prevent the animal from hurting those in the crowd.

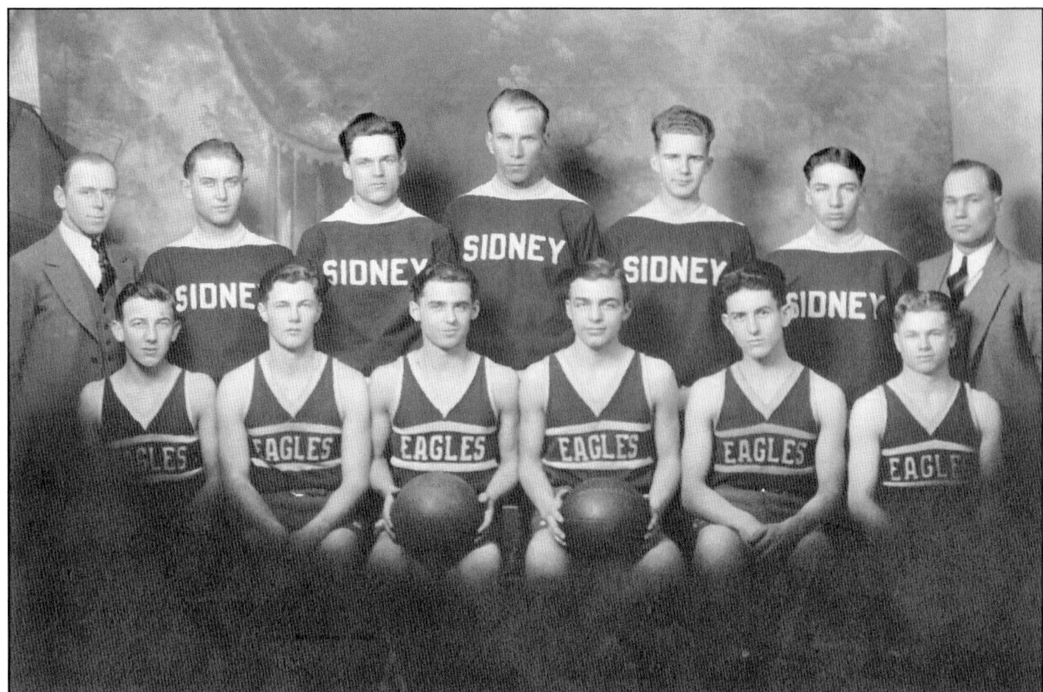

High school basketball was organized in Sidney in 1917. This photograph shows the 1932–1933 Sidney High School basketball team. Its record for the season was good and included 17 victories and 6 defeats. Most of the losses took place at the beginning of the season, which showed that the team improved over the year. It ended the season at a district tournament, taking third place overall.

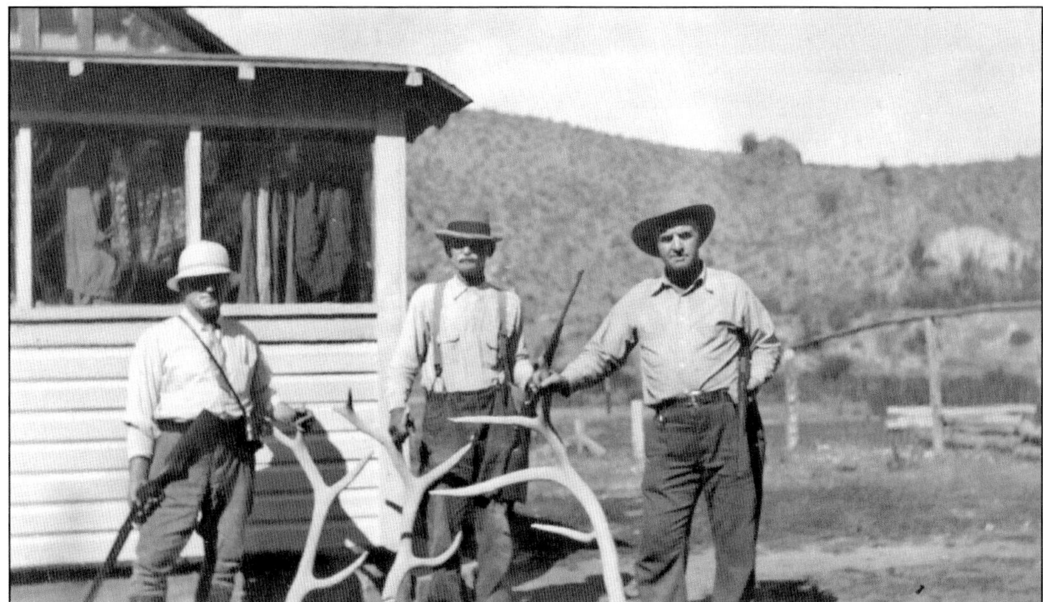

Hunting was and has continued to be a popular pastime for residents of Sidney. Not only did hunting take place around town, but members of the community also traveled to bag trophies. Here, from left to right, William Combes, Henry Hilger, and Fred Sullivan pose with antlers from their hunting trip in Hamilton, Montana, in the summer of 1934.

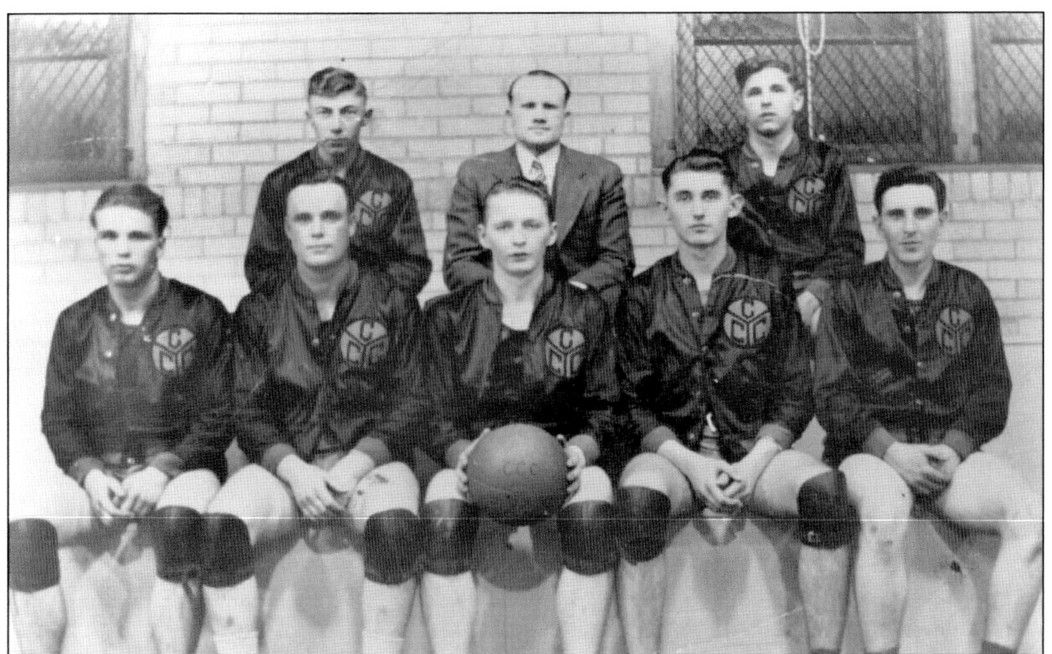

The Civilian Conservation Corps Company 2701 that added drains onto the Lower Yellowstone Irrigation Project had two camps. The main camp was just north of Sidney, and a sub-camp was located at what was called the Intake, near the headwaters of the project. The company participated in many recreational activities, including basketball, kittenball (now known as softball), baseball, and swimming. Pictured are the 1940–1941 National CCC Basketball Champions.

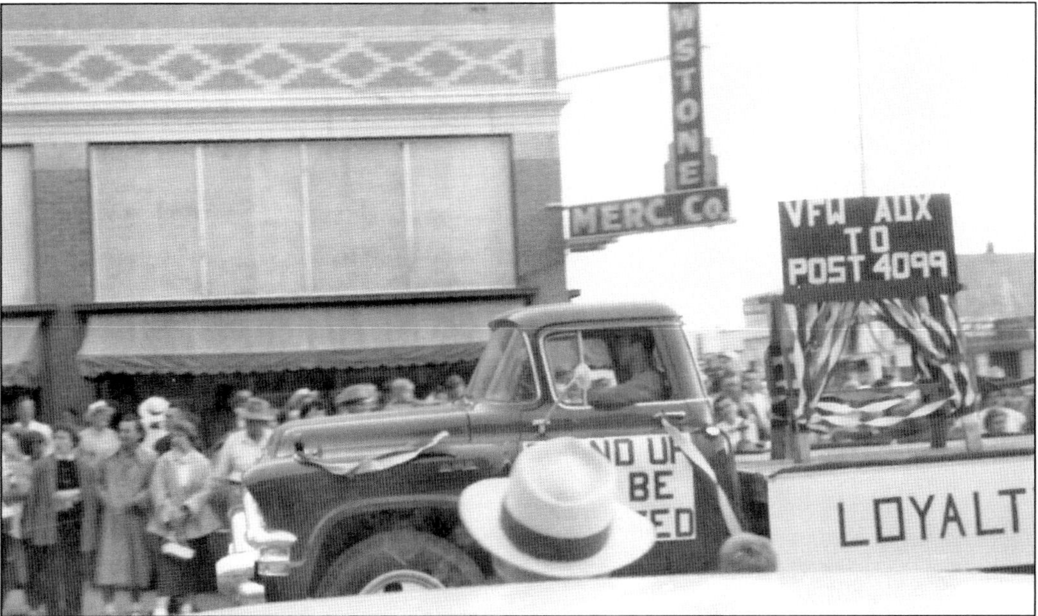

In 1946, the Lower Yellowstone VFW Auxiliary Post 4099 was formed in Sidney. Here, its Fourth of July float, on the back of a pickup, is driven by the Yellowstone Mercantile. The VFW auxiliary post is still very active today, contributing to many community service projects, including running the Flags of Honor room at Veterans Memorial Park.

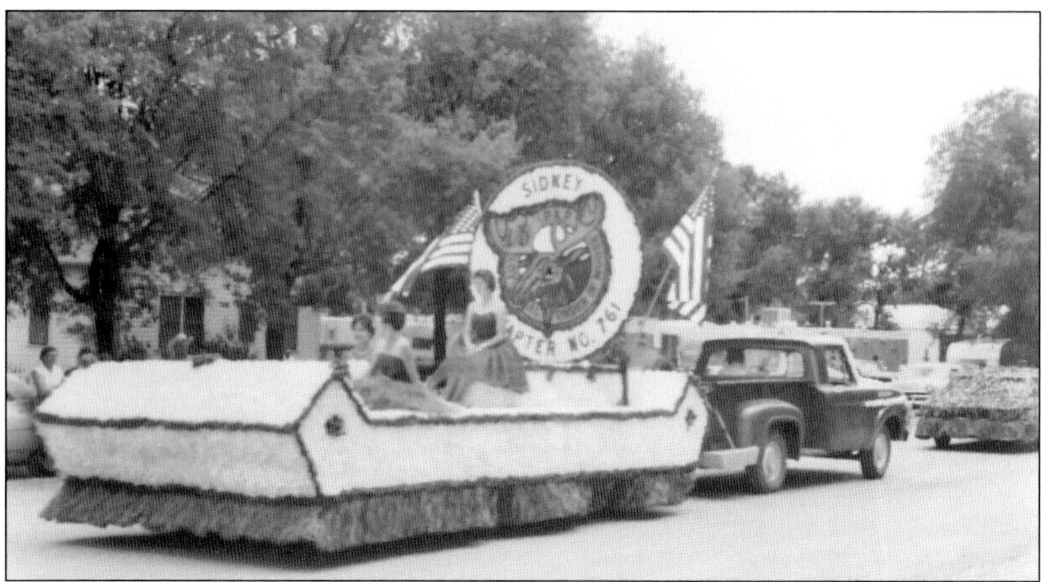

The Fourth of July was always a big deal in Sidney, and so were parades. Here, ladies representing Sidney's Loyal Order of the Moose chapter, which was formed in 1944, ride their float in the parade of 1963. Just seven days later, the local Moose chapter played host to the Montana State Moose Association Annual Convention. More than 500 members of the fraternal organization attended the three-day event.

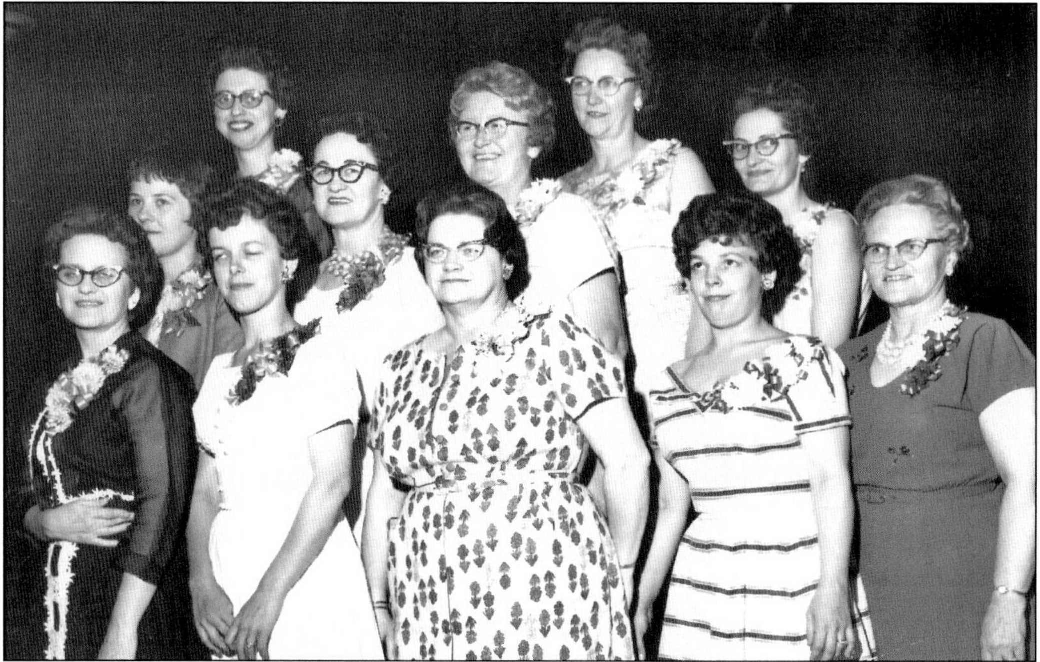

There has been no shortage of fraternal organizations in Sidney, but women have not always been welcome. In 1913, the national female auxiliary for the Loyal Order of the Moose was created. Originally known as the Women of the Mooseheart Legion, it is now known as the Women of the Moose. Sidney Women of the Moose, whose group was organized in 1945, pose here adorned with corsages.

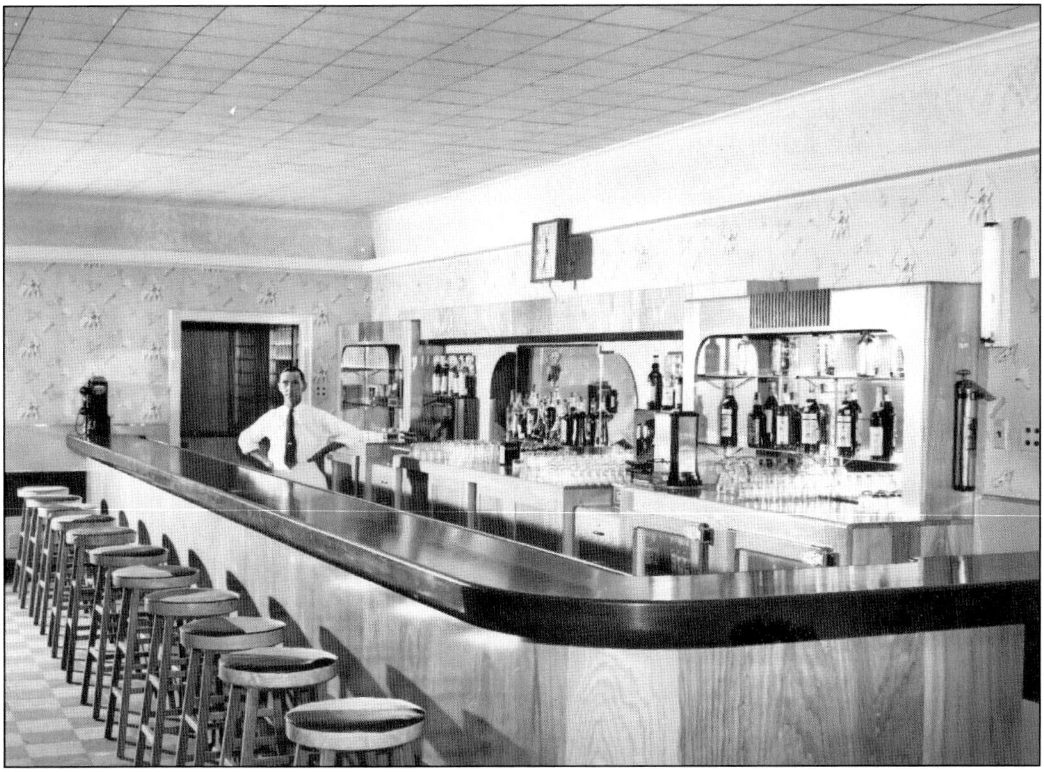

The Moose Lodge has long been a place where the members and residents of Sidney can take a load off and enjoy a drink after work. This photograph shows the bar in 1948. Walt Mende stands behind the bar. He served as bartender at the Moose Lodge throughout that decade.

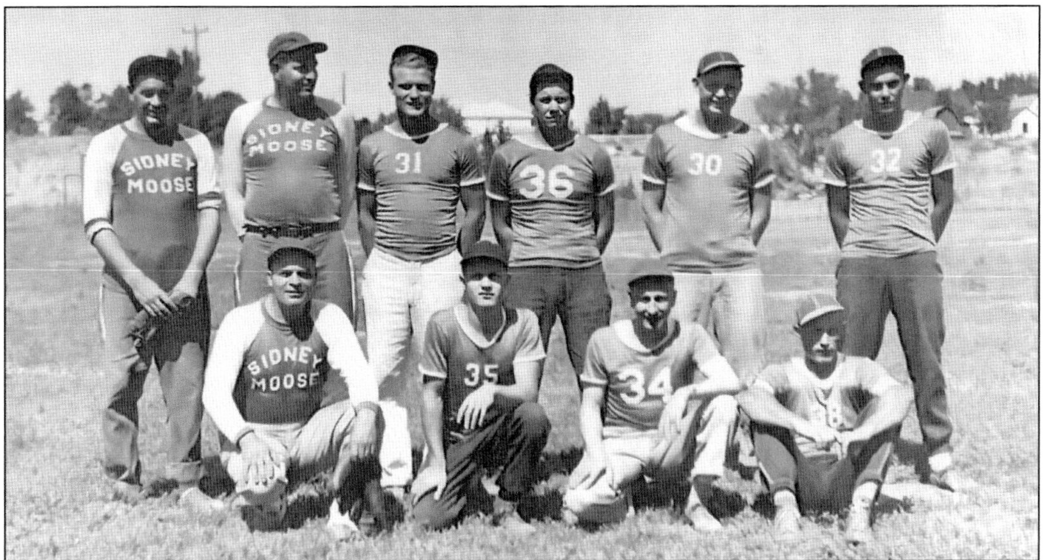

The Sidney Moose Lodge held its annual picnic on July 24, 1949, for all members and their families. The Moose had their own baseball team, shown here, and would invite Moose Lodge teams from surrounding communities to come to the picnic for a tournament. In addition to baseball, there was also a horseshoe tournament held for both men and women at the picnic.

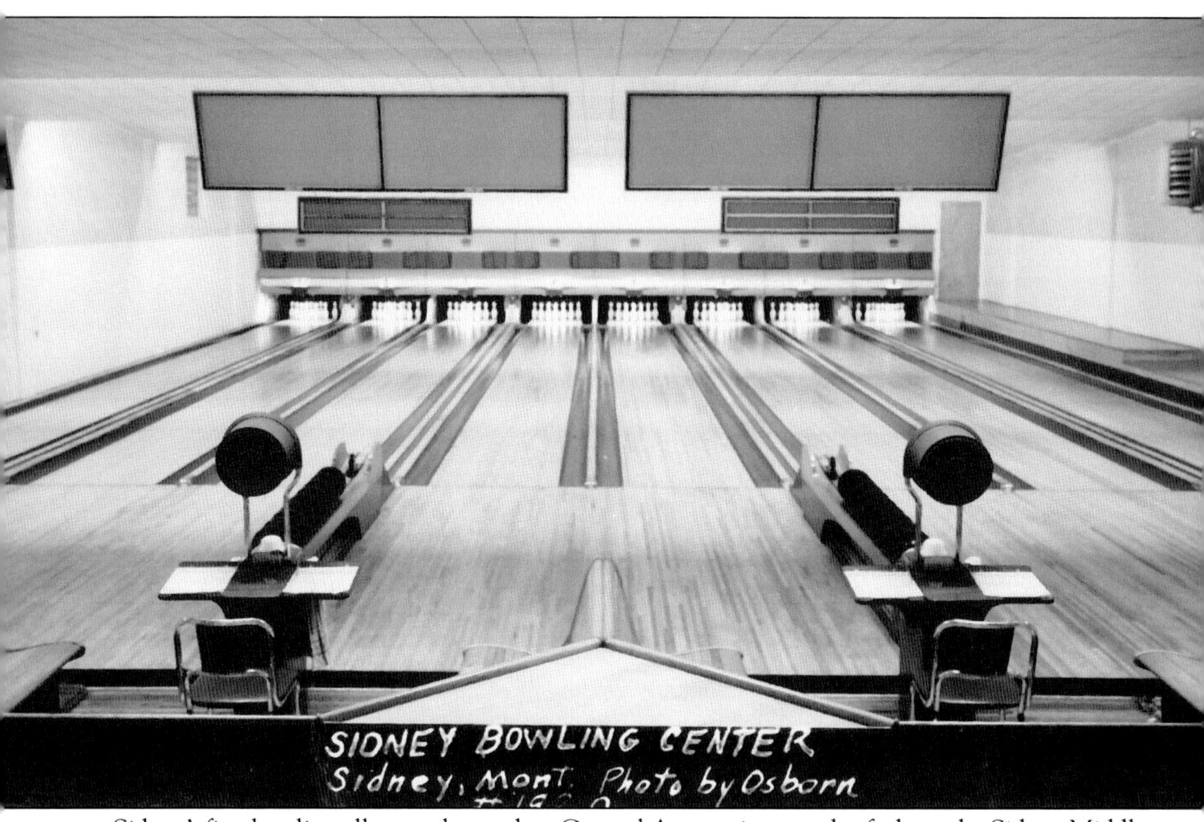

Sidney's first bowling alley was located on Central Avenue just north of where the Sidney Middle School is now. It was known as the Sidney Bowling Center. The center was opened in February 1949 and was owned by Dave Peer. In addition to a beautifully designed playing area, there were also locker rooms for both men and women and a lunch counter. In 1960, five local businessmen—Sam and Frank Maltese, Harold Mercer, and James and Robert Peterson—bought the alley from Peer. Mercer was appointed manager. The center was open long hours, from 10:00 a.m. to 2:00 a.m. seven days a week, year-round. The restaurant within the center was open extended hours, from 6:00 a.m. to 2:00 a.m. The Sidney Bowling Center remained in the ownership of the five men until 1979. That year, the Sidney Bowling Center was purchased by Ron and Mary Carter and Ross and Doris McCulloch. They renamed the business R&R Lanes.

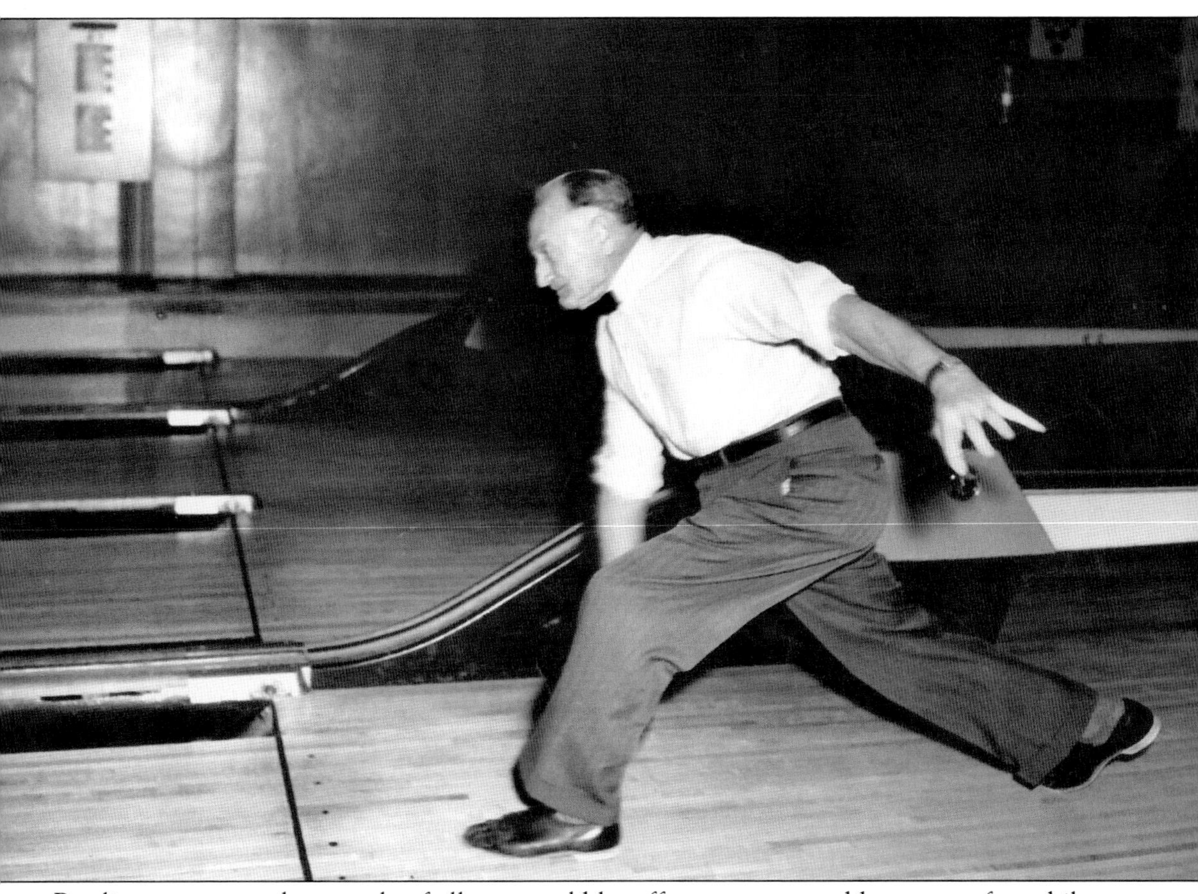

Bowling was a way that people of all ages could let off some steam and have some fun while doing it. Here, Dr. Ivan J. Peterson glides up the approach and begins to swing his arm to launch a bowling ball down the lane at the Sidney Bowling Center. Dr. Peterson was born in Wadena, Minnesota, in 1886. He went to the University of Minnesota, where he obtained a doctor of dental surgery degree in 1915. In 1918, Dr. Peterson moved to Sidney and opened his own practice. He continued to practice there for 47 years. Initially, Dr. Peterson preferred to play golf and spent his time at the local course. Soon, however, he came to love bowling even more. His love for the game did not slow down, even as he aged, and at the age of 76, he would still bowl up to three times per week.

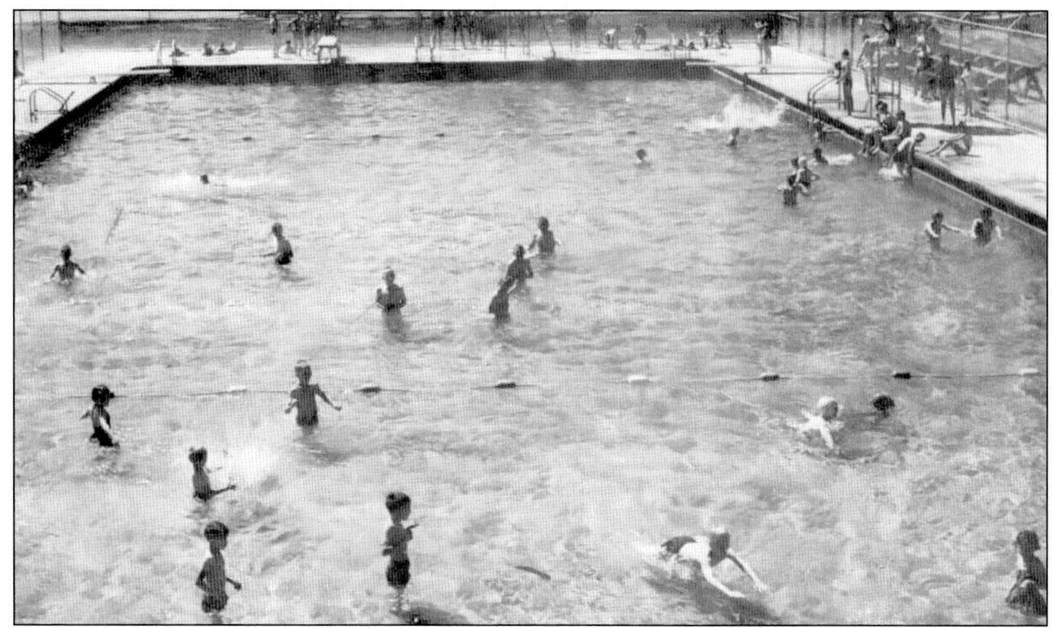

Taking a nice dip in a cool pool is most refreshing for northeastern Montanans. The pool in Sidney was built in the early 1950s. Originally, it was 50 yards long, but it was later converted to meters to comply with competition requirements. In 1975, the pool was remodeled at a cost of $100,000. A new filtration system was added, as was a heater to allow for a longer swim season.

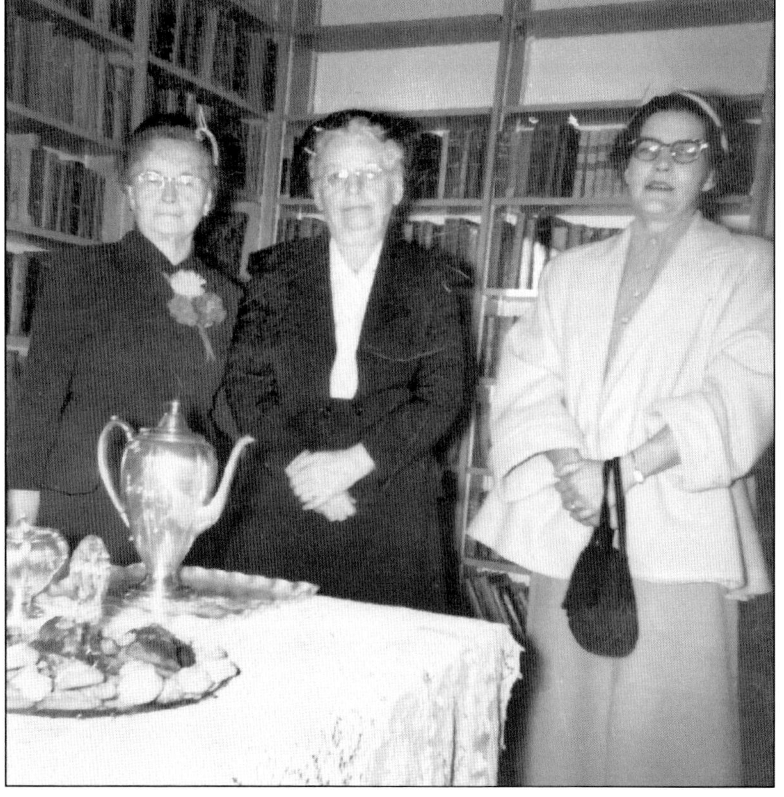

The citizens of Sidney appreciated taking time to socialize with their neighbors. In 1954, these three ladies took part in a tea that was being held at the library. Pictured are Antoinette Varco (left), one of the founders of the library; Charlotte Imes (center), past board member; and Elizabeth Thompson, library board member in 1954.

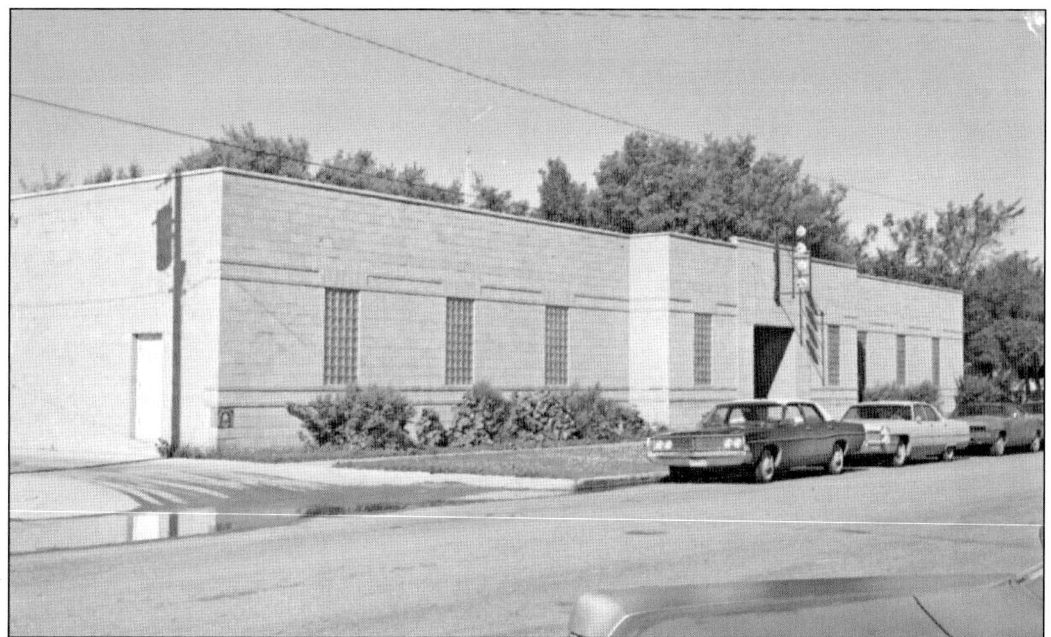

Sidney's Masons held their first meeting in April 1913 and were officially chartered on September 18, 1913. Meetings took place in several different locations over time, including the lecture room of People's Congregational Church, a room above Richland National Bank, and on the second floor of Yellowstone Mercantile Annex Building. A permanent Masonic temple was built in 1957 and dedicated on May 25, 1957, and the Masons still utilize it today.

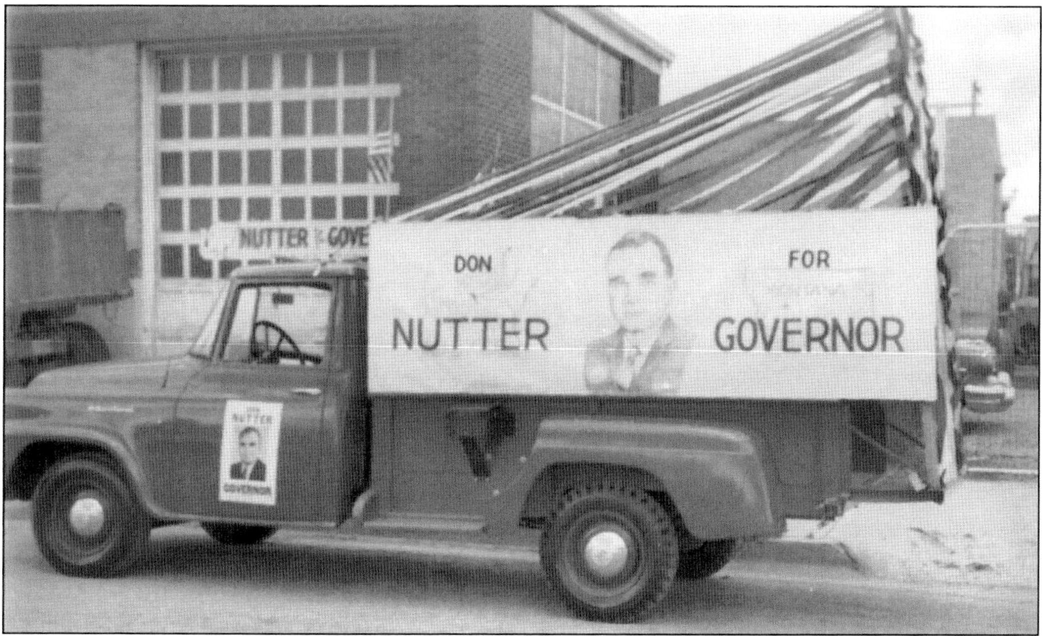

The townspeople of Sidney really rallied behind Donald Nutter during his run for Montana governor. Not only was the Republican Party headquartered out of Sidney, but there were also fleets of automobiles that were decked out with campaign signage. Here is a truck outfitted with Donald Nutter's campaign posters and other decorations in October 1960.

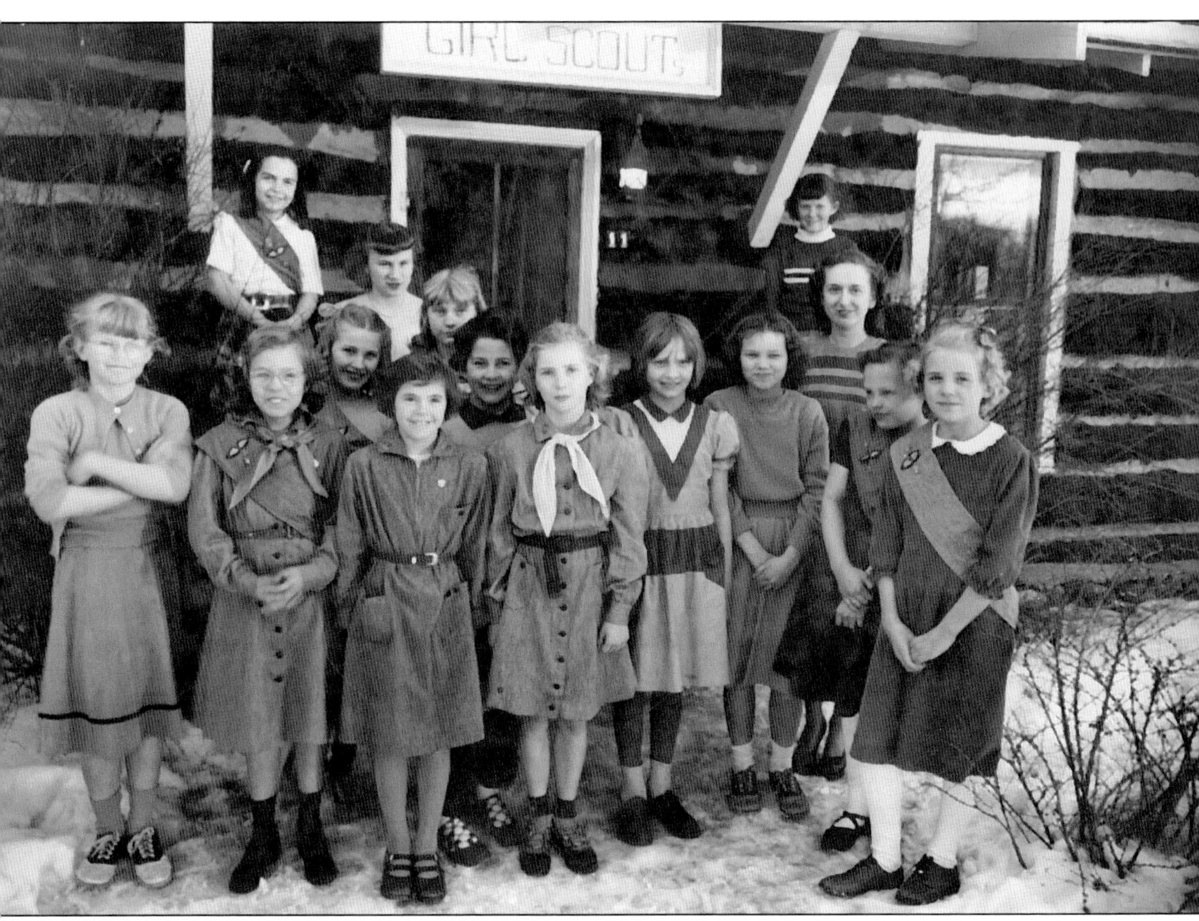

Girl Scouting has been popular in Sidney for some time, but it was not until 1932 that it really began to flourish. Originally, the Girl Scouts organized in 1922, when Charlotte Imes and Constance Nutt asked Mrs. Silas Gaiser to form in Sidney. In 1934, a log cabin was built using logs from Fred Estes's disassembled barn, which had been built in the 1890s. It was the third Scout cabin to be built in Montana, and the Girl Scout Council purchased grounds for the cabin at a tax sale the same year it was built. In 1953, the cabin was moved into Sidney, and a long room was built onto the back so that the Girl Scouts could have meetings without any rental costs. Here, a group of Girl Scouts from the 1960s poses outside of the Scout Cabin in Sidney. The cabin still stands in town today, next door to the MonDak Heritage Center. It was donated to the center in 1992 but is no longer in use.

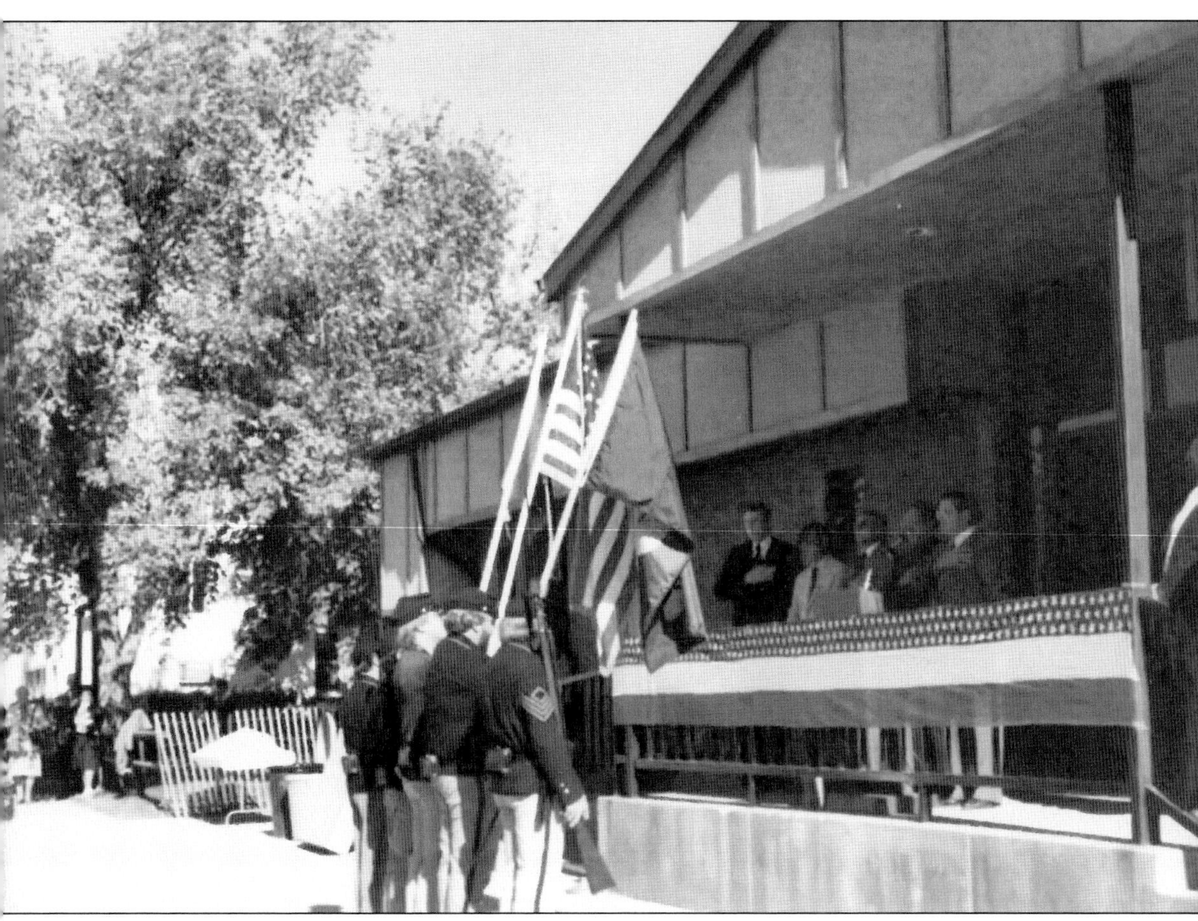

The MonDak Historical and Art Society was formed in 1967 with a mission that included preserving and contributing to the area's arts, culture, and heritage. In 1972, the organization opened the J.K. Ralston Museum and Art Center, which was named after the native Montana artist. The first museum was housed in the basement of the Community Memorial Hospital in Sidney. Just a year and a half later, the organization purchased the old People's Congregational Church, hoping to expand its museum. Continuing to grow, the society raised enough funds to build a new museum. In September 1984, a grand opening took place at the new building, called the MonDak Heritage Center. During the dedication, a flag presentation took place, which is shown here. The heritage center still operates today and houses archives and artifacts, including items that belonged to the first pioneers who came to Sidney in the late 19th century.

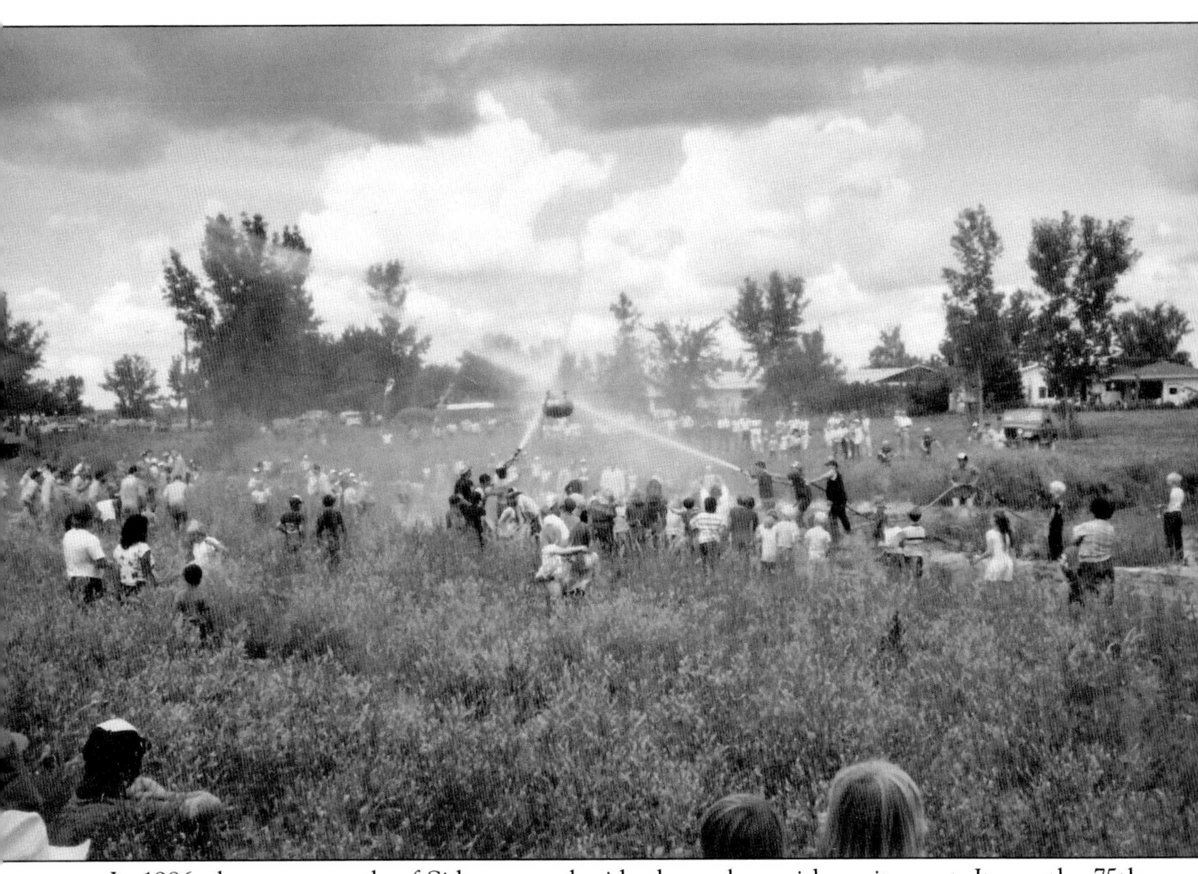

In 1986, the townspeople of Sidney were beside themselves with excitement. It was the 75th birthday of the town's incorporation, and everyone was planning a huge party to celebrate. Even though Sidney had been incorporated on April 21, 1911, planners decided to hold the event in July so that more people could participate. On Saturday, July 26, 1986, many events took place to celebrate the birthday, including a parade down Central Avenue and a historical presentation by the Friends of Fort Union, which took place in Petersen Park on the south side of town. One of the most highly anticipated events, however, was the Firemen's Water Fight. It took place at 1:00 p.m. in the south end of Petersen Park, across from the Lone Tree Creek. This picture shows crowds gathered to watch the teams of firefighters duke it out with their water hoses.

About the MonDak Heritage Center

The MonDak Heritage Center is one of the finest museums in the state of Montana and is the focal point of cultural activities in Richland County. Our mission is to engage, educate, and inspire our community by preserving and contributing to the area's arts, culture, and heritage.

The center houses a MonDak pioneer town exhibit in its lower level, with a street scene depicting an early MonDak-region town. Upstairs are two art galleries, two libraries, and a gift shop featuring the work of regional artists and area authors and other unique gift items. Proceeds from the gift shop benefit the center, which is operated by the MonDak Historical and Art Society, a 501(c)(3) not-for-profit, membership-based organization.

The MonDak Historical and Art Society was originally formed in 1967 and in 1972 opened a temporary museum known as the J.K. Ralston Museum and Art Center in the Community Memorial Hospital in Sidney. Named for a famed western artist and Richland County native, the Ralston Center operated until 1984, when the museum was moved to the MonDak Heritage Center, its permanent and present location at 120 Third Avenue SE in Sidney.